The Argumentative Theatre of Joe Penhall

The Argumentative Theatre of Joe Penhall

WILLIAM C. BOLES

McFarland & Company, Inc., Publishers
Jefferson, North Carolina, and London

LIBRARY OF CONGRESS CATALOGUING-IN-PUBLICATION DATA

Boles, William C., 1966 –
 The argumentative theatre of Joe Penhall / William C. Boles.
     p.   cm.
 Includes bibliographical references and index.

 ISBN 978-0-7864-5949-0
 softcover : 50# alkaline paper

 1. Penhall, Joe — Criticism and interpretation.   I. Title.
 PR6066.E4958Z65   2011
 822'.914 — dc22   2011005387

BRITISH LIBRARY CATALOGUING DATA ARE AVAILABLE

© 2011 William C. Boles. All rights reserved

*No part of this book may be reproduced or transmitted in any form
or by any means, electronic or mechanical, including photocopying
or recording, or by any information storage and retrieval system,
without permission in writing from the publisher.*

On the cover: scene from *Landscape with Weapon* (photograph by Catherine Ashmore)

Manufactured in the United States of America

*McFarland & Company, Inc., Publishers
  Box 611, Jefferson, North Carolina 28640
  www.mcfarlandpub.com*

For Leslie and Emma

Table of Contents

Preface	1
Introduction: From the Raves to the Stages of London	7
1. *Wild Turkey* and the New Man, the New Lad and the Penhall Male	25
2. *Some Voices* and the Failure of Care	40
3. *Pale Horse* and the Struggle to Mourn	59
4. *Love and Understanding* and the Demise of Relationships	77
5. *The Bullet* and the Stigma of Redundancy	98
6. *Blue/Orange* and Racism within the National Health Service	114
7. *Dumb Show* and Penhall's Women	135
8. *Landscape with Weapon* and Post–September 11 Drama	155
Afterword	179
Chapter Notes	183
Bibliography	189
Index	199

Preface

While a batch of fresh-faced, shock-inducing, cutting-edge, disgruntled, award-winning playwrights emerged on the stages and in the newspapers of London in the 1994 and 1995 theatrical seasons, I was sequestered in a carrel at the University of Tennessee, immersed in the research and writing of a dissertation that focused on an earlier group of young, controversial British playwrights from the middle part of the twentieth century. I would not become aware of this new renaissance of writing, a term used by some London reviewers to describe what they were seeing, until the fall of 1996, as I made preparations to take a group of 20 Rollins College students to London to study theatre for three weeks. As I began booking shows, I was suddenly coming across the names of playwrights unfamiliar to me, like Sarah Kane, Martin McDonagh, Mark Ravenhill and Conor McPherson. Intrigued, I sprinkled some of these new plays amidst the usual visits to the celebrity- and musical-heavy West End shows as well as the revivals offered by the Royal National Theatre and the Royal Shakespeare Company. During our stay in January 1997, we saw 20 plays, but I can only recall two of them: Mark Ravenhill's *Shopping and Fucking* (1996) and Martin McDonagh's *The Beauty Queen of Leenane* (1996). My undergraduate students and I were obsessed by these productions, and they became the two plays to which we always returned in our ensuing conversations. As a teacher, I was pleased with these new playwrights' abilities to make drama vibrant and intriguing for a college audience, a quality I am always seeking in plays that I teach in the classroom. As an academic, I was immediately hooked on the bold characterizations, the mature storytelling, the shocking and aggressive use of violence and sexuality, the surprising theatrical disruption of audience expectation and an all-around incredible energy that Ravenhill and McDonagh created. I instantly shifted my research attention to the plays and playwrights of this new era.

During following annual trips to London, as facilitator for students experiencing the variety of London theatre or as academic researcher, I sought out the works by these new writers, attending productions of new plays by Patrick Marber, Conor McPherson, Martin McDonagh, Mark Ravenhill, Roy Williams,

Simon Bent, David Eldridge, Jez Butterworth and others. It was during my sabbatical in 2001 that I saw a play by Joe Penhall, the National Theatre's transfer of the award-winning *Blue/Orange* (2000) at the Duchess Theatre. While of the same generation as all the new writers, Penhall was doing something different and far more challenging than his peers. He was addressing race, mental issues and power-mad doctors—all unexplored territory. As I continued to write about, teach and see plays by these new writers, I found myself constantly returning to Joe Penhall, as I read and reread his earlier plays that dealt with madness, business, friendship, family and the all-consuming nature of work and the plays that followed *Blue/Orange*, which suggested new territory as he turned to the dirty ethics of tabloid journalism and the nasty business of weapons manufacturing.

In a playwriting career of less than fifteen years, his plays demonstrated not only a remarkable maturity and growth as a writer, but also a dedication to challenging the elements of British society that he felt had been ignored by his peers and the journalists whose job it was to hold institutions accountable. A book-length study of Penhall's work is timely and necessary because of the leading authors to be associated with the burst of new creative talent on the British stage since the mid–1990s, he has received the least amount of scholarly attention, even though London newspapers at the height of the invasion of new writing identified him, along with Kane, McPherson, Ravenhill and McDonagh, as one of the five most important writers to emerge during this time period. The other four playwrights have all received scholarly attention over the last decade. A quick glance through the MLA directory in the summer of 2010 showed that of the five playwrights McDonagh and Kane have been the most popular subjects of academics, each with over forty items listed. Ravenhill and McPherson each have ten listings, and Penhall rounds out the group with only two listings (one of those is a page-long piece in a Japanese journal). In terms of book-length studies, the disparity between Penhall and his peers continue. Sarah Kane has had two books written about her by Graham Saunders, '*Love Me Or Kill Me*': *Sarah Kane and the Theatre of Extremes* (2002) and *About Kane: The Playwright and the Work* (2009). Conor McPherson has been featured in a number of books about contemporary Irish drama and was the subject of Gerald Wood's *Conor McPherson: Imagining Mischief* (2003). Mark Ravenhill has been featured in two book-length studies: Peter Billingham's *At the Sharp End: Uncovering the Work of Five Leading Dramatists: David Edgar, Tim Etchells, David Greig, Tanika Gupta and Mark Ravenhill* (2008) and John F. Deeney's *Mark Ravenhill* (2010). Martin McDonagh has had a number of book-length studies published on his works, including *The Theatre of Martin McDonagh: A World of Savage Stories*, edited by Lilian Chambers and Eamonn Jordan (2007); *Martin McDonagh: A Casebook*, edited by Richard Rankin Russell (2007); and *The New Grotesque: The Theatre of Martin McDonagh and Tracy Letts*, by Greg Thorson (2009). In addition numerous edited volumes have also appeared recently dealing with this time period of playwriting, including *British Theatre of the 1990s: Interviews with Directors, Playwrights, Critics and Academics*, edited by Mireia Aragay, et al. (2007), which contains the only academic interview with Joe Penhall[1]; and *Cool Britannia? British Political Drama in the 1990s*, edited by Rebecca D'Monte and Graham Saunders (2008), which draws many of its pieces from the In-Yer-Face and Beyond conference held in Bristol, England, in 2002. Recently, single title texts, examining plays from this time period, have also begun to appear, including a theatre guide to Sarah Kane's *Blasted* by Sarah Iball (2008) and Patrick Marber's *Closer* by Graham Saunders (2008). However, the prime source that covers this era is Aleks Sierz's *In-Yer-Face: British Drama Today* (2000). Sierz's text named and defined the theatrical movement that was afoot and covered the most important plays and playwrights of the period. Joe Penhall's first two full-length plays are discussed by Sierz. Clearly, a text that exclusively examines the plays of Penhall is notably absent, hence the importance of this work in bestowing upon Penhall's work its due recognition.

Penhall believes his plays should constantly test, provoke, engage and enrage his audience. His topical plays deal with the failure of a National Health Service policy of releasing schizophrenic patients into the community, the personal and familial devastation that comes with redundancy, the inability to mourn in our contemporary age, the presence of racism within the National Health Service, the peccadilloes of the tabloids and the shadiness of the military weapons industry. In this vein he has written one short and seven full-length plays, many of which have won awards and received critical acclaim; *Blue/Orange*, for instance, won an Oliver Best Play award, has been recognized as one of the best plays of the new decade of the century, and has been anthologized in *The Methuen Drama Book of Twenty-First Century British Plays* (2010), edited by Aleks Sierz. In addition, his plays have been produced at London's most important venues for new writing, including the Royal Court Theatre (three times), the Royal National Theatre (twice) and the Bush Theatre. Based on his theatrical successes, Penhall has also been given opportunities to make his mark writing for television and film. He adapted Jake Arnott's *The Long Firm* (2003) for British television and wrote an original three-part detective series called *Moses Jones* (2009). His film adaptations include his rewriting his own plays for the screen as well as writing the screenplays for *Enduring Love* (2004), based on the Ian McEwan novel, and *The Road* (2009), based on the Cormac McCarthy novel. Penhall has already established himself as an important playwright and with a number of scripts currently in production, including one with the venerable director Mike Nichols, he is on the verge of becoming an important writer for the filmmaking community, too.

This book will examine Penhall's plays by first providing the appropriate overlapping economic, cultural, political or literary context surrounding the play's subject matter (for example, the absence of mourning in contemporary

British culture or racism in British institutions) and then a close reading of the work and its characters in relation to this context. In such a way the macro- and micro-elements of the text are discussed. The introduction begins in the 1980s with Margaret Thatcher at the helm of the British government. Not only was Thatcher's government at its height of power and influence in changing many facets of the English establishment, but also a powerful youth culture, termed by some as Generation Ecstasy, was on the rise, enabling, in part, the theatrical renaissance of new writing that came in the mid–1990s. The introduction establishes the cultural atmosphere into which the new writers, like Penhall, arrived (he moved to England from Australia in 1990), discusses the theatrical version of Irvine Welsh's *Trainspotting* (1994) — which was, for some, the first In-Yer-Face play — and then places Penhall within the context of the major writers who emerged in the '90s, including Kane, McPherson, Ravenhill and McDonagh.

Chapter 1, which is about his short play *Wild Turkey* (1993), first discusses the rise of the New Man, whose characteristics were influenced by the women's movement, and then the New Lad, which encompassed an all-male attitude in direct contrast to the more feminine New Man. Penhall's play challenges these two dominant male stereotypes by focusing on an ignored but prevalent masculine position: the male who exists on the periphery of the capitalist system. Chapter 2 looks at *Some Voices* (1994), which was his first play to be adapted for film (2000), and which was written in response to the failure of the Care in the Community program instituted by the government to release mentally ill patients from hospitals to their families. Penhall was a firsthand observer of the social repercussions of this policy as he wrote articles about it when he was a reporter in Shepherd's Bush. The chapter discusses Penhall's own personal interactions with an acquaintance who was schizophrenic and then considers the play's depiction of a restaurant owner who must rebalance his life when his schizophrenic brother is placed in his care by the government. Penhall's follow-up to *Some Voices* was *Pale Horse* (1995), which is about the darkening spiral that the main character undergoes after the shocking death of his wife. Chapter 3, relying upon various theories (anthropological, sociological and philosophical) about mourning, discusses the nature of grief in the latter part of the twentieth century and then applies these theories to the main character's struggles to come to terms with his wife's passing. After first looking at David Mamet's *Sexual Perversity in Chicago* (1974) as a model of the contemporary depiction of the difficulty of romantic relationships, Chapter 4 details how Penhall's third play, *Love and Understanding* (1997), tied in perfectly to the theatrical zeitgeist of relationship plays, as his play overlapped with *Shopping and Fucking* by Mark Ravenhill and *Closer* (1997) by Patrick Marber. The chapter then compares and contrasts the three contemporary plays, placing Penhall in context with his peers in terms of their depiction of relationships and romance in the late 1990s. Whereas Chapter 4 places Penhall in the context of his peers, Chapter 5 compares *The Bullet* (1998), the most autobiographical of all his works, to works by three iconic figures from the twentieth century, Arthur Miller, Harold Pinter and Sam Shepard. The main focus of the chapter pursues not only the similarities and differences between Penhall's play and Miller's *Death of a Salesman* (1949) but also a more specific examination of the devastation that redundancy causes for the male characters and their families. The beginning of the chapter contrasts the use of the homecoming motif in Pinter's *The Homecoming* (1965) and Shepard's *Buried Child* (1978) with the opening pages of Penhall's play.

After Penhall completed *The Bullet*, the focus of his plays shifted from more domestic-oriented dramas to more public considerations of issues affecting British society. Chapter 6 covers *Blue/Orange*, about the fight between two doctors over the medical diagnosis of a black mental patient. This chapter contextualizes *Blue/Orange* within a discussion of race in Britain, ranging from the political and institutional oppression of black immigrants to Britain, stretching back to the 1940s, to the MacPherson report, which was released a year before *Blue/Orange* premiered and investigated flawed police proceedings after the murder of Stephen Lawrence, a young black man, by five white youths. The report found the Metropolitan Police Department to be rife with "institutional racism." In the ensuing months other government agencies found themselves under examination for racist policies. This chapter looks at how Penhall's play posits institutional racism at work within the National Health Service through its treatment of a schizophrenic black man. All of Penhall's plays are dominated by powerfully compelling male characters, while his females struggle for dramatic recognition, lack depth of character and are, cast-wise, dramatically outnumbered. Chapter 7 focuses on Penhall's female characters as *Dumb Show* (2004) offers Penhall's strongest female character in the guise of a sexy tabloid journalist who entraps a popular comedian. It discusses the strengths and weaknesses of the female lead, while juxtaposing her with other female characters from Penhall's earlier works. The final chapter explores Penhall's foray into post–September 11 political theatre with *Landscape with Weapon* (2007), which features a weapons designer who has created the next paradigm shift in warfare: armed drones. Starting with a summary of theatre's response to the September 11 attacks and the ensuing conflicts in Afghanistan and Iraq, the chapter places *Landscape with Weapon* in context to its peers, focusing on Penhall's decision to eschew the path of his contemporaries with a different perspective: an indictment of the military complex. However, the chapter argues that in the second half of his play Penhall goes even further than his contemporaries by changing his conversation from weapons to the institutionalization of torture by the British government, as it tortures two of its own citizens to gain control over the drone technology.

My work on Penhall's plays has been an ongoing project for a number of years; hence, some of the material herein has been previously published. Part of the material in the introduction was originally published in the online academic journal *Reconstruction* (Fall 2003). Part of the material in Chapters 1 and 2 has been reproduced, with permission, from *Drama and the Postmodern: Assessing the Limits of Metatheatre*, edited by Daniel Jernigan (Cambria Press, 2008).

Finally, a book such as this does not get written on its own. I am indebted to a variety of sources for fiscal, professional and emotional support. Thanks go to a variety of colleagues and administrators at Rollins College for the financial support to travel to England on numerous occasions to do research as well as release time from teaching to write the book. Thanks also goes to the variety of libraries and archives that have aided me, including the incredible support team at the circulation desk of Rollins' Olin Library who not only aided me with a variety of wide-ranging and at times far-flung Interlibrary Loan requests but also shared my summer enthusiasm for the Big Balls on *Wipeout*; the knowledgeable staff at the Theatre Archive of the Victoria and Albert Museum when it used to be housed in the bowels of the Theatre Museum in Covent Garden (sadly, no longer will theatre professionals have their research accompanied by the jubilant sounds of screaming schoolchildren visiting the London Transport Museum just outside the archive window); the Sound Recording department at the British Library, who aided me in hearing recordings of Penhall's play; the Royal National Theatre Archive personnel, who introduced me to a treasure trove of material about the two Penhall productions done at the Cottesloe Theatre; and, finally, the staff at the Newspaper Reading Room of the British Library in Colindale.

My foray into theatre and teaching would not have happened without three individuals: Harold Tedford, who first introduced me to the wonders of the London theatre; Dick Brucher, who inspired me to become a professor of dramatic literature; and Stan Garner, who demonstrated to me what it means to live the academic life. In addition, I want to thank the numerous students at Rollins College who have willingly waded along with me into the rich material from this era and the chair of the English department, Ed Cohen, who provided incredible support and encouragement over many meals of barbecue. My thanks also go out to Joe Penhall, who answered honestly and thoughtfully my many questions about the contradictions of the public record of his life. Finally, none of this would have happened without the emotional support, uproarious laughter and gentle nudging of my daughter Emma and my wife Leslie.

Introduction: From the Raves to the Stages of London

In *High Society: The Real Voices of Club Culture*, a book that purports to be the true story of ecstasy, raves and acid house, Simon of London described his experience of seeking out a Sunrise rave in a little country village on the 24th of June in 1989.[1]

> There were people standing in their gardens in their pyjamas and looking out of their windows in their dressing-gowns, wondering what the hell was going on: the sleepy village road suddenly had cars three abreast, all packed with sweaty, gurning kids with their music pumping. Nothing could have come the other way even if it had wanted to.... And there, silhouetted in the door, were two tiny figures. And even against the increasing daylight we could make out that they were uniformed coppers, and that each of them was holding a push bike! ... And the younger one had his helmet under his arm, and he wandered in looking totally gobsmacked — they had obviously never seen anything like it in their whole careers of policing a tiny, sleepy, suburban village [Harrison 141–2].

This musical gathering of raving youths would not be the last one to prompt gobsmacked expressions from local police officers, politicians and inundated villagers. In fact, with the success of the Sunrise rave that Simon described above, weekend outings provoking the same flummoxed reactions from local constabulary and denizens would become the norm rather than the exception, culminating in one incredible spring rave scene in May 1992.

The citizens of Castlemorton, a small village between Worcester and Gloucester, woke up one May morning to find themselves host to tens of thousands of ravers, who danced their time away to techno, acid house and jungle music, while enjoying the rush provided by ecstasy. One might ask, how does one manage to coordinate the arrival of, according to some estimates, 25,000 to 40,000 youths (many of them from London) in such an impromptu fashion? According to one source, identified as Harry,[2]

> No information was printed, it was all word of mouth. We didn't even know about the site until twenty-four hours before it all began. All these young people were able to group in one place, set up their own city, a police no-go zone. For a

government whose reason for being is to control people, here was a very frightening example of people saying: "We can and will do whatever we like" [Collin 220].

Harry's incredibly telling statement demonstrated the growing effectiveness, size, scope and attitude of the burgeoning nature of rave culture. Castlemorton became a prime demonstration of the strength of British youth culture as they appropriated the open areas around the town, creating their own temporary city where they were in charge and would decide on their own terms when the party would end. The usual institutional powers of the government held no sway over their newly created municipality. Castlemorton as well as other village and farm takeovers during the previous five years highlighted the now-empowered sense of youths who had grown up under a Thatcher-led government which had no compassion for its country's youth and their economic plight. Previous to Thatcher's election as prime minister, at age sixteen youths were eligible for government help. Thatcher's government upped the required age to eighteen and in the process displaced a slew of teens who suddenly found their means of survival seriously threatened.

By the time the five-day-long, impromptu Castlemorton rave came to its close, the John Major government, after consistently being humiliated by its inability to halt the weekend rave scenes and increasingly peppered with complaints from citizens of the beleaguered hamlets that became rave capitals for a weekend, began drafting early versions of a law, eventually to be titled the Criminal Justice and Public Order Act of 1994, to reign in the ever-growing contingency of youths dancing away in the British countryside by deeming rave music illegal. Matthew Collin noted that even though their legal reaction was not the first time the government had been moved to restrict behavior engaged in by youth movements, "never before, over years of post-war moral panics about the activities of teddy boys, mods, hippies and punks, had a government considered young people's music so subversive as to prohibit it" (223). However, due to the bizarrely vague manner in which the statute was worded, the government ended up defining a rave as a group of people who are outside and listen to music that was composed of "repetitive beats" (Keane 107). In effect, not only had the government made raves illegal, but they had also turned all outdoor weddings and receptions into law-breaking gatherings.

While the music (techno, acid house and jungle) plus the powerful effects of ecstasy provided youths opportunities for escape, they also provided opportunities for cutting-edge, wise, young risk takers to anticipate and profit from the financial opportunities of such a growing culture. While a definite sense of spontaneity existed with Castlemorton and other weekend raves, they did not happen on their own. In order for an event like Castlemorton and other large event gatherings to succeed, according to Collin:

> You needed lights, generators, projection screens, fairground rides, inflatable castles, a whole panoply of technological gimcrackery, and somehow you had to

assemble it all without being spotted. Then you needed a good lawyer to stave off the police and keep the landowner's resolve solid, and you had to make sure you'd advertised on the right pirate radio stations—otherwise they might well start broadcasting that your party was cancelled. But what you need above all was nerve—and the ravers ... had more than enough of that [98–9].

Such intricate supporting infrastructure for the spontaneous gatherings indicated that the youth movement was driven by savvy individuals, who relied on rapidly growing telecommunication technology, like phone message systems which could be used to announce rave locations, as well as the government's bulky, bureaucratic size working against it to secure the success of the weekend events. The rallying cry of self-individuality and action would be an important one for this new youth culture, which would become the most important youth movement in Britain since the 1960s. According to Jonathan Rutherford, "Rave culture has touched the lives of more under-25s than all the previous youth cultures put together" (17). To put Rutherford's comment into perspective, consider that one study estimated that up to 500,000 youths were going to clubs every weekend in Britain (Malbon 18).

As Castlemorton made clear, this group redefined the nature of the outdoor space of the countryside, making it their own. This appropriation was merely one component of a youth culture defining itself in opposition to what had come before. As in all cultural movements, the outsiders, in this case the Generation Ecstasy youths, became "us," while the authorities and their supporters were "them." Sociologist Sarah Thornton immersed herself in the rave scene and defined the two categories between the "us" and the "them."

Us	Them
Alternative	Mainstream
Hip/cool	Straight/square/naff
Independent	Commercial
Authentic	Falsey/phoney
Rebellious/radical	Conformist/conservative
Specialist genres	Pop
Insider knowledge	Easily accessible information
Minority	Majority
Heterogeneous	Homogeneous
Youth	Family
Classless	Classed
Masculine Culture	Feminine culture
	[*Club Cultures* 115]

Perhaps the most definitive text that captured the essence of the "us" of Generation Ecstasy and vilified the "them" was Irvine Welsh's groundbreaking novel *Trainspotting* (1993). Told through numerous perspectives, but mostly through the voice of Mark Renton, Welsh's novel introduced a group of heroin addicts and their struggles with life, work, romance, the big score, raving, football, the filthiest toilet in Scotland and, most of all, heroin. Lucy Hughes-Hallett in her book review in *The Sunday Times* remarked:

It gives voice to the silent, swaying figure at the back of the late-night bus, the one nobody wants to sit next to. It describes the lower depths from the viewpoint of the people who live down there. And despite the wretchedness of its subject matter, it is full of energy, the negative energy of anger but also the positive energy of youth and recklessness and of the author's vigorous intelligence.

Looking back on the excitement of the early '90s and the youth culture movement that was afoot, Matthew Collin wrote, "*Trainspotting* was *the* cult text of the nineties not just because of Welsh's literary talent, but because it had struck a deep chord with anyone immersed in drug culture" (28). Welsh explained the reason behind his desire to capture on the pages of his novels and short stories the sense of this powerfully emerging youth culture, telling National Public Radio's *Morning Edition* that the passions and energies of this group "have not been represented in writing because there's been such a kind of traditionalist, kind of Oxbridge, kind of imperialist strangle-hold on writing in Britain. So all I've really done is taken things that have been going on in different aspects of the culture, in music and art, and brought them into writing" ("Author"). Based on the success of the novel, Welsh became one of the leading spokespersons for this youth movement. "His characters were neither bohemians nor entirely conformist, but embodied the dissonance and contradictions between materialism and collectivism, between licit and illicit, that underpinned the nineties" (Collin 283). The energy and distinctiveness of Welsh's characters in *Trainspotting* could not be confined to just the pages of the novel as it was quickly turned into a play.

In March 1995 at the Bush Theatre Irvine Welsh's cult novel *Trainspotting* made its London stage debut, in an adaptation by Harry Gibson. The voice of Welsh's characters possessed the same truculent urgency and theatrical spontaneity as John Osborne's Jimmy Porter forty years previously. Gibson, remarking on the book's attraction to the youth of Britain, told *The Times*: "It's written from within the culture, where everybody's saying: This is us, listen to us" (Lavender). Like Osborne and the other writers of the 1950s before him, Welsh articulated the voice of the underclass, and similar to the characters in John Braine's *Room at the Top* (1957), Alan Sillitoe's *Saturday Night and Sunday Morning* (1958) as well as the stage's offering of *Look Back in Anger* (1956), these underclass figures had never before had the opportunity to have their voices heard in such a distinctive and powerful manner.

Having already achieved cult success through the groundbreaking, multi-narrator novel, the play already had a built-in, committed audience for the ensuing theatrical and later film adaptations. On the nature of Welsh's audience *The Village Voice* noted:

> Research by his publishers has shown that a hefty proportion of Welsh's audience doesn't read any fiction at all, apart from books by himself and kindred spirits like *Morvern Callar* author Alan Warner. Welsh regards postliterati as more competent readers than professional critics, because they have first-hand experience of

the subcultural realms he documents: drug-and-dance culture, crime, the black economy, welfare subsistence [Reynolds, "Filthy" 72].

So while the novel quickly became noted as a novel for those people who did not read, the play soon received the same recognition as a play for those people who did not attend the theatre.

Harry Gibson, who was looking for new material for the stage, went into a bookstore and was told about the success of *Trainspotting*. He adapted the piece, and unlike Danny Boyle's successful film version, which is an ironic coming-of-age story of Mark Renton as he comes off skag twice, has a dalliance with an underage girl, attempts to go straight in London selling dubious "prime" real estate and finally stiffs his three buddies by running away with 16,000 pounds from a heroin deal, the play is a much darker representation of the novel, including a harrowing scene of Tommy shooting up into his penis; an extended scene on the death of Alison's baby Dawn to cot death, malnutrition and neglect; the violence of Franco Begbie; the downfall of Tommy; and the emotional devastation of Begbie seeing his father in an abandoned railway station. The tenor, tone and direction are far less glitzy and powerful when compared with the film with its powerful soundtrack, furious editing and imaginative camera angles offsetting the story's horrors.

While one immediately is drawn to a comparison between the theatrical eruption provided by Jimmy Porter and Welsh's Scottish heroin users, the Scottish characters distance themselves from the familiar discontents of British leftist drama found in the plays of Osborne, Arnold Wesker, Edward Bond, Howard Brenton, David Edgar, Stephen Poliakoff and others. Instead, while Jimmy Porter ranted about the ringing of church bells, religious figures, the fading imperial nature of Britain and pompous Sunday editorials, Welsh's characters' rants are far more personal, far more primal, far more inscribed in the primordial ooze of basic existence. The playful game of bears and squirrels that Jimmy and Alison use to escape from the discord of their relationship and their world is replaced in Gibson's adaptation by heroin and the powerful effects the drug has, as Alison says after shooting up, "That beats any meat injection. That beats any fuckin cock in the world!" (26).

Where Osborne's seminal work of contemporary British drama started in silence, as Jimmy and Cliff sit behind their Sunday newspapers while Alison irons, *Trainspotting* opens with a theatrical explosion not only from the mouth of Renton with his profane and graphically descriptive language but also from his body that in his sleep released all of its contents onto his girlfriend's bed.

> Fuck! ... Ah woke up in a strange bed, in a strange room, covered in ma own mess. Ah hud pished the bed. Ah hud puked up in the bed. Ah shat masel in the bed. Ah slide outay bed. Ah pick up the duvet. Ah look down. The bed is a total fucking mess. The wee pink carnations on a white background're drowning in toxic brown pollution [15].

Our soiled hero tries to spirit the fecal-, vomit-, semen- and urine-stained sheets out of the house, but his girlfriend's mother will not let him. She insists on washing them for him, to which he protests greatly.

> Mrs Houston steals across the flair taewards us n makes a grab fir ma bundle. She widnae be denied. Ah pull it tae me, tae my chest; but Mrs Houston is fast as fuck an deceptively strong.... The sheets flew up in the air — n a pungent shower ay shite, alcoholic sick n vile pish splashed oot across the scene [16].

While Generation Ecstasy saw itself in these stories, older audience members at the Bush and at later performances in the West End felt that the play belched forth a similar "pungent shower ay shite, alcholic sick n vile pish splash[ing] oot." Benedict Nightingale in his review of the transfer production at Whitehall Theatre noted one such theatergoer:

> "Er, I suppose the second half is much like the first?" a tweedy old gentleman asked me in the interval. "We're wondering if it's really aimed at our age group." He was right on both counts, and left with his wife 20 minutes later, no doubt cursing a play-title deceptively reminiscent of happy boyhood days recording the numbers of puffers at King's Cross ["Mainline"].

And yet, the success of *Trainspotting* is well documented through its numerous productions[3] as well as the positive reviews the play generated despite the discomfort some of the middle-aged, middle-class reviewers felt about the material. Charles Spencer of *The Daily Telegraph* wrote that "in the claustrophobic Bush the moral stench is overpowering," but that "the power of Welsh's language ... makes the nightmare so vivid" ("Nightmare"). Spencer returned to see the play a few months later after it transferred to its West End home at the Ambassador Theatre. After seeing the production in the heart of London, he wrote the following:

> The West End has surely never played host to so extravagantly disgusting a play as *Trainspotting*.... It is, however, impossible to dismiss the play because there is no doubt that Welsh is a writer of real accomplishment and originality.... *Trainspotting* is not for the faint-hearted, but it is undoubtedly one of the most remarkable productions of the year ["You'll"].

The play again returned to the West End at Whitehall Theatre, the production where Benedict Nightingale met the disappointed tweedy man. His review captured the simultaneous discomfort and enlightenment that the audience experienced. He wrote, "Seeing it is like being asked to squelch barefoot through every bodily fluid known to man" but Welsh "leaves us with a vital, vivid picture of youth that, helped by drugs, joblessness and its own confusions, has succumbed to nihilism and a wild self-destructiveness" ("Mainline").

Accompanying the disruptive subject matter of the play also came the raucous, youthful, rave-going, E-taking, techno-dancing, football-frenzied, and non-conservative youthful audience. The appearance of this previously unseen brood in the lobbies and stalls of the hallowed West End made a powerful statement about the changing nature (at least temporarily) of the composition and vocal participation of London audiences. Michael Billington's review in the *Guardian* of the Ambassador Theatre transfer remarked that the audience was filled with youths who were "nattily clad and audibly enjoying this cult story of Edinburgh low-life" (10). Carole Woddis in *The Herald* wrote that the audience "loved the incipient anarchy of it, they groaned with the desperate degradation of it, and they thrilled to the dramatic urgency of it" (qtd. in Sierz 61).

The artistic directors and theatre managers, who had for years been trying to figure out how to entice younger audiences to the theatre, were ecstatic about the draw that the play provided to the theatres, but in the case of *Trainspotting* the old adage of "be careful what you wish for" proved to be all too accurate. Dominic Dromgoole, artistic director at the Bush Theatre, counted himself amongst those looking to change the audience dynamic at his theatre. "'We've got to get the kids in,' was the patronizing mantra that used to ring around theatreland. 'We've got to get them out of the clubs and the raves and the flicks and the internet cafes and get them back in the theatre. Harness all that energy and creativity.' We generally agreed until the first night of *Trainspotting*" (277).

In *The Full Room*, Dominic Dromgoole describes the night the kids arrived at the Bush and their appearance in the raised tier seats of the theatre made Dromgoole and his staff think twice about wanting these young audience members to ever to return to their theatre again.

> They were a fucking nightmare. They smoked cigarettes, joints, even heroin (something of a theatrical first that), they talked amongst themselves, picked fights, spilt drinks and created whatever mayhem they could. About three-quarters of the way through the first half, an old theatre nightmare was made manifest, when first one, then another two, then four, then eventually about forty, simply got up and walked out, passing right across the stage. The depression this induced was quickly alleviated when they all en masse walked back in. They'd just nipped out for a piss [279].

After the night ended a number of the Bush Theatre staff members huddled together asking, "The kids, how can we get them out? How can we get them back into the clubs, raves, etc. Where are all those nice people in sweaters?" (279). The onrush, though, had started. Streaming into theatres around the country came the raucous, rave-going, techno-dancing kids. Harry Gibson remarked on the influx of the new theatre goers: "We were told by lots of regional theatres that they'd never been so full for years" (Sierz 61). Perhaps even more significant was the play's transfer to the West End. The appearance and decorum of this previously unseen brood in the lobbies, stalls, dress and upper circles of the hallowed West End made a powerful and, for some, uncomfortable statement about the changing composition and philosophy of London audiences as well as the writers for the stage. Harry Gibson's remark to Andy Lavender etched out part of the rebellious attitude of these new theatre patrons: "The thought of doing [*Trainspotting*] in the West End gives you a sense of triumph and a sense of subversion.... It's kind of a buzz to know you're seeing this filthy piece of work in the home of [Agatha Christie's] *The Mousetrap*" (35). In effect, the staid, comported, mainstream, respectable, commercial West End British theatre, which in the 1980s and the early 1990s had been defined, for the most part, by the easy comedies of Alan Ayckbourn, the multilayered plays of Tom Stoppard, directors making their names on revivals, heady transfers from the Royal Shakespeare Company and the Royal National Theatre, and highly profitable and exportable British musicals, was now being inundated by an audience of alternative, rebellious, independent theatre goers and writers, who would become a dramatic staple for the rest of the decade. In 1998 *The Sunday Times* noted that because of all the new plays being written by young writers, "New and younger audiences ... bought tickets in the thousands accordingly" (Fanshawe, "Playing"). To put it in the parlance of Sarah Thornton's categorization of Generation Ecstasy, just as the raving "us" had evaded the powerful British government's attempts to crack down on their parties and invaded the countryside of comfortably staid "them," the theatrical equivalent of "us" had invaded the territory of the theatrically established "them." As seen earlier, from the late 1980s until the mid–1990s, governmental authorities attempted to squelch the rise of club-culture by shutting down clubs and countryside rave scenes, which sported thousands of E'd up dancers, and yet by the mid–1990s rave culture had muscled its way into mainstream culture through its musical, literary, economic,[4] political and theatrical influences. The defining moment for its co-opting by the mainstream occurred when Tony Blair adopted techno anthems into his campaign for prime minister.

Trainspotting's theatrical and economic success perfectly encapsulated and represented the dramatic turn of events that occurred on stage in the mid–1990s as the explosion of powerful new plays by young playwrights, many of whom were in their twenties, attracted a younger audience to the theatres. The energy, exploration and innovation found in the promoters of club culture also existed with these new playwrights. While club culture defined a pioneering musical, drug, economic and social movement, it also defined a turning away from the status quo established by British institutions and the clubbers' parents. The playwrights to emerge from this generation, like their raving peers, issued a challenge to a British theatre that had grown, according to some London reviewers, staid and boring. In 1991 Michael Billington, writing in the *Guardian*, declared the British theatre to be in a state of crisis. In previous decades the British theatre had been a hotbed of leftist theatre, producing plays by David Hare, David Edgar, Howard Brenton, Caryl Churchill, Howard Barker, Tom Stoppard, Edward Bond and Harold Pinter. Starting in the mid–

1970s, the theatre had witnessed the dramatic emergence of female writers and feminist theatre groups. The 1980s, though, were not friendly to the stage and throughout the decade it suffered. Margaret Thatcher's government cut arts funding, believing that the theatres should seek out their own resources and sponsors. At the start of the decade a burgeoning number of theatre troupes were doing innovative theatrical productions. By the end of the 1980s few were left standing. Important theatre spaces went dark, including the Royal Court Theatre Upstairs and the Cottesloe Theatre at the Royal National Theatre. Directors eschewed new material to instead focus on making a name for themselves through revivals of classic plays or scoring a hefty payday with a blockbuster musical that could be exported to Broadway and then the world. Sharing a similar perspective as Billington, Howard Brenton in his book *Hot Irons* (1995) wrote, "The British epic theatre with its issue plays that my generation of playwrights invented and wrote through the 1970s and 1980s has died on us. We need new ways of dramatising what people are thinking and feeling out there" (qtd. in Bayley, "Playwrights" 25). Just as the rave scene, in part, was a reaction to the boring club scene that had arisen in the 1980s with its stultifying focus on fashion and being seen, the theatre of the mid–1990s arose out of a reaction to the stultifying economic and creative environment that had occurred in the 1980s and into the first few years of the 1990s. Writing in the midst of the burst of new writing in 1997, David Edgar remarked: "Five years ago, sure, theatre was on life support. Suddenly, now, we're told, the stage has gone spicy. First nights are hip again. There are bratpacks, rude-broods and post–Tarantinians. There is even loose talk about a new golden age" ("Plays").

In reading the reviews of *Trainspotting* as well as similar-minded plays that followed, like Sarah Kane's *Blasted* (1995) and Ravenhill's *Shopping and Fucking*, the middle-aged, white, middle-class theatre critics were excited about these fresh theatrical voices releasing the somnambulant theatre from its Thatcher-induced slumber through their focus on violence, graphic sexuality and drug experiences; however, they were also a bit wary of the new group of audience members invading the West End in search of the theatricalization of their own stories, experiences and fears. The new playwrights were telling stories that highlighted the conditions and behaviors of those people that the stage had neglected. Harry Gibson explained that that was precisely part of the attraction of *Trainspotting*: "Irvine doesn't sanitise or romanticise. The seedy things that happen in toilets, shagging your brother's pregnant wife at his funeral ... we know such things go on, but they're not talked about" (Curtis, "Spotting"). Welsh explained further: "I think that a lot of people are sick of the kind of representations of the world that we live in as a kind of bland *Four Weddings and a Funeral* sort of place — they want something that says a wee bit more about the society we actually live in and a wee bit more about the different cultures within that society that tend to be ignored" (Mac-

Donald). Mark Ravenhill shared the same philosophy with the magazine *Midweek* about the characters that dotted his plays: "You only have to wait for a bus in Camden for ten minutes to come across the people I'm writing about in the play. What surprises me is Londoners who claim to have no knowledge of this kind of life" ("Curtains Up"). Like J. M. Synge who went to the Aran Islands and wrote about what he saw, these young playwrights looked outside their flats and found inspiration in their friends, families, raves, pubs, city streets, public transportation and clubs, writing the truth of what they saw. In turn, the young theatre goers visited West End theatres in droves, especially because the Royal Court was based there while their Sloane Square digs were being refurbished, to see similar works by young playwrights who were telling their stories on the stage including Kane's *Blasted*, Ravenhill's *Shopping and Fucking*, Jez Butterworth's *Mojo* (1995), McDonagh's *The Beauty Queen of Leenane*, Ben Elton's *Popcorn* (1996), Nick Grosso's *Sweetheart* (1996) and David Eldridge's *Serving It Up* (1996).

Like the ravers who were unhappy with the state of the club scene and the ability to enjoy themselves in the way they wanted to, the plethora of writers all shared a common interest in writing for the stage because of their dissatisfaction with the British theatre's inability to address the issues and concerns so central to their own generation. James MacDonald, director of *Blasted*, offered a perspective similar to Brenton's, stating, "I think writers like Kane are reacting to a new complacency and to a lack of risk-taking in the theatre. We've lost the culture of protest" (Hemming, "Look" 17). Anthony Neilson, another new writer to emerge in the 1990s, also commented on the reason why new plays, like *Trainspotting* or in his example *Blasted*, had become *de rigueur*: "I think *Blasted* spoke for a generation which has a dulled, numb feeling — not apathy, but a feeling that nothing you do will make any difference" (Hemming, "Look" 17). In explaining part of the genesis of his own plays, Martin McDonagh expressed a disdain for the British theatre offerings that surrounded him as a youth, especially the ones that had a distinctly tilted political perspective. "I grew up with it being kind of dull and political, and lecture-y.... You don't need to pay 10 quid to be lectured to.... I always felt that as long as you tell good stories, people will be more interested than they will in whatever political question is going around that month or that year" (Kramer 72). David Edgar also noted the ability of these writers to use established conceits of the theatrical landscape and spin them to their own liking, stressing that "the new writers are often pulling off a cunning postmodern trick, by subverting genres that none the less remain accessible on the level of the familiar" ("Plays"). Amelia Howe Kritzer offered a different perspective on the direction of these writers, noting the political component shared by them.

> They show a concern over issues of rationality, character development, and maturity, within the context of the failures of families and society to provide effective

structures of protection, guidance, social integration, and opportunity.... They appeal to public conscience to recognize and help the victims of ruthless cuts in social welfare programmes [47].

Finally, Matt Wolf perhaps summed up the dual nature of these plays in his discussion of *Shopping and Fucking*. He wrote, "Still, nothing in the play is as sensationalistic as its knowing come-on of a title, which may be why the West End audience this summer went into the Gielgud theatre so many hipsters and came out shaking off a singular vision of hell" (45). As Wolf notes, while the plays may have been attracting new audiences to the theatre, they were not letting them off easily. These plays did not glorify their generation; they challenged them, aesthetically, politically, socially, economically and culturally.

The emergence of so many new writers with an eye toward redefining so many facets of the theatre prompted some theatre critics to herald the arrival of a new renaissance of British drama. Obviously, with the proliferation of these new writers and their attention-getting plays, critics tried to be the next John Russell Taylor, who coined the phrase "Angry Young Men" to sum up the works emerging in the mid–1950s. They wanted to be the critic who, in one neat phrase, defined a literary movement and captured the essence of this new, exciting era of theatre which only seemed to grow with each new premiere at theatres like the Bush and Royal Court. In the process a number of labels were attempted, including the New Brutalists, the New Nihilists, the New Lads Play, the New Angry Young Writers, E Generation plays, Smack and Sodomy Kids, the Theatre of Disenchantment, the Theatre of Urban Ennui, Maggie's Kids, and Thatcher's Children. While all the titles made for good copy in the London papers, none accurately captured the myriad direction of all the plays, and, no doubt, part of the problem resided in the presence of so many playwrights having pieces produced. In addition to the playwrights already mentioned, these were some of the other writers associated with the movement: Joe Penhall, Patrick Marber, Phyllis Nagy, Jim Cartwright, Judy Upton, Simon Bent, Judith Johnson, Rebecca Prichard, Tracy Letts, Nick Ward, Roy Williams and Ayub Khan Din. Finding one common theme in the works of over twenty writers proved impossible, since all were covering various aspects of the British experience. David Edgar addressed this issue as he noted that these monikers failed to capture the spirit and movement of all the new plays precisely because there were just too many diverse types of plays emerging, including "gay plays such as *My Night with Reg* and *Beautiful Thing*, boys' bonding plays such as Tim Firth's *Neville's Island* and Patrick Marber's *Dealer's Choice*, lads' plays such as *Mojo* and Simon Bent's *Goldhawk Road*, girl-in-a-boy's-gang plays such as *Shopping and Fucking*" (Edgar, "Provocative" 27).

And, not surprisingly, the playwrights themselves did not put much stock in the varied titles. McDonagh, when asked about the attempts to group all the writers together under one heading, said: "That makes it sound as though we all know each other and sit around in cafés all day chatting" (Kramer 72).

Their theatre was as much concerned with the politics of the state (like Bond and his contemporaries) as it was with the politics of the stage. For them, no topic, no subject, no action, no condemnation was a theatrical taboo. Hence, the diversity of the subject matter explored in these plays: pornography in Anthony Neilson's *The Censor* (1997); homosexual rape, oral sex, hand jobs, ecstasy-induced states, rimming, capitalism, the phone sex trade and anal penetration with a fork in *Shopping and Fucking*; physically abusive fathers and the generational recycling of violence to their sons in Judy Upton's *Bruises* (1995); an act of rape committed by children in Rebecca Prichard's *Fair Game* (1997); cybersex in Marber's *Closer*; mental incarceration, verbal abuse, torture and murder in McDonagh's *The Beauty Queen of Leenane*; and the failures of National Health Service policies with regard to schizophrenics in Penhall's *Some Voices*. One of the more telling anecdotes about the effect of all the groundbreaking plays and subject matter being performed on stages around London was relayed by Dromgoole, who followed the producer Michael Codron out of a production of Samuel Adamson's *Clocks and Whistles* (1996) and overheard the following conversation: "'I liked that very much,' [Codron] said. Then, after a pause, he whispered, 'Was it any good?' 'Yes. Yes, it was … very good,' his friend replied. Michael looked happy, 'Was it? Oh good, I am glad.' I was delighted, not by the approval, nor by the insecurity, but by the suggestion that no one knew the rules anymore" (1).

Eventually, though, one critic did find a way to create a dichotomy of rules to help name the movement. "In-Yer-Face," which was crafted by Alexs Sierz, became the accepted moniker as well as the title of his era-defining book on these writers. Sierz defined what an In-Yer-Face play was:

> the language is usually filthy, characters talk about unmentionable subjects, take their clothes off, have sex, humiliate each another, experience unpleasant emotions, become suddenly violent. At its best, this kind of theatre is so powerful, so visceral, that it forces audiences to react: either they feel like fleeing the building or they are suddenly convinced that it is the best thing they have ever seen, and want all their friends to see it too [5].

Perhaps the most defining play of the era to create a feeling "so powerful, so visceral, that it forces audiences to react" was Kane's *Blasted*, which caught the public and the media's eye due to the major loathing the London theatre critics bestowed upon it. Their reviews were swift, brutal and dismissive. Charles Spencer from the *Daily Telegraph* termed *Blasted* "this nauseating dog's breakfast of a play," while Nick Curtis of the *Evening Standard* dismissed the work as "an artful chamber of horrors, designed to shock and nothing more." Paul Taylor of *The Independent* was perhaps the most descriptive in his assessment of the play: "Sitting through *Blasted* is a little like having your face rammed into an overflowing ash tray, just for starters, and then having your whole head held down in a bucket of offal." Clearly, the critics missed the politics of the piece as Kane queried what would Britain be like if Bosnian-like war atrocities occurred in Leeds. The graphic depiction of violence drew immediate parallels to Edward Bond's *Saved*,[5] which thirty years previously had provoked the same howls of protest, derision and ensuing media debate about the corruption of British theatre due to the graphic depiction of a baby being murdered on stage. The media launched a debate about the merits (or lack thereof) of the 23-year-old's play, and the fact that a woman was the writer of such material distressed a number of figures to no end.

Like Kane, her fellow writers were fascinated with the omnipresence, dangers and contemporary romanticizations of violence. Their plays provided a new examination of the violent facet of contemporary society which had become the norm for their generation, not only in the pop cultural iconography of films like Quentin Tarantino's *Reservoir Dogs* (1992) and Oliver Stone's *Natural Born Killers* (1994), both of which were cited by some commentators as major influences on the "In-Yer-Face" writers, but also in the news. Kane remarked: "I open up my newspaper and find headlines about murder and killing—the landscape is violent and [*Blasted*] is set within that. *Blasted* is about the effects of violence" (Roberts 25). Jez Butterworth, whose play *Mojo* drew immediate comparisons with Tarantino's work, eschewed the connection between him and the filmmaker, stressing that unlike Tarantino he does not think violence is funny. Instead, Butterworth said, "I'm interested in the devastation that [violence] causes, in the ways people *experience* violence" (Yates 11). In remarking on the prevalence of violence in his play, Anthony Neilson argued, "I think it's offensive when you don't feel appalled by violence" (Hemming, "Look" 17). Whereas Edward Bond in *Saved* used violence as a means to deconstruct capitalism's reliance on violence (suggesting an economic, governmental and political connection), these younger writers explored the personal stakes and ramifications of violence on the state of the individual as well as a commentary on society as a whole. In addition, the use of violence also provided a challenge to the conceits of the stage. Kane discussed the visceral power of Bond's play and its influence on her theatrical vision: "When I read *Saved*, I was deeply shocked by the baby being stoned. But then, I thought, there isn't anything you can't represent on stage. If you are saying you can't represent something, you are saying you can't talk about it, you are denying its existence, and that's an extraordinary ignorant thing to do" (Bayley, "A Very Angry" 25). Kane's sentiment was a basic principle of these new writers. The purpose behind their plays was to liberate and redefine the nature of the theatrical discourse of the British theatre and in so doing, they influenced the larger state of the British theatre.

Theatre managements saw an untapped financial potential in all the violence that the new plays sported. One of the most underrepresented and relished demographic was the male audience member under the age of 30, who rarely attended theatre but had the disposable income to do so. The success of the violence laden plays by Kane, Welsh, McDonagh and Ravenhill did not go unnoticed by the larger theatrical outlets, especially the Royal Shakespeare Company, which had its London home at the Barbican. In October 1997 the RSC unleashed a marketing campaign riding the violence of these new plays with the aim of attracting young male theatre goers to three Shakespearean plays *Coriolanus*, *Henry V* and *Hamlet*. The poster advertising *Coriolanus* featured a blood-spattered man. For *Henry V* the ad executives equated the battle of Agincourt with the drama and excitement of an away football game, but with the noted distinction that for Henry V and his undermanned "squad" "away games were like life and death" (Midgley 3). Finally, for *Hamlet*, the Prince of Denmark held Yorick's skull as if it were a football. In addition to the usual theatre advertising to be found in the Underground, the RSC placed ads in the sports pages of the London papers, thus immediately reinforcing the sports photos, headlines and scores with the Shakespearean plays and their titular characters. The ad's appropriation of football imagery also suggested to the male football fan that the Bard's plays feature the same excitement, drama, intrigue and rivalry of a Mersee side derby between Liverpool and Everton or the intensity of a match between Tottenham and Arsenal.

One playwright, who emerged at the same time as all these new writers and was prominently grouped with Ravenhill, Kane and McDonagh, was Joe Penhall, a journalist turned playwright. The impetus for his initial plays came from a similar influence as his peers—the streets around him. In his case as a reporter in Shepherd's Bush, many of the people he encountered comprised the ever growing and struggling multicultural population of London. Not finding success through the newspaper articles in order to draw attention to their plight, he turned to the stage. In this way he used the theatre to highlight the mental illnesses so visibly present in the London streets with his first full-length play *Some Voices*. His initial plays also dealt with lower-class, struggling, psychologically injured characters and the unsettled environment in the world around them. *Wild Turkey*, his first and only short play, examines the economic struggles of shop owners in Mile End and the brutality that exists in its streets after the shops close up. In *Some Voices* a pregnant woman is threatened by her brick-wielding boyfriend and later the attacker is struck in the head with a hammer. Another character douses petrol all over his brother's kitchen and himself, threatening to set himself and the space on fire. In *Pale Horse*, his second full-length play, the main character visits a sado-masochistic club/restaurant where food and abuse go hand in hand and later aids in the burying of a body of an abusive boyfriend of one of his employees. Clearly, the elements of sex and violence so prominent in the work of his peers also appear in his plays. And yet, London commentators saw something in his writing that differentiated him. Simon Fanshawe described Penhall as "a writer whose plays are unashamedly formal, even conservative in their structure, whose themes are deeply humane and who is talked about increasingly as having enough fashion-free depth to outrun the rest." However, upon a deeper examination of his writing one sees that Penhall's plays did not fit the tenor of the In-Yer-Face writers. (Just as if one looks more deeply at the other plays, they too begin to show characteristics that deviate from the prescribed pattern described by Sierz.) While the graphic nature of the litany of abuses that occur in his peer's plays provoked outrage and concern, his plays are comparatively tame. His plays do not feature graphic sexual acts. While there is violence, it is muted (usually occurring off-stage before and after scenes) as he is not interested in creating a shock effect around the violent actions of his characters, as was so prominent in Kane's *Blasted* and Ravenhill's *Shopping and Fucking*. The sexuality, violence and language are all tempered in deference to larger political ramifications and intentions behind his work. Unlike Kane and Ravenhill's experiences with the reaction to their plays, Penhall's meaning was never overwhelmed by the shock factor of the material.

Perhaps the most striking difference, though, when one looks at Penhall and his peers is his background. Unlike almost all the other In-Yer-Face writers, he was not a direct product of Thatcher's government, since he spent his formative years growing up in Australia rather than in the England of the 1970s and 1980s that experienced so much unrest. Penhall was born in the United Kingdom on August 23, 1967, as the youngest child of three to a dentist father, who put himself through medical school working a number of different jobs, including being a plumber, and a physiotherapist mother. His father was born in Durban, South Africa, to a Newcastle miner, who moved to South Africa to mine for gold, and a Scotswoman. His father became a conscientious objector to the South African policy of Apartheid and left his birth country, moving to England. When he was 23 years old, he burned his South African passport in protest in Trafalgar Square. Penhall traced his name back to tin miners in Cornwall. "I went to a tin miner's museum in Cornwall once and found records of one John Penhall (aka John Penhale) who was a miner and writer. He wrote the first ever book about tin mining" ("Q and A"). Penhall's tenaciousness in and about his plays reflects that same hardscrabble, diligent and hardworking attribute needed by miners to survive in such a difficult atmosphere.

When Penhall was four years old, his family packed up all of their belongings and moved to Perth, Australia. His family then moved again. This time to Adelaide, Australia, where, with the exception of a few months return to England when he was nine, Penhall remained until he left to attend the Sydney School of Art in 1988. He eventually left Sydney as well, moving to England. The moving back and forth between Australia and England as well as the changing locales within Australia had a significant effect on Penhall. When asked to describe his childhood, his adjective of choice has been that he had a peripatetic childhood. This sense of movement and never really finding one location as an element of one's sense of identity would become an important element of many of his male characters, who throughout his plays seek some defining moment, person and/or position (albeit physical, economic, social or familial) that will finally end their peripatetic wanderings, which take not only a physical form but also a psychological one as well.

With the exception of "being Pommy-bashed" by his Adelaide schoolmates (Maxwell), Penhall's early years were relatively happy.

> I grew up in a wonderful, joyful, affectionate seventies nuclear family. Very physical and demonstrative. When I was about four, my mum used to take me to work, to cookery classes, everywhere. She'd wear Pru Acton T-shirts and play the Beatles and cuddle me to her breasts, bundling me into an old Renault 4 and whisking me off to watch her perform physiotherapy or cook coq au vin. My dad coming home from work was the high point of my day ["Introduction" xiii-xiv].

However, when his father later lost his job, the idyllic happy home faded as the pressures upon his father to support his family weighed upon the entire familial atmosphere of the Penhall home, which later became an important influence on *The Bullet*, the most autobiographical play of his entire collection.

While Penhall has made his reputation as a writer of award-winning plays, compelling television dramas, and finely crafted film adaptations of successful novels, he also is a talented artist and musician, both skills he developed as a teen in Australia. Part of his attraction in moving to Sydney to go to art school was because he found he had a talent for silk screening, photography and cartoons. In addition to this artistic talent, he was a talented musician, having trained for a number of years in classical guitar, and for the three years prior to moving to Sydney he had written music and played in a number of bands, none of which were successful. However, he later found an overlap between his playwriting and musical skills, composing the music for the Bush Theatre production of his play *Love and Understanding*; co-writing some of the music for *Moses Jones*, a detective serial he wrote and produced for the BBC; and collaborating with Nick Cave, who scored the film *The Road*, which Penhall adapted for the screen from the Cormac McCarthy novel. In addition, after his initial success as a playwright, Penhall collaborated with Pete Townshend of The Who on adapting *Quadrophenia* into a stage musical.[6] The planned musical never came to fruition as the project was put on hiatus when Townshend and The Who returned to touring. Penhall's hope in going to art school was that he would not only be able to improve his artistic skills, but also connect with fellow students interested in forming a rock band, but he left after a semester because the student body "turned out to be full of vegetarians in Reboks" ("Q and A") and was "so bloody inarticulate" (East). Even though the art school rock band did not materialize, he found other musicians with whom to form bands, but like in Adelaide, none met with much success.

While Penhall had seen a few plays while in school in Adelaide, Sydney gave him his first real taste for theatre. A nearby fringe theatre called the Balmain Loft presented a season of Joe Orton plays, which was an early influence for him. In addition, during his formative years in Australia he also devoured the works of Charles Bukowski and Jack Kerouac. And while Penhall found the philosophy of these writers enticing and he did his own drifting from Adelaide to Sydney to finally London, he also did not completely embrace the mantras of their writings. Once on his own in Sydney, he worked diligently to support himself, albeit in a number of different ways. While he was able to make some money from the gigs his various bands booked, he also tried his hand at diverse jobs, ranging from kitchen work to journalism. In Sydney he wrote for one publication, *On the Street*, for about two years and was a production editor for *Australian Doctor Weekly*, where he found professional recognition of his artistic abilities, having photographs and some cartoons published. His latter job would later prove to be serendipitous, as a number of Penhall's plays would critique the medical world by examining the debilitating state of patient care, the exhaustion and ethics of doctors and the questionable policies of the National Health Service. The topic of mental health was also a driving catalyst for many of his plays, as Penhall admitted, "It's one of the few things I both really care about and find enigmatic" (Hemming, "It's a Mad" 11). His works would cover a variety of topics relating to the mental breakdown of its characters, including schizophrenia in *Some Voices* and *Blue/Orange*; the widening depression of a widower dealing with his wife's death in *Pale Horse*; the self-destructive behavior of a best friend in *Love and Understanding*; and the complete destruction of an inventor's sense of self due to torture in *Landscape with Weapon*. In addition, being the son of two parents who worked in the medical profession inculcated in him a sense "that doctors were somehow unimpeachable" (Logan). His plays, though, would dispel this notion, as his plays note that "there's as much salaciousness and dishonesty [in that profession] as anywhere else" (Logan).

When he moved to London in 1990, he originally gave himself a deadline of only four months to succeed. While living on the dole for a little bit of time, he attempted once again to get a band together. Once again his band did not meet with much success, but Penhall credits this time in London as a boon to his musical skills, which improved considerably. He also tried his hand at various nowhere jobs and restaurant gigs, including running a pizza bar. He was eventually successful in finding a paying, successful career, landing a job as a journalist with the *Hammersmith Guardian*.[7] The various stories that he covered and the beat he traveled, which included West London's Shepherd Bush, prompted his adrenaline to run. On any day of the week an editor would tell Penhall that "there's a double murder on Shepherd's Bush Green, go and get the skinny on it" (Ellis). For the burgeoning journalist it was an extremely exciting time. In addition, covering the diverse and multicultural socio-economic area of Shepherd's Bush provided Penhall with voluminous material to whet his theatrical interests, including "the man who laughed so much he fell off a wall and killed himself; the Polish couple who blew each other's brains out on Shepherd's Bush Green because they were going to be made redundant at the same time" (Ellis). The stories and people he met were compelling and he admitted that "it was the beginning of me writing plays" (Ellis).

What was it, though, that attracted him to plays over other genres? Penhall acknowledged that a play allows you to "get things off your chest. Plays are kind of confessional and testimonial. You can't write it unless it connects deeply with your psyche and your life. If you have an axe to grind and a big mouth the theatre is the place to be" (Horsburgh). In addition, he wanted to create characters similar to those persons that he covered in Shepherd's Bush, characters that "live and breathe in a way that got in people's faces and made them feel. Theatre was the obvious place to do it" (Ellis). Finally, Penhall enjoyed a good argument and he found it impossible to have one with his newspaper editor, fellow guests at a dinner party, or with the "three dozen Nigerians and a mad Scottish chef" (Litson) with whom he worked at a restaurant. Instead, Penhall realized that the "best way to have those arguments seemed to be in the theatre" (Litson).

Having grown up in Australia, he saw London from the eyes of an outsider, and thus spotted injustices where other citizens saw the status quo, the prime example being his shock about the plethora of homeless people on the streets. His sense of the injustice of their treatment became one of the influences for him to write *Some Voices*. This experience with his first full-length play gave him the opportunity to define his theatrical philosophy surrounding his role as a playwright and the intentionality of his written work. Both had to be "a thorn in the flesh" of not only the audience members, as he hoped to prick their sense of social injustice (Rees, "Vexed"), but also the various institutions that control the life of British citizens. His plays have embraced this mantra as he has aimed to point out the wrongs of society, including the contemporary failure of institutions and the community to provide the support for those mourning; the emotional and psychological toll redundancy plays upon the individual and families; the destructive nature and unethical actions of tabloid journalism; and the dicey ethics behind weapons manufacturing. Penhall remarked on how his writing provided him with an opportunity on saying what needed to be said. "I love detonating a story in a room and watching the effect it has" (McLauglin 5). In discussing the writing of *Blue/Orange* and its confrontation of racism in Britain: "I knew that the subject was dynamite. But I knew it had to be said. It was either going to go off in my face or it would work and open up this whole issue and start people talking" (Smith). Since 1993 Penhall has been writing plays that have provoked the arguments in which he so wants to be engaged. In embracing such a confrontational position, he has successfully become London theatre's own "thorn in the flesh."

1

Wild Turkey *and the New Man, the New Lad and the Penhall Male*

Mike Newell's *Four Weddings and a Funeral* (1994) turned the British New Man into a global phenomenon. The reason? Newell had found the best typification of the New Man in the stuttering, eyelid-twittering, moppish hair features of Hugh Grant, who prior to this lead romantic role had appeared as a supporting player in the art house-oriented films *Maurice* (1987) and *Impromptu* (1991). This Richard Curtis–written film brought Grant to the attention of the world and, more importantly, Hollywood, making him an international star. In the film his character Charles watches his friends marry around him while he pines after an American woman, named Carrie, who keeps flitting through his social circles at various matrimonial ceremonies and one funereal event. This film crystallized what would become the most representative characteristic of the myriad romantic leads that Hugh Grant would play: his complete and utter inability to articulate his feelings to his romantic interest. He stammers, stutters, pauses, erms and ehms, lankily and uncomfortably shifts his body and looks everywhere but at the woman in question, as in this memorable quote from the film when he announces his love for Carrie.

> Ehm, look. Sorry, sorry. I just, ehm, well, this is a very stupid question ... but I just wondered, by any chance, ehm, eh, I mean obviously not because I guess I've only slept with 9 people, but-but I-I just wondered ... ehh. I really feel, ehh, in short, to recap it slightly in a clearer version, eh, the words of David Cassidy in fact, eh, while he was still with the Partridge family, eh, "I think I love you," and eh, I-I just wondered by any chance you wouldn't like to ... Eh ... Eh.... No, no, no of course not ... I'm an idiot, he's not ... excellent, excellent, fantastic, eh, I was gonna say lovely to see you, sorry to disturb.... Better get on....

While it makes for a funny scene, it also demonstrates Richard Curtis and Hugh Grant's pinpoint reimagining of the New Man as a festering gob, who is so delicately structured and so overwhelmed by his more experienced female companion (his reference to having slept with nine people is in contrast to her admission to him that she had slept with 32) that he is reduced to relying on the shallow lyric from a Partridge Family song to express his feelings rather than directly stating his affection for her. In addition, he never allows her to answer his questions but instead answers for her. Their entire relationship is summed up through his speech, including the fumbling courtship and the ignominious break-up.[1] Grant and Curtis would continue to collaborate in documenting the utter romantic ineptitude of this British male type with *Notting Hill* (1999), where Hugh Grant's character once again stutters his way through a relationship with another American woman, this time an internationally recognized movie star, and then again in *Love Actually* (2003), where in an extremely unlikely display of romantic inability, Hugh Grant's prime minister character becomes smitten with one of the Downing Street staff members. In assessing the significance of these romantic roles Andrew Spicer writes that "the independence and strength of the women in these films allow Grant ... to adopt feminine qualities. This is manifested in his insecurity and compliance..., his lack of ambition and his desire for stability and heterosexual union, thereby fulfilling his supportive New Man credentials" (187). While Hugh Grant is the face of this cinematic recreation of the British New Man wilting in response to his strong female co-stars' characters, the initial emergence of this male type in the 1980s was also in response to a woman, but not a romantic leading lady, but instead to one of the most powerful women in the world.

The predominant figure looming over the landscape of Britain in the 1980s was Prime Minister Margaret Thatcher, whose influence redefined the country's internal features politically, economically, socially and culturally, while also prompting the re-emerging identity of Britain as a player on the world stage. While a British woman controlled and fostered the world's new perception of the island nation, cultural changes were afoot in relation to the country's male population. British men, like their country's world image, were undergoing a facelift as a visible portion of them metamorphosed into the New Man. And just who was the New Man? He was actually a type comprised of two bifurcated personalities. Tim Edwards in *Men in the Mirror*, his book on male fashion, noted that "as a result of the impact of second-wave feminism in particular, men and masculinity were under attack, and a new form of masculinity that was more caring, nurturing and sensitive — or, alternatively, more narcissistic, passive, and introspective — was developing" (39). There was the nurturing, sensitive man, who, according to Edwards, was best captured iconographically through a Calvin Klein ad for the cologne Eternity that featured an infant being held by a man (39). The magazine *Arena*, which produced its first issue in the midst of the rise of the New Man and focused on fashion, entertainment, sport and females, described this male type as "sensitive, charming, [and] considerate. He hoped one day to own an Audi and an

Armani. But he'd do the housework and not be afraid to shed a tear" ("Our Decade"). This nurturing male, while still actively invested in attaining material goods, hence the Audi and Armani reference, was heavily influenced and swayed by the rhetoric of the women's movement.[2] The other side of the New Man, though, the non-nurturing, narcissist male focused on style and fashion. Edwards notes that for this iteration of the New Man, "those with the looks, the income and the time on their side have never had it so good in terms of the opportunities which the expansion of men's style and fashion have to offer them" (134). While the sensitive male could be found around the country, the prime location for the fashion-focused incarnation of the New Man was London where the booming economic opportunities of the monetarist system put in place by Thatcher's government was enjoyed most among City types.

However, it was not just the "loadsamoney"-oriented businessmen and middle-class fathers and husbands who were experiencing this transformation. It was the younger generation as well. Rather than being influenced by the rise of feminism, though, these males were being chemically converted into the New Man by the nightclub drug ecstasy, especially during the height of the rave years in the late 1980s and early 1990s. In *Generation Ecstasy* Simon Reynolds noted that ecstasy intensified "the pleasure of physical expression while completely emptying out the sexual content of dance" (247). The "emptying out of sexual content" would prove to be a significant contributor to the changing dynamics of the sex scene in the clubs precisely because of the drug's powerful side effect on males. Specifically, as Reynolds wrote later, "E is notorious for making erection difficult and male orgasm virtually impossible. A real dick-shriveller, it also gets rid of the thinks-with-his-dick mentality, turning rave into space where girls can feel free to be friendly with strange men, even snog them, without fear of sexual consequences" ("Rave" 88). Because of ecstasy, the club scene no longer fulfilled its social purpose of providing a predatory space for the hunting of female patrons, as it did in the 1970s and early 1980s. Instead, the club and the men who frequented it became absent of threat. Ben Malbon's *Clubbing* addressed this changing dynamic. He interviewed one female raver named Carol who remarked, "you can talk to hundreds of blokes and there's nothing in it all…, whereas if you're going to a pub and a bloke comes up and talks to you or you go over and talk to a bloke they automatically think you fancy them" (42). According to club-going journalist Louise Gray, "People were very cuddly, and that was very nice: you could be cuddled by complete strangers in a totally nonthreatening way, 'cos you knew nothing was going to happen" (Reynolds, *Generation* 63). The predatory nature of the club male vaporized under the drug's influence, and in his place materialized the male "cuddler." And this dramatic shift in the masculine demeanor led some social critics to remark that ecstasy not only took away the predatory, sexual drive of males, but also contributed to their increased social feminization. Reynolds noted: "There's a sense in which E, by feminizing the man, allows him to access *jouissance* independently rather than seek it through women. Hence the self-pleasuring, masturbatory quality to rave dance" ("Rave" 89). With acid house's and raves' seemingly exponential growth every weekend came the reciprocal increase in the "feminization" of males every weekend night.

However, Imelda Whelehan, author of *Overloaded*, doubted the actual existence of the New Man. She argued that the New Man "was a media vision of what pro-feminist men would look like" and it was "not surprising that we see elements of this negative reaction coming across in men's magazines" (61). In particular, she referenced *Loaded*, founded in reaction to the male fashion obsession found in *GQ*, *Arena* and *Esquire*. Mick Bunnage, one of *Loaded*'s original writers, argued that the magazine was "being really honest about being blokes and how rubbish blokes are about everything.... There's so much more fun to be had getting drunk, fucking about and making stuff up" (Southwell 28). In addition, Mary Ann Hobbs, who worked at *Loaded* before becoming a Radio One DJ, noted that "the nineties started with *Loaded*.... All that desperate uptight eighties hypocritical rhetoric crashed.... *Loaded* fucked it up the arse!... There was nothing genuine about New Man eighties idealism" (Robb 43). As the New Lad emerged, this attitude would become a prevalent one.

Even as Hugh Grant was promoting the British New Man on screens to audiences around the world, the New Lad was energetically emerging as a slap back at the fashion-loving, nurturing sense of a feminized masculine self. John Beynon in *Masculinities and Culture* remarked that this new male type rejected the New Man philosophy of men "as the fragile sex" whose "sensitivity and emotional literacy [should] be at the heart of the new masculinity" (93). Tim Southwell, co-editor and founder of *Loaded*, which became the touchstone of New Laddism, wrote that his magazine's message was "don't take us too seriously, we're blokes and we're useless.... We like football, but that doesn't mean we're hooligans. We like drinking but it doesn't mean that as soon as the pub shuts down we turn into wife-beating misogynists. We like looking at pictures of fancy ladies sometimes but that doesn't mean we want to rape them" (100–1). Rosie Boycott, who co-founded the feminist magazine *Spare Rib* and later became an editor at *The Independent* and then *Daily Express*, shared a similar perspective in describing what kind of man British women wanted: "Women can't bear the idea of a bloke, who goes to the supermarket and buys the nappies. It provokes a deep-seated mistrust. You want to be equal in the office, but who wants equal sex? Sod the PC. Let's just do what turns us on" (Southwell 105). In essence, *Loaded* and its like-minded newsstand brethren of *FHM* and *Maxim* reminded the demographic of lads about the important tenets of "tits, booze and bums" (Calcutt 271), all of which had been, for the most part, suppressed by the New Man with the rise of feminism and the cultural conditions of Thatcher's England. Whelehan though saw problems with the New Lad's cocksure attitude toward women. She described him as "almost always white; part soccer thug, part lager lout, part arrant sexist" (58). In addition, "from a feminist position it is difficult not to interpret the new lad as a nostalgic revival of old patriarchy; a direct challenge to feminism's call for social transformation by reaffirming — albeit 'ironically' — the changing nature of gender relations and sexual roles" (6).

The New Man philosophy of bettering oneself and recognizing the partnership with women had officially crashed and burned. This New Lad, as described by Andrew Calcutt, was part of a "generation who did not know how to become men, so they acted out a pantomime version of traditional masculinity, topped with a cheeky smile to let you know they were only joking" (271). Whelehan concurred with Calcutt by noting that the moniker of New Lad came from "an epithet used to describe behaviour associated with adolescence, such adolescent behaviour has come to determine men's natural state of being, and women are implicitly asked to accept it" (9). Despite the dismay of some about the returning rise of patriarchal fervor, the New Lad quickly assumed a firm grip on the British public and media. In fact, "By the summer of 1994 *Loaded* was synonymous with irreverence and laddishness was in the air as a backlash against 1980s over-dressed, narcissistic new man.... Lads' programmes dominated television ratings, most notably *Men Behaving Badly* and *Fantasy Football League*" (Beynon 111). The lyrics of Brit pop, which was "invented, played, written about and bought by white middle-class males" (Calcutt 108) and featured bands like Oasis, Pulp and Blur, reinforced the behavior and posture of the New Lad. Clearly, the public was more open to seeing "boys being boys" rather than men behaving nicely.

In addition to appearing on television, in the magazine stalls and on the best-seller list of novels,[3] the New Lad was also making his appearance felt on the British stage. For the previous two decades the British theatre had been a bastion of groundbreaking work by female playwrights, like Caryl Churchill, Sarah Daniels, Pam Gems and Timberlake Wertenbaker, who challenged the traditional nature of the patriarchal view of the British stage. However, by the mid–1990s the British stage was awash with lad-friendly plays, including Anthony Neilson's *Penetrator* (1993), Nick Grosso's *Peaches* (1994) and Jez Butterworth's *Mojo* at the Royal Court; Simon Bent's *Bad Company* (1994), Tracy Letts' *Killer Joe* (1995), and the theatrical version of *Trainspotting* at the Bush; and Patrick Marber's *Dealer's Choice* (1995) at the Royal National Theatre. In December 1995, Phyllis Nagy, an American playwright who had relocated to London and found great success with *Butterfly Kiss* (1994), and Mel Kenyon, a theatrical agent for Nagy as well as Sarah Kane, wrote a condemning and genuinely fearful op-ed piece for the *Guardian* about the present state of the cultural landscape. The two penned that the rise of the New Lad on stage, in magazines and on television

> is only one of the symptoms of a much more serious underlying illness: the fact that violent misogyny is alive, kicking and applauded throughout England. For

women in their thirties, who grew up with feminism, a fervent belief in equal opportunities and a sneaking suspicion we might be rather brighter than the boys, to realise that misogyny was never really conquered but simply lay low until it was ready for a counter attack is terrifying [2:7].

Unsurprisingly, their letter did little to quell the tide. In the months after the letter was published post-feminist plays continued to proliferate, including productions of Bent's *Goldhawk Road* (1996) and Conor McPherson's *This Lime Tree Bower* (1996) at the Bush as well as Martin McDonagh's *The Beauty Queen of Leenane* and Mark Ravenhill's *Shopping and Fucking* at the Royal Court. In 1997 David Edgar noted the proliferation of male-oriented plays and remarked that "these plays address masculinity and its discontents as demonstrably as those of the early 1960s addressed class and those of the 1970s the failures of social democracy. And [with the success of Marber's *Closer*] there is a sign that plays about boys being boys have yet to run their course" ("Plays"). All of these productions over a four-year period continued to solidify the appearance of the lad in his various guises on the stage. Perhaps one of the most representative writers who captured the voice of the New Lad was Nick Grosso, author of *Peaches, Sweetheart* and *Real Classy Affair* (1998). At the end of Act 1 of *Peaches* Frank reveals a similar philosophy as expressed by Tim Southwell and his *Loaded* buddies.

> I tell ya, sometimes *I* feel like Bogart — one guy and 57 babes. The way I see it, there's only one of you, and about six million babes in this town — so whichever way you look you're outnumbered. So you better get to work. There's no point being old and saying you lived a little, talking about the way — you gotta talk about *babes* when you're old, tell your grandkids about it. Fuck the fucking war! [36].

As Aleks Sierz's *In-Yer-Face* so thoroughly documents, the mid–1990s ushered in a brief, but potent, era when young male playwrights (and a few female playwrights) dominated the London stage and through their plays they reflected the daily world surrounding them, and the appearance of the New Lad was a dominant and prominent feature of their storytelling.

Many critics, including Aleks Sierz, lumped Joe Penhall in with his contemporaries as an "in-yer-face" writer and a creator of "lad"-like work.[4] Such a designation as being part of that cultural movement toward laddism and the glorification of their misogynistic characteristics was incorrect in describing the early plays of Joe Penhall. Unlike his "In-Yer-Face" contemporaries, Penhall's plays were not interested in documenting the rise and boyish acts of the New Lads, but instead delved deeper into the pressing situation facing men who did not fall into easy, culturally chic classification of British masculinity. They depicted men who struggled with their uncertainty about their place in the world economically, socially, familially and politically. After discussing the two types of cultural definitions of masculinities that emerged in the 1980s and 1990s and considering the permutations and importance of those respective movements, John Beynon in *Masculinities and Culture* concluded: "While there is widespread acknowledgement that masculinity has changed considerably during the 1980s and 1990s, there is, I believe, no longer any clear consensus as to what the new man actually stands for" (120). And that interest in the uncertainty of a man's status is precisely at the heart of the early plays of Penhall.

More than likely, one reason for the absence of this mindset behind his plays is precisely because Penhall moved to London in 1990 from Australia, missing all the movement around the emergence of the New Man. According to Penhall, once he arrived in London he was far more worried about earning a living rather than tapping into the cultural zeitgeist of the time as he worked a number of menial, low-paying jobs before finally landing a newspaper reporter position. With that kind of personal working experience at the forefront of Penhall's early years in London, it is not surprising that the focus of his first plays was on the exertion of lower-class males to survive in London in the 1990s. Foregrounding this difficulty he focused on relationships between friends, brothers, families and lovers in relation to the world of work. This direction of Penhall's writing was noted by Dominic Dromgoole, the artistic director of the Bush theatre during the explosion of new writing in the mid-1990s. He wrote in *The Full Room* that Penhall "prefers the epic within the domestic" (222). Penhall refused to endorse the contemporary trend of the shallow, "bird"- and football-focused New Lad. Instead, he created richly textured, at times Chekhovian, male characters with deeply seated complexities. Penhall admitted that his male characters were "quite psychologically feminine blokes.... They don't even understand women half the time. They're not pursuing money or power or pussy — what they're trying to grab hold of is something that's quite small and delicate, almost existential" (Hoggard 6). His characters represent those males of the 1980s and early 1990s who found themselves in a crisis of masculinity because the new definitions of masculinity did not conform to their economic and social situation. Beynon remarked that among the lost generation of males who found themselves unclaimed by the cultural cliques "[m]any remain bad at acknowledging and expressing feelings and are trapped between old-style, machismo and nurturing 'new man-ism'" (72). If the New Man was represented by Hugh Grant's romantic comedy characters and the New Lad was found on the Tube peering out from behind the open copies of *Loaded*, *FHM* and *Maxim*, then the men that Beynon described and Penhall captured were best represented by the cultural touchstones of men in films like Ken Loach's *Riff-Raff* (1991), Mark Herman's *Brassed Off* (1996) and Peter Cattaneo's *The Full Monty* (1997), where lower-class characters struggled to hold on to their jobs and make a mark economically, socially and familially by re-establishing themselves and their masculine characteristics of breadwinner and family man within their community. This crisis of position plays prominently throughout his first three plays and it is in *Wild Turkey* where his male characters struggle not only with their role in society as successful and professional members of the economic landscape but also as members of a community of men.

Before becoming a playwright full time, one of the menial jobs Penhall had after moving to London from Sydney was the manager of a gourmet pizza place. The neighborhood surrounding the restaurant was home to a local criminal, who was infamous for using a claw hammer to attack people. On one occasion the thug's teenage son burst into the dining area of the pizza parlor with a loaded air pistol. Penhall explained what happened next: "When [the teenager] got the hiding he deserved, his father came around, pulled a knife and wrecked the place in the middle of the night" ("Re: E-mail"). That incident provided the impetus for *Wild Turkey*, his first play, which premiered at the London New Play Festival at the Old Red Lion Pub in 1993.[5]

Upon first glance, one might consider the piece to be a shortened British version of David Mamet's *American Buffalo* (1975), as the play, like Mamet's, focuses on the oppressive nature of capitalism on choices made by three lower-class males and their ensuing interactions with various criminal activities.[6] Both plays ask: what is more important: economic status or friendship? *Wild Turkey* focuses on Stu, a burger bar owner who has relocated his business to a socially and economically challenged location; Ben, his best friend, who also serves as an unpaid restaurant employee as well as the live-in security guard of the premises; and Danny, the outsider of the group, who provides handyman assistance as well as procures items needed by business owners on the street through evening thieving forays. The play takes place over a twelve-hour period from the close of business to the opening the next morning. As the play opens, Ben and Stu close up while discussing the paltry day's earnings and the questionable safety of their new neighborhood. A bloody Danny arrives, relaying a story of almost being run down on the street and his retributive beating of the car's driver. However, Danny's encounter follows him into the restaurant in the guise of a giant of a man, who demands liquor, threatens all three men, and then beats up Danny after recognizing him as his assailant. The first act ends with Stu discovering his car has been stolen. The second act opens the next morning with the discovery of a break-in, including the theft of the cash box, which contained all of the previous day's earnings, and the destruction of the front windows. Danny returns, claiming to have found Stu's stolen car, now completely wrecked. Stu soon realizes Danny's culpability in the theft of his car, and in order to protect himself Danny attempts to turn Ben against Stu. However, in the process inadvertently reveals that he was the one who stole the cash box and destroyed the premises. When Stu returns from dealing with the police, Danny hits Stu in the head with a baseball bat, smashes more of the restaurant and leaves. The play ends with Stu and Ben beginning to put the restaurant back in order, so they can open for business.

While the piece premiered at the New Play Festival, no London critics wrote a review of the production. The closest remark to a review occurred in Jeremy Kingston's review of other productions at the festival, when Kingston admitted he missed Penhall's *Wild Turkey*, which he described as "a jaunty, raunchy tale of life in a burger bar."[7] The only reviews which exist for the play stem from its premiere in Sydney, Australia, at the Old Fitzroy Theatre in 1999. Colin Rose of *The Sun Herald* dubbed it "a juvenile piece of writing," while Carrie Kablean of *The Sunday Telegraph* noted that while it was his first play, it was not a play "on which to base his reputation."

Wild Turkey begins what will be a continuing interest on the part of Penhall in having his plays revolve around work as the setting and main focus for his characters. In their work experience they struggle to stay afloat economically, socially and psychologically. This experience can be a challenging and difficult one to face, and, according to Nigel Edley and Margaret Wetherell in their study *Men in Perspective: Practice, Power and Identity*, "Many men, then, are in a situation where … their *real* experience of work is one of powerlessness" (103). Stu's sense of control over the restaurant faces a triple threat of economic, geographic and security issues. Despite his position of being restaurant owner and his proud claim of being a capitalist, he battles mightily to make a profit. For unexplained reasons, Stu has moved his restaurant from a successful location in Battersea to this new economically depressed location in Mile End. He reminds Ben, "We had it all, Ben. Didn't we? The Clam Bake. Nice little restaurant. Friendly clientele. Happy people" (215). His new digs are not as glamorous or successful.

As the play opens, Stu counts the take for the day, only 95 pounds, all of which he stores in a shoebox that he encourages Ben to hide under his bed upstairs. Partly defining the economic difficulty is the neighborhood in which they now find themselves. While they have control over the menu, they have no control over the outside world and its hampering influence upon them and their business. The play's opening highlights the tension and difficulty involved with Stu's business placed in the midst of a rough neighborhood with new, unpredictable neighbors:

> BEN: Some feller completely off his head. Just screaming into the night....
> Don't go out there.... Just some nutcase....
> STU: You're right. Just abusing the world in general.
> *He peeks through the door.*
> *He's vomiting now.*
> *He returns and sits with a sigh.*
> Look at it out there. A fuckin' jungle [214–5].

Grosso's *Real Classy Affair* shares the same attitude about the shape of the streets of London,[8] as Billy and Stan discuss the theme for Stan's proposed restaurant.

> BILLY: I'd go continental … to make people forget they're in England.
> *Stan looks bemused.*

STAN: why dya wanna do that?
Billy points outside.
BILLY: have you been out lately?
STAN: yeh.
BILLY: then you know.
STAN: know what?
BILLY: know England is on its *knees*!
Stan looks bemused.
STAN: it's just a bit *cold* that's all.
BILLY: Stan, this land is going to the *dogs* and when it *does* the few lucky punters in your bistro will survey the continental décor and have a *lot* to thank you for believe me [100–1].

In addition to the crazies outside, there have been recent break-ins at other businesses and Ben has been held up in the restaurant by a man with a knife. While Stu's concerns are economic in nature, Ben's sense of powerlessness rests in his constant state of fear. After being held up once, he fears more reprisals. He has lost any sense of comfort and self-confidence in protecting himself and the premises. He confesses his fear to Danny, who tells him: "You don't wanna be scared, mate. Life's too short to be scared. You wanna get out there, show 'em what you're made of. You wanna keep a big lump of four-by-two by your bed and if there's any trouble you take it down and show 'em the business end" (241). Stu, though, pooh-poohs Ben's concerns (and, in turn, his masculinity) about being held up by reminding him that it was a blunt knife, "blunt as a baby's arse" (207). While Ben presses that more robberies are likely, Stu is less worried, telling him that the incident was a one-off. However, Ben continues to press, asking Stu to acquire a grille on the windows as well as a safe, all of which Stu refuses to do. In this difference of opinion about the safety of Ben's person and the premises and the daily earnings exists the crucial disjunction between the two as Ben's concerns are vetoed by Stu's finances. And Ben confronts Stu on this point exactly, "I'm saying the money is becoming ... you are becoming ruled by the money side of things. By business." To which Stu replies, "I am sorry for being a capitalist" (208). True, Stu views all by the bottom line of money, but he simply cannot afford the security measures proposed by Ben. Instead, he offers Ben all the protection he will need: a baseball bat, instead of the four-by-two proposed by Danny. And while economically the baseball bat, which Danny had previously given to him, is a *gratis* item against his budget, he is not completely guided by economics. Friendship is crucial for Stu, and this element drives his refusal because if a safe and grille are acquired, then Ben will be out of a job, which Stu does not want to happen. He explains, "It's in your best interests for us not to get security.... And it's in your favour that we are at risk, twenty-four hours a day. Seven days a week. We need you.... You are the only person I can trust in this life. You are a friend instead of just another nutpot employee" (209–11). For Stu, despite the economic struggles that he faces, he still believes fervently in his restaurant and the fact that it is rooted upon the building block of his friendship with and reliance on Ben. For him, there is a benefit of being part of a community and Ben and Stu contribute to it. For him, his restaurant goes beyond merely the till. He tells Ben: "We are doing something good here.... We are doing something important.... We cook hamburgers.... We are entrepreneurs.... It's the new thing" (211). Despite Stu and Ben's altruistic mantra about running a restaurant, the economic struggle, high-risk neighborhood, and the lack of security highlight the precariousness and possible powerlessness of both of their economic positions.

However, the greatest threat to their capitalistic dream comes from yet another force upon which they have no control: another person. The real representation of male powerlessness rests with Danny, who, unlike the other two, lacks any economic foothold, even a precarious one like Stu and Ben's. Completely on his own, he relies on businesses on the street to want either the stolen goods of dubious quality he acquires or his ability as a handyman, previously playing the roles of locksmith and cobbler for Stu. Based on Stu and Ben's conversation, it appears that Danny is successful in both services he provides to the street as they talk about him confidently and even a bit jealously because of Danny's seemingly enticing position of freedom in the neighborhood as a freelancer. His arrival at the restaurant also suggests power in his position as they await him and keep looking outside for his arrival. However, undercutting their words about Danny's prowess is the fact that throughout the first part of the act Stu and Ben struggle to get the stolen television from Danny to work so they can watch a boxing match.

With his entrance, as he yells, "Fucking fucking fucking fucking SHIT!" (216), which is reminiscent but not quite as vituperative and misogynistic as Teach's first entrance in *American Buffalo*,[9] Danny appears to be powerful and in control as he relays a story about a car nearly running him over and his response of viciously beating up the driver. The power and presence inherent in his entrance actually indicates the start of his downfall as the malfunctioning television is immediately brought up and Stu demands: "I want a new TV.... And a satellite dish. Now don't fuck me about" (218). As soon as the issue surrounding the television is solved, a loud, threatening hammering starts on the restaurant door. Danny assures them that no one can get into the restaurant. "They can't pick that lock—not after I fixed it. Nobody can.... They're not coming in. Nobody's coming in here. I defy anybody to—" (219), and then, of course, defying the authority of Danny's statement and his craftsmanship, someone enters. In this case a giant of a man, looking for his attacker. As the large man enters the restaurant and demands a drink, Stu and Ben cower before him. Danny though stands up to him but quickly finds a knife being held up to his neck. The giant forces Danny to lick his boots—"What kind of a man are you? Licking the piss off my boots" (225)—and then throws him across the room into the tables. The giant departs, leaving the three men to face the violence and anger that entered and then just as quickly exited the space. Through the pressure of Ben and Stu, Danny reveals that the giant was the man he had beat up outside, causing him to pursue him to Stu's restaurant for revenge. Stu and Ben are overwhelmed by the violence and the danger in which they were put. They blame Danny for bringing him to their place of work and tell him if anything else happens to the restaurant it will be Danny's fault. Danny, though, doesn't see it that way. At first he questions the masculinity and power of Stu and Ben. "You people are women" (229). He then takes a different tack and likens their experience with the giant as similar to a band of brothers in the war.

> DANNY: We fought together tonight. Side by side. Doesn't that mean anything to you?
> STU (*puzzled*): No.
> BEN: No.
> DANNY: You don't know what that means?
> STU: No.
>   *Slight pause.*
> DANNY: I don't either ... but believe me, it's meaningful [230].

Danny's attempt to cement a bond between him and the two men fails. He is an outsider, when it comes to the dynamic between the men in the restaurant. He provides a service and is welcome when he provides it, but his impulsive actions of violence and unpredictable behavior, like the citizens on the street outside the restaurant, constantly keeps him from being part of their community. As Stu tells Ben, Danny "used to fix things, now he fucks them up" (264). Danny comes from the world of the street, while Ben and Stu are from the world of business, and ultimately both cannot co-exist in Stu's restaurant.

The second act only reasserts the continuing difficulty Danny experiences. He longs to reassert himself with Stu, after his embarrassing display the night before. He enters, claiming to have found Stu's smashed up, stolen car, even though he is extremely vague about where he actually found it. Seeing the destruction in the restaurant from an overnight break-in, he uses the crime as a way to move his way into the good graces and stable community of Stu. He appropriates Ben's fear of more violence as a means to break up the relationship between Stu and Ben, offering himself to Stu as a much more solid line of defense for the restaurant than the hesitant Ben. "I don't mean this in any bad way ... but ... he's a berk. He don't know what he's doing.... I can always help you out. Till this blows over" (246). For Stu, even though he is angry with Ben's inability to confront the burglar during the break-in, his commitment to Ben and his role in the success of the restaurant is paramount to Danny's attempts to sway him. His allegiance of friendship to Ben is far greater than to Danny. When pressed further, Stu offers the final defense of his decision to stick with Ben over Danny.

STU: Look man, I'm just trying to run a business.
DANNY: And that's all that matters is it? Your business.
Pause.
STU: Yes [247].

The need for a definitive placement within the concept of an economic status is paramount for Danny because of his failures with the television he sold Stu, his beating by the giant man and the dismissal of his importance in the light of Stu running a business. Danny is in need of verifying his abilities, having completely had his ego and personal representation undermined. Adding to Danny's powerlessness is the fate of his brother, Ives, who has escaped from a mental institution.[10] Throughout the first act Danny desperately tries to find his brother and, lacking a car of his own, ends up stealing Stu's car in order to drive around town looking for him.

Danny's mental and economic condition of increasing powerlessness in the face of all the incidents surrounding him reflects the same characteristics Edley and Wetherell noted about the struggle of men in the 1980s and 1990s who struggled to define themselves through an economic identity. They wrote that "divisions in experience between the private and the public, and the institutionalisation of competitiveness cause a process of 'depersonalisation'.... Men become focused on maintaining an increasingly precarious masculine authority, and familiar with violence both as a strategy, and as the potential object of the violence of others" (101). This strategy of violence comes to the forefront for Danny as he realizes, due to Stu rejecting his verbal arguments to replace Ben, he has lost the one grasp he had at attaining a sense of economic identity and responsibility. The powerlessness of Danny's situation the night before manifested itself through the violence of crashing Stu's car, breaking into the café, destroying the front windows and finally stealing the miniscule proceeds from the night before. However, with this rebuff his violent streak has yet to be completed.

After talking to the police, Stu accuses Danny of all of the crimes befalling his establishment, asking, "Why did you do this to us, Dan?" (259). Danny at first denies any wrongdoing but then explodes: "You people are parasites. You are your business. You don't deserve this ... all this ... you don't deserve anything!" (260). He then takes the baseball bat and hits Stu in the head. In defense of this brutal attack, he tells Ben: "He betrayed his friends.... Thinks he's above us. Thinks cos he's got a bit of paper ... a thing saying he's in charge, saying he owns a thing, it makes him alright. Better than us" (260). Amelia Howe Kritzer noted the importance that economics plays in the works of the new writers of the mid–1990s. She suggested:

> Significantly, these plays attribute more of a role to economics than to politics in structuring the lives of members of their generation.... Material culture forms the basis of recognition, even for the most deprived and isolated of the characters. The playwrights, to various degrees, condemn materialism, identifying it as a

source of exploitation, but the characters in their plays fail to free themselves from the habits of materialist consumption [64].

Danny completely encapsulates this sense of investment in materialism and the recognition that comes from possessing objects and status, even if it involves working at Stu's restaurant. Both Ben and Stu possess a status of solidity on the street, while he is a nomad moving between all the various establishments, relying on them to keep him afloat. Unlike them, he is not in control of his own economic possibilities.

Over the course of the play Danny's masculinity is systematically deconstructed, and like Teach in *American Buffalo*, who, upon losing status with Don, takes a pig iron to the junk shop while vituperatively critiquing the world around him: "There Is No Law. There Is No Right And Wrong. The World Is Lies. There Is No Friendship. Every Fucking Thing" (Mamet 103), Danny takes the baseball bat and proceeds to destroy the café in frustration at his stagnant position. While doing so, he rants: "The fire brigade ... Batman and Robin! THEY WON'T COME. YOU DON'T COUNT. THIS PLACE IS WORTHLESS. YOU ARE WORTHLESS. YOU'RE ALL WORTHLESS ... nothing ... nowhere ... I AM NOT NOTHING.... I thought we were friends. Silly me. My mistake" (263). Danny's breakdown, like Teach's, perfectly solidifies a male psyche lost amidst a world of changing expectations of masculinity. His focus on his status of not being "nothing" reifies everything he has been struggling to overcome. Thrown off by Stu, rejected by Ben, beat up in front of the two of them by the giant, unable to save his mentally ill brother, he finds that he has no power or place in his immediate surroundings. Made to lick the giant's shoes, he has become nothing. In addition, his focus on the loss of friendship with Ben and Stu points importantly to his struggle and place with other men. As Spicer notes, "Underclass men are adrift in a society represented as hopelessly run-down. Their male confidence is eroded because they lack the traditional strengths of working-class masculinity: a secure place as the principal breadwinner ... and comradeship with mates at work" (188). Danny possesses none of these attributes. When Ben questions Danny about his behavior, he is at a loss for words to explain his dilemma of status. He does not possess the ability to articulate his concerns and struggles. All he has are his violent actions. Because of his behavior and inabilities to provide a cooperative presence within the economic framework of this street, he finds that there is no longer room for him within the confines of the capitalistic community. Danny's fate then is exclusion as he leaves the restaurant, having lost his tenuous position there.

Whereas Mamet ends *American Buffalo* with the community of men inside and outside the junk shop still intact, Penhall suggests that male camaraderie and support is not so easily mended. The forgiveness present in Mamet's play is not present here. The actions have become too serious to be so easily dismissed. Don's shop in *American Buffalo*, after all, is a junk shop. When Teach trashes the space in a rage, he is merely attacking junk. Danny though destroys furniture and the working accessories necessary to the success of the business. In addition, he trashes the livelihood of the business and its physical usefulness by destroying the front windows. He has made the business untenable, while Teach's rage does not prohibit the continuation of Donny's business. In addition, after he hits Bobby in the head, Teach is still considered a vital part of the community as he drives Bobby and Don to the hospital.[11] In *Wild Turkey* that sense of community and camaraderie cannot be re-established as too much damage has been done.

Despite Danny's failure to assimilate into this male economic community, the play still reifies the importance and unifying nature of the capitalistic creed for those who are enmeshed within its parameters. Stu, wounded from the hit he sustained from the baseball bat, must begin his day and continue on because of the delicate economic position of their restaurant. However, before they can begin Stu admits to Ben that he was wrong in believing that Ben was at fault in the robbery. Stu's suspicious thoughts about Ben had all been placed there by Danny in an effort to convince Stu to get rid of his live-in security guard. He acknowledges his error, stating, "It's just me an' you" (266). In order for them to succeed, there must be a reckoning and an acknowledgement of the importance of their friendship and business relationship. At the close of the play Stu and Ben restart their day by re-subscribing to the principles of work and the sense of community that work instills in them and gives definition to their day and life.

> STU: All I wanna do is my job.... Is that, do you think that's such a bad thing?
> BEN: It's a good thing Stu. It's alright. We cook the food.
> STU: Yes.
> BEN: We do the job.
> STU: We do the job
> BEN: It's okay.
> STU: Yeah [75].

This reification of the world of work not only solidifies the position of Ben and Stu in light of Danny's tirade and destruction, but also in defining a means for males to their place in society. They sustain their identity for another day in their world of economic uncertainty. The reestablishment of the work society by both Ben and Stu and the repetition of the phrase "We do the job" stresses that work comes before all else and for them is the most important element at stake in their world.

2

Some Voices *and* the Failure of Care

Whereas *Wild Turkey* was inspired through a mix of David Mamet and the vandalism of the pizza parlor Penhall managed, *Some Voices* stemmed not only from his journalistic observations but also his encounter with an acquaintance who was diagnosed with schizophrenia. The influences for his first full-length play ranged from a relationship he had forged in Sydney with a former rock star to his personal and professional revulsion at the irresponsible disruption of the communal dynamics of his Shepherd's Bush neighborhood by a Thatcher governmental policy which released hundreds of schizophrenics into neighborhoods like his own all across London.

As mentioned earlier, Penhall hoped to form a rock band with his fellow students at the Sydney School of Art, but, disappointed with the quality of the student body, he left after a semester. However, he still pursued his rock and roll dream by playing guitar for a number of local bands, including one called The Immediates, and even after a decade had passed since Penhall had been a part of the group, he still "cringed at the memory of the suit-wearing band" (Morgan). He confessed that even though The Immediates "had a residency at a place in Zetland ... I don't think anybody ever saw us" (Morgan). Being part of the music scene, though, allowed him to mingle amidst Sydney's musical circles and it was in this way that he at one point encountered Jeremy Oxley, the founder, composer and lead singer of the 1980s Australian rock group Sunnyboys, whose self-titled first album is considered to be one of the best Australian rock albums ever. Over a four-year period (1980–1984) the Sunnyboys were one of the most prominent bands in the country and at their height in 1984 they played before a crowd of 70,000 adoring fans in Melbourne when they opened for The Police, who were also at the pinnacle of their success.

Not surprisingly, as is the story with numerous bands, the Sunnyboys plummeted from their apex with just about as much speed as their ascension. While part of their trouble involved the ubiquitous problem of the mismanagement of finances, the larger force behind the break-up was Jeremy Oxley's unpredictable behavior. Penhall, as an outsider, saw Oxley's post–Sunnyboys behavior up close. He told the Australian newspaper *The Age*: "He could play like Hendrix when he was pissed as a newt, and could write the most incredible songs. Then you'd go to a bar with him and he'd get beaten up. Snooty Sydney people thought he was a loser, it just broke my heart" (Roberts). Pete Oxley, Jeremy's brother and bass player in the band, explained the nature of his brother's condition: "Jeremy suffered from schizophrenia since probably 1982.... After we stopped playing he spent sort of eight years just going insane basically and a lot of people just thought he was an arsehole. He was drinking a lot and taking every drug under the sun but what he was trying to do was medicate himself because he hears voices" (Oxenbridge). During this period, Oxley refused medical and psychiatric help and, in turn, he could not control his behavior, which would, at times, become violent. In Canberra he tried to punch through a glass window in order to get to the person on the other side. In Sydney his sister, Melanie, caught him using a razor to cut his arms. He claimed he was making tattoos. After having his jaw broken in a bar fight in 1988, his sister remarked that the medical establishment was partly to blame for her brother's continuing condition, "He comes into the hospital, wild-eyed and with a broken jaw — it should have been obvious to them there was a psychiatric problem ... [but they] let him discharge himself after a few days" (Guilliatt). While his family members and those close to him recognized the serious problem that Oxley faced with his self-damaging behavior, his actions struck outsiders as merely the behavior expected of a privileged rock star.

Penhall's initial encounter with Oxley — they would, for a period of time, become drinking buddies— occurred as the rock star was far removed from his success. The discovery by Penhall that Oxley's seemingly selfish actions were actually a result of schizophrenia would be his initial influence when he began writing *Some Voices*. Penhall explained that at first he thought Oxley "had gone mad under the weight of his own genius, drink, wild women," but when he discovered the diagnosis was actually schizophrenia, "I was haunted and abashed" (Hoggard). That haunting would continue for a number of years until he finally transferred his dismay about Oxley's situation into print.

After leaving Sydney, Penhall moved to London and after holding a number of low-paying jobs (like the restaurant manager position that inspired *Wild Turkey*), he was hired by the *Hammersmith Guardian*, where he reported on all facets of the Shepherd's Bush area for two years. Penhall noted that this was an exciting time for him, "reviewing the Kinks and then doing a murder on Shepherd's Bush Green" (Rees, "Vexed"). By reporting in this urban community, he also saw numerous disturbing demonstrations of the National Health Services' philosophy about Care in the Community, which released patients early from hospital care and placed them with medically unqualified family members. In a Platform talk in 2000 at the National Theatre, Penhall described the policy as "flinging people out and letting them fend for themselves."[1] As a reporter, Penhall received multiple leads from community members about former mental patients who were released and failing to succeed: "I wrote a couple of news stories but beyond that I had no remit. It was frustrating that people would just turn that page" (Ellis). In addition, he was learning more about the nature of the city and the power of mental illness on not only the stricken individuals but also his specific Shepherd's Bush community. In his introduction to the first volume of his plays, he noted that the challenge to his community played a crucial part in providing the larger framework for the play's surroundings. "*Some Voices* was about the difficulties of assimilating in the metropolis.... [Shepherd's Bush] was full of former mental patients and Irish and Kiwis and Croatians and drunks and drifters in amongst the media types" (ix-x). In addition, he explained: "*Some Voices* is about showing how, because of a simple physiological illness, a perfectly ordinary nice man has wound up a ranting lunatic on a wasteland with people beating him up or giving him a wide berth" (Klein 78). Based then on his experiences with the failure of his reporting on Care in the Community to evoke an uprising from his readers, his personal learning curve on the difficulties facing his community members and his firsthand observation of Oxley's behavior, he began working in earnest on an early version of *Some Voices*, which featured a schizophrenic main character who was released through the Care in the Community program to the auspices of his estranged brother. Early in the play the fortitude of Penhall's position can be found in the character of Ives, a twenty-year veteran of the mental hospital, who sums up the medical professionals who surround him: "They pretend to care—they profess to know how to be in the business of caring, which to me, sonny Jim, is no different to a butcher professing to know how to operate on the brain" (5). In recognition of the everyday experiences on his reporter beat, he set the play in the heart of Shepherd's Bush.

The early drafts of *Some Voices* were read by Penhall's friend, Brian Coucher, an actor, who eventually directed a staged reading at the Battersea Arts Centre. After revising the play a number of times after the reading, Penhall began shopping his first full-length play to various London venues. He first submitted the script to "the [Royal] National [Theatre], who turned me down which enraged me, then the Bush, who turned me down, which enraged me even more because I lived in Shepherd's Bush, and then the Hampstead Theatre, which didn't particularly surprise me" (Litson). He finally received a positive reaction from the Royal Court and, surprisingly, he turned them down when they expressed an interest. Penhall explained: "It's nice that it sounds ballsy, but it was probably just naivety" (Maxwell). He was tired of the games played with him by the previous theatres. "They all do the same things: if they like you they get you in for a cup of stewed tea and patronise you for an hour" (Maxwell). Penhall did not want to travel to Sloane Square for a cup of tea only to be told "thanks again." "I said all that to Stephen [Daldry] and asked how serious he was, and he said, 'Well, we can't get into bed before we've had the foreplay'" (Litson). But, Daldry, like Dominic Dromgoole at the Bush Theatre, was well aware of the growing mood and strength of the new up-and-coming playwrights and he had a plan to highlight their talent by reopening the unused Upstairs Theatre, dedicating its space to the production of new plays by young talent.

Based on Daldry's response, Penhall finally went in and had his cuppa with the artistic director, who optioned the play and then placed Penhall in the Royal Court Theatre's Young Writers program, where he received guidance from Caryl Churchill, April de Angelis and Hanif Kureishi.[2] Penhall appreciated the opportunity offered by the program. "The Royal Court has this ethos: they really think they can teach you to write," Penhall said. "You could sit around stroking your chin having philosophical conversations about your favourite writers and it was a lot of fun" (Horsburgh). In addition to entering the program, Penhall quit his newspaper job and bought a bottle of Scotch to celebrate the fact that he was now a playwright. With this recognition Penhall decided not to return to Australia. He had made it as a playwright.

Penhall, though, was not the only playwright being courted by the London theatres via conversations over Earl Grey tea. Due to the influx of National Lottery money into cultural programs and institutions as well as Daldry's recommitment to the Royal Court Upstairs stage, the Court undertook in the fall of 1994 a firm stance behind the importance of new writing by producing a seminal, and highly influential, season of new plays in their upstairs space. The first play to open the season would be Penhall's *Some Voices*. However, the Royal Court's bet on young writers was not an easy sell for its audience. Daldry explained that upon his arrival at the Sloane Square theatre, he found that "audiences felt new writing was a bit like molasses or a pill you had to take. The big change was getting new writing out of 'it's good for you,' out of the 'should'—'you should go to the theatre,' 'you should fund it'—and into being the life blood of British theatre" (Aragay and Zozaya 11). Daldry's instincts, though, were correct and the season tapped a level of excitement and pent-up anticipation from London audiences. By the time the season had run its course, the nature of contemporary British theatre would be completely redefined as critics would herald the emergence of a new Renaissance of British playwriting. From September 1994 until September 1995 the following plays premiered at the Upstairs Theatre at the Court: Penhall's *Some Voices*, Nick Grosso's *Peaches*, Judy Upton's *Ashes and Sand* (1995), Sarah Kane's *Blasted*, Michael Wynne's *The Knocky* (1995), Judith Johnson's *Uganda* (1995) Anthony Neilson's *Heredity* (1995), Phyllis Nagy's *Disappeared* (1995) and Simon Block's *Not a Game for Boys* (1995). No doubt because of the strength of these new plays, the exuberant press coverage that was being generated and the success of the Court's commitment to new writers, Daldry decided that for the first time in forty years the Royal Court would produce the first play by a new writer, Jez Butterworth's *Mojo*, on the main stage. The only other writer to hold that distinction was John Osborne in 1956 with *Look Back in Anger*.

Some Voices opens on the day Ray, having been diagnosed as schizophrenic and institutionalized for 28 days, will be discharged by the National Health Service under the auspices of the government's Care in the Community policy. Ray is released into the custody of his brother, Pete, whom Ray has not seen for many years. Part of the condition of Ray's freedom involves taking his medications and meeting regularly with health service personnel. Despite the continual efforts of Pete to keep Ray on course, Ray refuses to follow the medical directives. A few days after his release, Ray intervenes between an arguing couple, Dave and Laura, and is beaten up by Dave. Laura cleans up Ray's wounds and soon thereafter they run into each other at a pub. They escape to the seashore to get away from their respective problems. At the end of the first act Laura and Ray make love in a field.

The second act opens with Ives, one of Ray's former psychiatric inmates, and Ray making a ruckus in Pete's kitchen. Pete throws each man out, and Ives ends up on the street, where he dies in Ray's arms. Having been thrown out by his brother, Ray moves in with Laura, but when she learns the truth that Ray's unpredictable actions and deteriorating condition are actually due to his schizophrenia and not just a personality quirk, she kicks him out and goes back to Dave. Ray visits her at her flat, where Dave then physically attacks Laura. In defending her, Ray takes up a hammer and hits Dave in the head. Ray hurriedly retreats to Pete's restaurant where after dousing himself and the space with petrol, he threatens to set everything afire. While Pete tries to talk down his brother, Ray reveals that he hears voices that just make no sense to him. In the final scene of the play Ray has been placed in a hostel and Pete teaches him how to make an omelet.

Ian Rickson, the play's director and later Daldry's successor as artistic director of the Court, described working on the play as "a very invigorating journey. You do not quite know what you will end up with, but you know you are connecting with something very deep in the play" (Aragay and Zozaya 21). In addition, he pronounced a fondness for the play, admitting that among all the theatrical productions he had directed, it was one of the pieces of which he was most proud. Rickson commented: "The play has a compelling and mythic power, ever reaching outside itself for escape, resolution and feelings. I love the play's roughness and spirit.... The last scene [Ray teaching Pete how to make an omelet], for example, is sublime" (Little and McLaughlin 298). Rickson and designer Rae Smith created a memorable theatrical environment by completely reimagining the attic space. Smith said: "What was interesting about that was using the decrepit environment of the theatre upstairs to echo the decrepit environment of the schizophrenic.... In the production, Lee Ross (Ray) just stumbled around from one room to another—the rooms didn't really have any parameters for him" (Little and McLaughlin 298–9). This physical transformation forcefully and viscerally struck the London critics. Aleks Sierz described the space in *In-Yer-Face*, writing that "the walls were stripped right back to the brick, which was painted black, and a huge round institutional window, which opened onto the outside world, was revealed.... Near the end, after the petrol scene, Ray stands by it again, and a ray of bleak light comes in" (211). Kate Bassett's opening night review in *The Times* also noted the highly physical nature of the production in the newly reopened space where "nothing escapes you. Life's details are thrown into disturbing relief. Just the way Ray's T-shirt, translucent with paraffin, clings to a body on the verge of burning itself up, becomes sharply upsetting." Dominic Dromgoole, director of the Bush Theatre, who initially passed on *Some Voices*, attended a performance, where he "had one of the best evenings of my life" (221).

As the start of Daldry's experiment with new writing, Penhall's play, which premiered in September 1994, began the season auspiciously as *Some Voices* received strong opening night accolades from the reviewers. David Benedict of *The Independent* noticed an element that distinguished Penhall from other young writers, writing that he "is unfashionably unafraid to tackle serious things seriously," while Kate Bassett noted the play is "as sparkling as it is bruising." Michael Billington, the *Guardian* reviewer, remarked that Penhall "offers a graphic picture of a west London world full of the walking wounded, and writes with grim humour." Sarah Hemming called *Some Voices* a "beautifully written piece," which approaches a dark topic "with a light touch and liberal doses of comedy. The love scenes are tender, the fights are scary, and the play frequently veers towards tragedy, only to pull back, pinning you to your seat. Best, however, is the fact that it is not black and white." Irving Wardle of *The Independent* noted Penhall's play "puts him alongside the late David Mercer as an authentic dramatist of schizophrenia." In addition, he recognized the strength of Penhall's writing by signaling out Ives' "pounding authoritarian speeches, with their comic implosions of the apocalyptic and the humdrum and their flights of schizophrenic poetry." He found them to be "the most eloquent passages" of the play. Finally, John Peter in his *Sunday Times* review was the most effusive in praise for the new writer's first full-length work: "This is the most thrilling playwriting debut in years.... Penhall is writing about the insecurity and maladjustment of urban society; its fear of other people's solitude, its lack of imagination, its need to control people being disguised as care." At the end-of-the-year, Penhall and his play were both recognized. *Some Voices* won the John Whiting Award, given annually to the new play that best addresses issues related to contemporary society. Penhall also made *The Independent*'s end of the year list as one of the playwrights to keep an eye on, along with fellow Royal Court new writers Nick Grosso and Judy Upton. In 2000 the play was made into a feature film, using Penhall's screenplay, and starred a pre–James Bond Daniel Craig as the schizophrenic Ray.[3]

As in *Wild Turkey* Penhall once again features a struggling restaurant owner, but in this case he expands his focus to men struggling to solidify their status within the dynamics of class. This concept is expressed by Ives, an escaped mental patient and the brother of Danny from *Wild Turkey*, who dies on a London street abandoned and unrecognized: "I do not like to hear people say money is no obstacle because money is the obstacle. I don't need to be told as long as you have your health because you buy your health and so it is a question of as long as you can afford it. I'm not stupid. I can think. I can see the people that pass me by" (49). Penhall's interest, like in *Wild Turkey*, continues to focus on those males who have been passed by, who are not part of the larger economic boom, so accurately expressed by the New Man of the 1980s, and not part of the New Lads of the 1990s who have the money to spend on magazines, football gear and tickets and multiple pints at the local pub. As Penhall revealed, "If you are ill or bereaved or disadvantaged or unemployed, then you are invisible.... If you are not perceived to be normal, with a nice job and a nice wife, family and place in society, then you can fall through the cracks and life becomes impossible" (Klein 80).

Ray has been released into the custody of his brother Pete, who has been consumed with running his restaurant, which is more successful than Ben and Stu's attempt in *Wild Turkey*, but now has second thoughts about his investment in being a savior to the restaurant that their father previously ran. As Pete tells his brother, "Maybe my wife left me because I was this selfish cunt who wore a pinny and tossed salads all day for other people. Maybe I should never have tried to save dad or his greasy old caff or his doomed fuckin' life cos that would have just been responsible" (68). Amelia Howe Kritzer argues that Pete's investment in making the restaurant a success can be seen as "exemplifying the Thatcher ideal of self-reliance" (48). And while Kritzer is correct, Pete's situation has at the same time become troublesome and questionable because, as Nigel Edley and Margaret Wetherell noted, "Capitalist production is organised around a series of divisions between home and work, between work and leisure, private life and public life. Experience is thus compartmentalised as people move between these different spheres" (101). With Ray now present in Pete's life and reliant upon his brother's help, Pete struggles to maintain the divisions between the various compartments of his world. It now inescapably blurs together as he worries about Ray infringing on his ability to effectively manage and run the restaurant. A particularly telling scene early in the play demonstrates Pete's difficulty as he tries to manage his staff in the dining area of the restaurant (while he is busy in the kitchen), cook meals, control the outflow of food and counsel Pete all at the same time. He ends being unable to think straight with all the various responsibilities he must navigate. He will be the first of many Penhall males who is stretched too thin and unable to find a moment of peace for himself. At one point he tells Ray that he would love to just give up all his responsibilities (the restaurant, the family honor, caring for Ray), but he does not, "Because I am obliged, Ray ...

to do this thing for you. It is what I have to do.... The measure of a man ... in this life is whether he can do ... what he thinks he has to do" (68). His understanding of the concept of doing what one thinks one should do ultimately allows Pete to sift through all the aspects of his life and determine what is of greatest priority for him: his family.

Nevertheless, Pete has done well with his restaurant as he lives in a neighborhood where, according to Ray, the neighbors drive around in "fancy cars" and drink champagne. In addition to noticing the materiality of his brother's neighbors, Ray latches onto the falseness that they represent: "I've seen them go where the sunbeds are and come back orange" (52). Ray finds his brother's rich neighbors repulsive and his brother's place in it a betrayal of their working-class background: "What's the matter, Pete, you grown out of the Bush? You in a different bracket now so you don't notice things any more?" (52). Pete's response is of one who has lost a sense of class designation between individuals. He tells Ray that his neighbors are just people. Driving Ray's anger are the two divergent paths the brothers have taken. Ray has long been a loner, disappearing for numerous stretches of times. When he would eventually resurface, he would be in jail in a new location of the country. Pete, though, has stayed close to home, worked hard and achieved a modicum of success. The contrast between the brothers plays out through the location of their various scenes. Ray constantly moves amidst the city and it inhabitants, and his scenes take place on the street, at the beach, in a pub and in Laura's flat. However, Pete always appears in spaces that are enclosed, as he is trapped in his kitchen, producing pesto pies and curly sausage, while yelling into an intercom to his wait staff about the food that needs to be pushed. In fact, his only interaction comes through the intercom at work and his discussions with his brother Ray and the people he brings into his brother's flat. The arrival of Ray back into his life moves him out of the rut of the restaurant, but he finds it difficult and perplexing to deal with his brother, who refuses to take his pills, lies about meeting with the various persons deigned to help him return to society and cannot help himself from getting involved in the problems of others.

Even though the issues of class introduced in *Wild Turkey* are continued in *Some Voices*, Penhall's first full-length work is, at its heart, a family play that examines the struggling relationship between two brothers as they confront the pressures of their past, Ray's mental illness and Pete's newly appointed familial responsibility. In addition to promoting Penhall's critical position against the reinsertion of the mentally ill into society as represented through the fate of Pete and Ives, the play also criticizes the personal investment Care in the Community demands of family caregivers, and, in this case in particular, the demands placed upon the relationship between brothers. The situation with their relationship is, obviously, much more fraught than simply sibling rivalry because they have not seen each other for a number of years due to

Ray's previous behavior of disappearing for stretches of time and then turning up incarcerated and needing his family to rescue him from his altercations with the police.

Pete, who is now required by the government to care for his peripatetic brother, fosters a great deal of resentment and hostility toward Ray because of the responsibilities that have fallen upon him since his brother last disappeared, including taking on the burden of the restaurant that his father ran so that the familial connection to the business is maintained, all to the detriment of his marriage as he spent more time in the restaurant than with his wife. He tries to justify his reasons for the focus on his work rather than his spouse: "I just ... had this weird idea that the thing to do was to go to work and do an honest day and pay a few bills.... I don't see what's wrong with that" (68). In addition, Pete has watched Ray take on the traits of the father who left the family, leaving their mother to raise the two sons on their own. In abandoning his family, Ray misses out on all the aspects of a family life, including being the best man at Pete's wedding, attending the funeral of their mother who died of cancer and failing to support Pete during his divorce. Through their actions, Penhall stresses that generational recycling is inescapable for both of these brothers as they end up professionally and personally emulating their father, which is something that Ray has feared happening. He recounts for Pete a memory he retains of their father. "I just notice how filthy he is and unshaven and how he stinks and he wears ... like an old blue safari suit.... And I think ... I think ... I'll be like that one day" (82). While this connection between fathers and sons is a passing element of this play, Penhall's later work *The Bullet* will explore the inescapable repetitive connection between fathers and sons.

However, in terms of fraternal relations Ray views Pete's picking him up from the hospital as a moment of exhilaration as well as a chance for reconnection, giving him a good feeling about the re-establishment of their relationship. His return into Pete's life bestows upon him the renewed sense of freedom and opportunity to begin again by escaping into the folds of his family, which is clearly established through a reverie Ray shares with Pete, when, as boys, they played by a river bank near the local brewery, racing sticks down the river and admiring the brewery horses. Signaling that their reconnection will not be as smooth as Ray imagines, Pete has no recollection of the event ever happening and then states that he has to leave for his restaurant, cutting off any chance for shared memories. Before Pete leaves, he attempts to solidify Ray's sense of commitment to his post-release treatment and his first meeting with a health professional, who will "sort out the thingie for your whatsit.... She'll fix you up with that fella.... The fella they recommended for the whatsit" (11–2). His linguistic inability to discuss his brother's condition is a prelude to his overall inability to comprehend how to care for and guide his brother through the days, weeks and years ahead, as made clear when he later tries to follow through with his brother on his upcoming visits to the various medical authorities in the NHS system.

Not only does Pete have the difficulty of learning an entire new language of technical terms and doctors, but he also faces the unpredictability of what his brother will do next, which in the course of the next scene involves him getting beaten up. Ray encounters Dave threatening to beat up a pregnant Laura with a brick because he believes she has a piece of jewelry that he needs. While Ray manages to snow his overwhelmed brother for a time about taking his pills and going to meet with the medical practitioners, he does not fool Dave, who knows the streets of Shepherd's Bush and the various people populating them, as he keeps them in check with threats and violence. For Ray's troubles, as he tries to stop Dave, Ray gets a forehead to the nose and a warning to stay away. Over the course of the play Penhall suggests through the behavior of Dave that there is a thin line between the mental condition of Ray and the violently aggressive actions of Dave. Ray tells Laura that Dave is similar to the fellows "walking around wired, angry, wound up ready to ping" (22). His description of Dave could just as easily be applied to the past patients released in the Care in the Community program, and Penhall will return to an echo of "the wired, angry, wound up ready to ping" character with Christopher in *Blue/Orange*.

After Ray returns with a bandage on his nose and a black eye, Pete realizes that the situation he faces with his brother will be a challenge, especially with a restaurant demanding his constant attention. Ray's presence in his life changes everything. Worried enough as he is about his restaurant, he now is obligated to be caregiver to his ill brother. Pete tells Ray: "I signed a bit of paper to get you out of that place ... and I put that in writing we go through a whole procedure and you don't ... appear to give a shit" (25). Pete's frustration highlights the struggle between the two differing brothers. As Sierz notes, Ray and Pete "embody the conflict between freedom and responsibility, permissiveness and home-making," respectively (212). In addition, according to Kritzer, the two brothers become representatives of what is problematic with Margaret Thatcher's England. Kritzer writes:

> Thatcher's insistence that [extreme] needs should be taken care of within families has resulted in a dysfunctional brother threatening to overwhelm the functional one, endangering his stability and productivity. With a subtle duality of perspective, *Some Voices* allows the audience to see schizophrenia both realistically as a mental illness that affects individuals and metaphorically as an indicator of social breakdown [48].

For Pete, Ray's behavior indicates that nothing has changed since Ray left the family years before. History continues to repeats itself. When they were younger, their mother dealt with the familial and social consequences of Ray's behavior, but now Pete has become both parent and brother for his sibling. All of the inherent responsibilities associated with Ray's behavior have fallen to him, and in turn his brother threatens everything Pete has worked to create.

In the scene where Ray appears with the bandage on his nose, Pete is a whirling dervish of multi-tasking — trying to figure out his brother, cooking meals for the diners upstairs and upbraiding a server through the intercom and the diners in the room. The latter two work elements he has managed to mentally and physically balance. Ray's presence alters that and is highly disruptive. As they talk in the kitchen, Pete tells his brother to just stop misbehaving, acting "screwy," and instead just act normally, thinking that Ray's behavior is something that can be willfully started and stopped, as if he has the ability to control the factors that influence his behavior. Ray, though, takes great exception to his brother's simplification of his situation.

> RAY: Nothing 'sent' me screwy, Pete. Nothing sent me.
> PETE: I just don't understand it that's all I just ... don't understand.
> RAY: Nobody understands it.
> PETE: Why can't you just ... pull yourself together?...
> RAY: How do I pull myself together, Pete? Is there a string or something that people just pull on every time they're in the shit? [26].

Pete talks to his brother like a parent would to a misbehaving child, who, unlike Ray, has the ability to fix his errant actions, like cleaning up a messy room. Pete later echoes the ubiquitous parental comment, when he tells Ray, "Do I have to stand over you morning and night every night for the rest of your life?" (51). Pete's struggle with his position is precisely what drove Penhall to base the play around the failure of Care in the Community. The government shuffled off Ray to the care of his brother without providing any type of guidance, attention or instruction as how deal with his mental and physical conditions.

The above conversation between the two brothers documents the two sides of this problematic situation. Pete attributes Ray's actions to controllable outside forces, like consuming too much drink which then provokes getting into fights, as Penhall saw with Jeremy Oxley, with the end result usually being a beating or incarceration. These behaviors in Pete's mind are within the parameters of one's self-control. He believes that Ray can just fix it all by himself by just pulling himself "together." Ray, though, has come to realize the uncontrollable aspect of his condition and his plaintive and repeated statements of "nothing 'sent' me screwy" are his unsuccessful attempts to explain to his brother that his behavior cannot be contributed to anything definably tangible. No one element encapsulates his condition and it cannot be solved just through willpower. The two brothers though speak at cross-purposes, with neither one being understood clearly due to Pete's lack of education on Ray's condition, Ray's inability to describe his own internal struggles and the palpably fraught history between the two of them. Pete, though, does indicate a glimmer of recognition about the importance of his role in his brother's life. After hearing his brother's comments about his lack of control over his condition, he acknowledges his disadvantage in dealing with his brother's woes and he tells Ray: "You have to be patient with me, I have to be patient with you" (27). While the play focuses on Ray's various personal, romantic and physical struggles in the weeks after his release from incarceration, Pete's role is equally crucial. Penhall's play suggests that no progress can really be made until Pete experiences a true epiphany about the state of Ray's condition. Once he does so, then he will be able to help his brother. While the play charts the steady decline of Ray, it also documents Pete's slow process in coming to understand exactly what his brother means when he says that "nothing 'sent' me screwy."

Pete has always followed one goal: to take over from his father and save the restaurant. In addition, he has played the role of the stalwart son, who has succeeded in contrast to Ray's peripatetic movements around the country and in and out from jail. He is the tried and true one and does not have time for the unpredictability and nature of Ray's condition. If Ray takes his pills, sees his counselors as the medical community has said and follows everything he is told, then everything will be all right. Pete blindly places his belief in the system that the National Health Service has established for dealing with the patients they have released. In his mind they are the experts and know exactly how the system should work and the steps that the patient should take. He encourages Ray to follow all the established protocol. "You go and see the woman and you do what she tells you to do.... And you do what I tell you to do.... And you do what they told me to tell you to do" (29). However, Ray, from his own experiences, knows that following the rules when it comes to his mental condition will not ease his woes. Pete also puts his faith in the power of the pills prescribed to Ray by his doctors precisely because the authority figure of the doctor has prescribed them. They are the authorities, they make the rules, so they must be followed. However, Ray understands the effect of the pills better than anyone. While the pills may put his condition in check, they also provide a much different aspect to the world around him, keeping him in a state of discomfort, including a state where colors are all wrong. All things green appear faded. Yellow no longer has the same hue. Even the sun and the sky, under the influence of the drugs, no longer have their normal colors. The sun has turned white, while the sky is silver. In addition, the space around him seems to constrict as he complains that his bedroom walls are closing in around him.

The brothers' encounter in the kitchen of the restaurant after Ray's beating by Dave will be the last time they are alone together on the stage for an extended period of time until the final two scenes of the play, which focus exclusively on them. Perceiving the relationship with Pete as tenuous and unproductive as all he tells him to do is take medicine and attend appointments, Ray decides to pursue an alternate relationship, making friends with Laura, with whom he has no history and, perhaps, more importantly, is someone who is as equally troubled as he is. She is pregnant, abused and, after her last encounter, separated from Dave. Ray feels a kinship with Laura and wants to spend time with her. Since she does not know about the state of his mental condition and thinks his off-handed comments and odd behavior are merely quirky eccentricities, he also does not have to worry about her challenging him about missing appointments and not taking his medications. As they talk in the bar, he questions her about family and whether she has any siblings. When she reveals that she has sisters, Ray tells her: "That's good because you have to be able to like your family. You have to be able to trust them but mainly you have to like them. And sometimes you just don't. Sometimes you don't trust anybody" (32). For Ray trust becomes a crucial element of his connection with others. Their relationship is childlike as they both want to ignore their own fragile states and the disciplinarians in their lives, for Laura, the dangerousness of Dave, and for Ray, the patronizing paternalism of Pete.

In order to escape their stressors, they go to the beach. This brief respite, which occurs at the end of Act 1, is an important moment of the play as it is the only time when Ray manages to escape from the city and its travails, which Penhall criticizes in *Wild Turkey* and *Some Voices*. In his introduction to the first volume of his plays, Penhall wrote: "Anybody who spends time in a city doing anything other than going to work and coming home understands the soullessness of city life" (x). And this attitude is present in *Wild Turkey* with the vicious world outside of Stu's burger bar and in *Some Voices* with Dave's brutality, Ives' ignored death on the street by citizens of Shepherd's Bush and even the fast-paced nature of Pete at work as he struggles to keep up with the orders coming down from his customers. When Ray encounters Laura at a bar a few days after the confrontation with Dave, he describes his neighborhood as rife with violence and incivility. His encounter with Dave was not the first time he had been treated to such disdain and anger. He does not understand the mentality of the English populace that responds to him so negatively and with such hostility—"Pardon me for being so bold as to exchange a look in the street while I'm going about my business, pardon me for daring to speak to you because we do not speak to each other" (23). Ray and Laura's seaside day trip allows Ray to escape from the tremors and dangers of the city which only exacerbate his schizophrenic tendencies. Pete Oxley revealed a similar situation with his brother Jeremy, who had forsaken living in the city to instead be in the rural setting outside of Brisbane: "The city's a very stressful place and the country has a bit more space to breathe. That's good for the sensitive souls I would say" (Humphries). Ray's confrontational sense of the city can be found in his reaction to the customers in the supermarkets. He tells Laura: "Haven't they got anything better to do except drag their fat arses around with their fat husbands and their screeching kids?" (62). Ray's contentment at being at the seashore temporarily lifts not only the darkness off Ray and Laura but also the play as the two enjoy nature and the beach, so they are not embedded in the London society that is so difficult and draining on them. Finally, the first act and the respite culminates in a field where Ray and Laura make love, immersed in only each other with no other concerns and for the first time in the play Laura feels safe.

Where the first act rises to the play's apex of happiness with Laura and Ray making love in a field, the second half of the play charts Ray's mental disintegration as his anti-social behavior and violent emotional swings increase. Pete realizes that in order to save Ray he will have to change his own attitude toward and treatment of him. The first sign of Ray's descent occurs in the second act's first scene through his conversation with his brother and Ives, who has escaped from the mental institution. Throughout the scene Ives sings and talks about coming from the Planet Vega. Pete, fed up with the noise and the drinking, finally blows his top when Ray tells him that he has told Ives he can stay. Ives, offended, leaves, and Ray and Pete are left alone. Pete tries to get Ray to take his pills, but Ray refuses. Instead, Ray announces he wants to move out and go and live with Laura in order to escape from Pete and his elitist neighbors. What is revealing is that Pete has always believed that Laura was merely a fictional creation stemming from Ray's mental condition. For the first time he has an inkling that perhaps Laura and the things his brother tells him are actually true. Despite this moment of realization, Pete decides to rescind the conditions set down by the health service and which he agreed to follow. He is willing to make Ray someone else's responsibility and he recommends that they should go talk to Ray's health service minders about making a change. Ray though claims to have already gone and asked his counselor if he could live with Laura, even providing a little bit of descriptive detail to his encounter by recounting that the woman he saw had a mole on her lip. Pete though finds Ray's comments completely preposterous, expressing his disbelief at what his brother has told him. Not knowing for sure whether Laura exists or not and scarcely believing that his brother actually talked to the authorities, he is nevertheless willing to give up on his relationship with his brother and his obligation to him after only a few scant weeks. As Ray tells him, it is a better situation this way since "you have a business to run" (54), placing himself as secondary to Pete's true obligation.

A few scenes later Pete meets Laura for the first time and during their conversation Laura learns the truth about Ray's condition. First, Ray makes rude and achingly mean statements to her about her baby when it kicks, telling her, "Kick him back. Give yourself a ... do it yourself abortion" (65). Through Pete she learns that Ray's unpredictable behavior is due to his schizophrenic condition rather than just a personality quirk, as she had at first thought. In addition, she learns that he has not been taking his medication, explaining why his attitude has become more varied, and as Ray continues to make belligerent statements about her and her baby, she storms out to get away from him, leaving Pete and Ray alone again. Ray has now exhausted all potential avenues for care. His treatment of Laura, refusal to take his pills, and verbal attacks on Pete break the final ounce of connection he has with his brother. Pete tells him: "I'm coming to the end of my rope here. I'm right at the end.... I can't fucking do it any more" (67). Pete sends Ray out of his house and onto the streets to survive on his own. He has completely divorced himself from his commitment to his brother. Both have reached the bottom of their tolerance for one another. A violent encounter with Dave will finally bring them back together.

Pete's epiphany that he needs to focus on his brother occurs after Laura and Ray defend themselves against a jealous and vengeful Dave by hitting him with a hammer, sending him to the intensive care unit. Pete joins Laura in hospital waiting room. He reveals, what he had long suspected, that Ray has not been going to his assigned appointments with the various assigned medical authorities. While Pete might be inclined to blame his brother for this lack of following the rules of his release, his blame of his brother wilts when he confronts NHS personnel with their confusing blizzard of papers and forms. As they wait to hear about Dave's condition, he tells Laura about his experience with an NHS administrator, who does not even have a record of Pete and his condition. When he asks why, he finds himself enmeshed in the bureaucratic intricacies of irresponsibility and apathy. He is told that they do not know about Ray. The worker explains:

> "Because he didn't fill out the form." "What are you talking about?" I say. "I filled out the form." "No, you filled out *your* form," they say. "He's supposed to fill out his form and take it to a different building." "I filled out the fucking form," I say. "I did everything to the letter." "No," they say, "you filled out the form to say he filled out his form. If he didn't fill out his form then it's null and void" [76].

The bureaucratic figures are more concerned with adhering to the lockstep governmental procedures instead of following up on the mentally ill patients who have been released into the community. His plea to Laura — "Where are the people who make the rules? Where are they hiding — can't they see what's happening?" (76) — no doubt captures the same sense of frustration that Penhall and various members of Shepherd's Bush felt when the Care in the Community program commenced. Pete realizes he has pawned his brother off on a bunch of strangers and put faith in a failed governmental policy rather than relying on himself to ensure that his brother receives the medical attention he needs. Pete's Kafkaesque experience allows him finally to see the situation as it truly is. As Kritzer argued, *Some Voices* "highlights the gaps in those services caused by inadequate funding and bureaucratic rigidity" (48). The only help his brother can receive is what Pete himself can provide. He cannot rely on Thatcher's policy, especially when bureaucratic paper pushers play the game of pronouns when it comes to distinguishing the difference between "your" and "his" forms.

Among all the new writers to appear at the Royal Court, Penhall was not the only one to castigate British institutions and the government. Penhall's take on the National Health Service's failure in *Some Voices* was echoed by ensuing new plays in the upstairs space, including Upton's *Ashes and Sand*, Kane's *Blasted* and, in the next season, Ravenhill's *Shopping and Fucking*. Upton's *Ashes and Sand*, which premiered directly after *Some Voices*, indicted a misogynistic police force unable to control a girl gang's vicious rampage through a coastal community as they robbed and attacked visitors at a local pier. In one scene the bored police officers use a nude centerfold as a dart board, indicating the amount of respect the institution holds for its female citizens. Kane's *Blasted*, which premiered a few months after *Some Voices*, rebuked the newspapers' obsession (and in turn the public's) with sensational tabloid journalism. Her male protagonist Ian is a newspaper reporter who, in the midst of a British civil war, is more interested (as is his tabloid employer) in a sensational murder that occurred to a British backpacker in Australia than the death and destruction which surrounds him. A soldier, who has forced his way into Ian's hotel room, pleads with Ian to use his journalistic profession to tell his story.

> SOLDIER: Tell them you saw me.
> Tell them ... you saw me.
> IAN: It's not my job ... I do other stuff. Shootings and rapes and kids getting fiddled by queer priests and schoolteachers. Not soldiers screwing each other for a patch of land.... Not you. Filthy, like the wogs [48].

Like Estragon with the little boy in Beckett's *Waiting for Godot*, the soldier demands an acknowledgement of his existence, identity, self from Ian. He needs to be recognized in a world that has spun out of control. However, like the boy, Ian does not make it his business to worry with such reportage. His goal is the sensational and not the tragic.[4] Ravenhill's *Shopping and Fucking* attacks the ineptitude of child social services agencies that are unable to aid Gary, who has been continually raped by his guardian.

> I went to the council. And I said to her, look, it's simple: he's fucking me. Once, twice, three times a week he comes into my room. He's a big man. He holds me down and he fucks me. How long? she says. About two years, I say. I say he moved in then six months later it starts. I told her and she says "Does he use a condom?"... I tell her he's fucking me — without a condom — and she says to me ... I think I've got a leaflet. Would you like to give him a leaflet? [40–1].

Similar to Penhall, Ravenhill captures the sheer ineptitude of paper pushers who ignore the pleas of the victims as they, automaton-like, just go through the motions of their jobs. In all of the cases the existence of compassion is gone. Individuals are left to fend on their own, in whatever capacity they can muster. In situations like the ones in *Blasted* and *Shopping and Fucking* there is nothing beyond the government agency onto which the victims can latch. However, Penhall's play is different from his peers in that Ray does have a safety net, which is precisely the epiphany Pete reaches. He is the only one who can aid his brother.

Having reached this realization about the commitment he must make to his brother, he searches for Ray, finding him in the kitchen of his restaurant, where Ray has spread petrol all over himself and Pete's kitchen and now holds a lighter, ready to engulf it all in flames. Facing such a possible conflagration of emotions and physical threat, Pete eschews his regimented, tough parental, just "get 'er done" philosophy. A new tack is necessary with his brother. Once again the two brothers are alone, facing one another. With Pete's realization of Ray's serious condition, he now asks him questions, hoping to find solutions, instead of making pronouncements in the hopes of forcing a solution upon his brother. He asks: "It's the ... it's the voices, isn't it?... They've come back. (*Ray nods.*) What are they saying?" (81). No longer being dismissive, Pete now asks to understand and Ray, sensing the change in his brother, explains what he is experiencing with the voices: "They scare the shit out of me. They say very fucking weird things I can tell you. Things even too weird for you to figure out, Pete" (82). While Pete and Ray finally come to understanding one another, Penhall also pushes the audience further with the dramatic possibilities of Ray's condition. Just as Pete, and the audience, thinks he has annulled the threat of Ray setting fire to himself, by taking away the lighter, Ray pulls another one out of his pocket and the process repeats itself. In fact, the tension exponentially increases, as Ray has armed himself with four lighters. Penhall acknowledged: "I was conscious of having two or three violent climaxes, three very emotional climaxes, so the audience were absolutely exhausted at the end. I wanted them to be absolutely exhausted because that's what schizophrenia does to you.... I was dragging people beyond their sense of endurance" (Sierz 214). Once Pete relieves his brother of the lighters, he puts his "arm around Ray to comfort him" and later "pats him on the shoulder, drapes a couple of dishcloths around him and carefully mops him dry as they speak" (83). His act of compassion and caring is also the first time in the play Penhall indicates any kind of physical contact of brotherly affection between the two. Pete has finally come to appreciate the seriousness of his brother's condition and made the conscious investment in aiding him.

Like the end of Act I where Laura and Ray make love, the play ends on a moment of comfort and stability as Pete teaches Ray to make an omelet. The restorative final scene of the play is ironically inspired by Sam Shepard and his warring brothers play *True West*.[5] In that piece one brother, a criminal, and the other brother, a struggling writer, challenge each other to take over each other's profession. The writer brother steals all the toasters from the neighboring houses, hiding them in the kitchen, where the entire play takes place. Throughout the play's third act toast is continually being made. Penhall was inspired by this mix of realism and theatricality and since "making something on stage is incredibly compelling" (Hoggard), Pete teaches his brother to make an omelet. And in so doing, the warmth and caring of the scene transfers to the entire Upstairs theatre audience, which can smell and hear the cooking butter, the browning of the vegetables and the final creation of the breakfast meal. It is a powerful, humanizing and uplifting conclusion. Sarah Hemming, writing for *The Independent*, described this moment as "one of the most healing scenes in recent drama" (2:11). Aleks Sierz remarked that "when the theatre was filled with the smell of the omelette that Pete cooks for Ray, it felt as welcome as a homecoming" (211). Even though Mark Ravenhill was discussing the optimistic endings of his plays *Shopping and Fucking* and *Some Explicit Polaroids*, his comment that "human beings can never be completely isolated — they will always try to form groups, to socialize themselves" is applicable to many of the plays from the middle of the nineties, including Penhall's first two plays (Montforte 93). After the violence has ended and the struggles for social position and masculine identity have been ultimately exhausted, Stu and Ben in *Wild Turkey* find a common bond with one another in support through the regiment of work. Equally, Pete and Ray also bond through Pete's instruction about how to make an omelet, which is something that Pete does in his job every day and, therefore, allows him to find a way in which to merge the two distinct worlds of business and family together. Their fighting, Pete's sense of obligation and Ray's resentment have vanished and now the two can communicate simply and caringly over a moment that is not grounded in defining one's place in society, not grounded in trying to fulfill an expectation instilled through familial animosity and not grounded within the pressing, chaotic world of London. In this hostel, in this room, in this moment between two brothers, the expectations and pressures of the outside world are replaced by a caring, nurturing moment of brother helping brother with no stigmas attached.

And yet there is a less positive alternative reading to the ending of the play. While it does end in a moment of bonding, sharing and an absence of anger between the two brothers, who throughout the play have argued and found fault with one another, it also highlights that for these characters they ultimately have only themselves upon whom to rely. By the end of the play all the characters have separated. Ives is dead, Dave is in a coma, Ray lives in a hostel, Pete is in his home alone and Laura has moved away. Hanging over the warmth of breakfast is the sense of impending loneliness. While it does end in a comforting moment of cooking and bonding between the two brothers, it also ends in the partitioning of them from one another. Ray needs to live in the hostel. He cannot coexist with his brother in his house. What then distinguishes Penhall's ending from his contemporaries' endings, which are based in the need for community, is the fact that this closing scene depicts Pete *teaching* Ray how to cook a meal because Ray is going to have to exist on his own and cook for himself. When he stayed with Pete, his brother fed him. That can no longer be the case. While Ravenhill's two plays and even Kane's *Blasted*, which ends with Ian and Kate sharing food and drink together, offer a sense of closure between the characters with these final communal closing scenes,

Penhall's piece suggests that when schizophrenia is involved community and bonding is not possible. Despite the presence of violence, oppressiveness and uncertainty in the worlds of Kane and Ravenhill, one can still find some optimism, but Penhall suggests though his work that the powerful effect of mental illness will squelch any hopes of comforted closure. After all, when Laura discovers that Ray is mentally ill, she immediately leaves him and goes back to the abusive Dave. Even though they shared a few weeks of happiness together, the stigma of schizophrenia is too powerful a disease to allow for happiness. Ray, though, believes she will return to him after going away to have the baby and praises her lovingly to his brother: "You'd love her all over, everything about her. Her face, her legs, her arms, her shoulders, her feet, her toes, breasts, hair, hands. (*Beat*) Knees, neck. Her laugh, she had a blindin' laugh, Pete, which was because of her eyes, she had very dark blue twinkling eyes" (89). Pete tries to break the news to him that she has left him for good, "She ... she doesn't really want to see you again. For a while" (87), but Ray does not understand the subtext of his brother's words. Instead he provides caveats of them not reconnecting until both of them are feeling better. So while the comforting smells of breakfast wash through the playing space, the audience is left with the final image of the heartbreaking innocence of Ray believing that Laura will return to him. It is a devastating moment, but also a final comment from Penhall that in this new world order of mental illness crafted by the National Health Service all is not and will not be well. As Ray tells his brother, "Sooner or later we're all on our own for a while" (89).

3

Pale Horse *and the* Struggle to Mourn

One of the most important contemporary examinations of mourning in Britain was conducted by Geoffrey Gorer, who in the 1960s interviewed a wide sample of citizens about their relationship to and experience with death and published his findings in the seminal *Death, Grief and Mourning* (1965). Part of the power of the text is Gorer's highly personal preface recounting his own experiences with death, grief and mourning. His first remembrance of death commenced with the interruption of his playing in the streets with his friends as funeral processions would go by. Decorum and social expectation dictated that they demonstrated their respect for those who passed. He wrote that as a youth, when they were playing in the street, they

> had to keep an eye out for them and take off our hats or caps for the whole time that the funeral procession passed us; it was very *rude* not to, and showed a lack of respect for people in their great trouble. And when people were dressed in mourning—they might be visitors or servants or shop-assistants—we had to be quiet, and not fidget or make a noise. As small children we learned that mourners were in a special situation or state of mind and had to be treated differently from others, with more consideration and more respect; and I think our education on this subject was typical of that period [xvi].

His description fosters an image of an entire community coming together as one when the mourning processional passes through as well as the training of its youth to respect the sanctity of the mourning period, unlike our contemporary times where funeral processions of automobiles are seen as annoying and highly disruptive to getting to a destination on time or through the next cycle of the traffic light. This sense of recognition of respect within the community for the deceased and grieving family members played an integral part in maintaining a stable ritual around mourning. Peter Homans noted: "The community provided the foundation for what Philippe Ariés calls a 'public' understanding of mourning and death. 'Public' meant that the surrounding, commonly shared community took upon itself, in the form of its rituals, much of the burden of mourning that would otherwise have been overwhelming" (6).

In a later portion of Gorer's preface he recounted when his relationship to death moved from being merely a casual, cap-doffed observer on the side of the road to being one of the members of that processional parade. "I do not remember how soon I was given black ties and had bands of crêpe sewn on to the sleeves of my suits; but I remember the first days I wore those insignia of woe feeling, despite my unhappiness, somehow distinguished, in nearly every sense of the world. I was set apart; and this was somehow fitting and comforting" (xviii). Gorer's observation is significant as he noted that being in a state of mourning delineated him from others and, while there was sadness attached to this emotional and social position, there was also a comfort in being part of a ritualized pattern of behavior which had its own rules and expectations (for example, the dress code of black ties, suits and bands of crêpe).

However, this sense of comfort was not to last because this almost tranquil, calming sense of the socially defined nature of mourning from when he was a child began to change throughout the century. In his first examination of grief and mourning, "The Pornography of Death" (1955), he noted that death was no longer a subject that was present in the everyday lives of the community. Instead, "death had superseded sex as a taboo subject and one surrounded with a morbid and furtive fascination for many people" (xxv). He argued in *Death, Grief and Mourning* "that the majority of British people are today without adequate guidance as to how to treat death and bereavement and without social help in living through and coming to terms with the grief and mourning which are the inevitable responses in human beings to the death of someone whom they have loved" (126). According to Gorer, the shift occurred because the onus moved to the individual having to cope with the death of a loved one on one's own rather than having the ability to rely upon a societal framework that aided in the process of mourning, like Gorer had experienced as a child. "Today it would seem to be believed, quite sincerely, that sensible, rational men and women can keep their mourning under complete control by strength of will or character so that it need be given no public expression, and indulged, if at all, in private, as furtively as if it were an analogue of masturbation" (128). Why did this change occur? Thanatologists have noted that previously the death of a loved one happened in the home as the dying figure was surrounded by family and community members. However, the removal of the dying figure away from familial confines and into hospitals precipitated the change in how mourning came to be handled. In his seminal work *The Hour of Our Death*, which examined death across cultures and over a millennium, Ariés wrote that in contemporary times

> the community feels less and less involved in the death of one of its members. First, because it no longer thinks it necessary to defend itself against a nature which has been domesticated once and for all by the advance of technology, especially medical technology.... The community ... has been replaced by an enormous mass of atomized individuals [612–3].

Peter Homans built upon Ariés' argument by positing that mourning practices have changed so dramatically because of "the erosion and fragmentation of community caused by the processes of modernization" (1).

One of the main figures influencing the act of mourning away from the church and community support network and toward the sole individual was Charles Darwin, who noted that one could study the mourner and her emotions through the nature of science. Homans remarked that Darwin "removed it from the control of the traditional sites of mourning practices, that is, from the influence of the clergy and their churches. Mourning gradually came to be recognized as an internal, and principally psychological, activity" (7). In turn, this shift in mourning practices aided in developing the practices of trained psychologists and psychiatrists. And, not surprisingly, a major influence on that migration was Sigmund Freud. Specifically, Freud redefined the nature of mourning as an internalized experience, making the community no longer an important or even necessary part of the mourning process. He also contradicted the long-held mindset about how one adapted to the death of a loved one. Previous thought about mourning posited that over time the pain of the loss would slowly evaporate. The longer the mourner was away from the deceased the better the mourner would begin to feel. Freud, though, saw this issue of time actually much more internally complicated. Freud wrote that "in mourning time is needed for the command of reality-testing to be carried out in detail, and that when this work has been accomplished the ego will have succeeded in freeing its libido from the lost object" (252). He also noted, "Mourning impels the ego to give up the object by declaring the object to be dead and offering the ego the inducement of continuing to live" (257). By the time Gorer's study appeared in the 1960s, the influence of Darwin and Freud had truly trickled down to the masses. The community's as well as the church's role in mourning had lessened considerably.

Precisely this point about the difficulty of mourning due to the failure of the community is at the heart of Penhall's play *Pale Horse*. At one point Charles and Lucy, the two main characters, discuss the repercussions of secretly burying a man who Lucy killed in self-defense rather than notifying the authorities. Charles argues against it.

> CHARLES: People will miss him.... People will come looking for him. People ... in the community.
> LUCY: Who? [127–8].

And to Lucy's question Charles has no answer. Charles, who experiences the shock of his wife's death, experiences the strain and failure of finding succor from his immediate community. Lucy's question of "Who?" echoes Charles' own search for the "who" amongst the members of his community who can answer his questions about death and provide any type of ritual of comfort.

Even though Gorer's study is over 45 years old, it reinforces what other thanatologists have observed, which is that mourning has shifted from a communally supported action into a much more individualized and private act that requires an individual's own adaptation to the grief process rather than the larger context of a community providing a barometer of support. In other words, mourning has become swept under the carpet, excised from public viewing. As Gorer notes, "Mourning is treated as if it were a weakness, a self-indulgence, a reprehensible bad habit instead of a psychological necessity" (131). It is precisely this aspect of mourning, as an individual's struggle rather than as a community-supported ritual, that drives Joe Penhall's *Pale Horse*.

A year after *Some Voices* appeared on the Upstairs stage of the Royal Court, Penhall made his second appearance in the Upstairs theatrical venue. After having previously focused on a burger bar and an Italian restaurant owner, Penhall completed his trilogy about struggling food service owners with *Pale Horse*. Returning to the Upstairs Theatre along with Penhall was the director Ian Rickson and Ray Winstone, who had played the put-upon-brother Pete in *Some Voices*. He now was cast in the lead role of Charles, the bar owner and recent widower, in what is Penhall's bleakest play. The title *Pale Horse* stems from the Four Horsemen of the Apocalypse. The fourth horse to appear, a pale horse, held the rider Death, who, along with the other three figures, brought darkness to the world. In order for the actors to understand the darkness of death, Rickson had his performers meet a grief counselor, vicar and mortician, who, according to Penhall, was "over-keen" and "wheeled in his favourite corpses" (Ducas). The visit had its intended effect on the actors as "Ray [Winstone] came into rehearsals next day white as milk" (Little and McLaughlin 321). While the darkness of death prominently hovers over the entire play, Penhall has also created a world bereft of order and sense. Unlike *Wild Turkey* and *Some Voices*, which featured steadying figures in the forms of Stu and Pete, *Pale Horse* eschews this mollifying structure of offering a character who holds steady in the midst of the chaos of the world. Instead, Charles desperately searches for an anchoring position for his grief.

Returning to the food service/bar industry in London, Penhall this time sets much of the action in the struggling bar owned by Charles. In the play's first scene Charles learns that his wife has been killed by a bus. The rest of the play charts his downward spiral over the next few weeks as he struggles to mourn for her. Despite his grief, his business must continue and he hires a new barmaid, Lucy, who had previously worked for his friend at a restaurant/club/bar where S&M is the main item on the menu. Her former boyfriend, who runs the restaurant and is Charles' friend, comes to Charles' bar to harass her for leaving him, and she kills him. Charles ends up helping her hide the body, and the first act ends with them burying the corpse in a field. Through their shared secret Charles and Lucy become friends and then lovers, but when Lucy and a bar customer, who hits on her, get into a dust-up, Charles erupts into a pale of violence and badly beats the customer. Hoping to find a solution to his behavior, he seeks out the vicar who held the service for his wife and ends up roughing him up as well. The play ends with Charles, wearing a shirt covered in blood, standing by his wife's grave as constables arrive to take him away.

While the piece is driven by Charles' personal anguish in confronting his grief, another layer exists highlighting a world inherently obsessed with and subsumed by violence. *Pale Horse* features an incredibly grim world, and since so much of Penhall's work is driven by a reworking of his own experiences and those of his friends, it is noteworthy to remark upon a piece he wrote for the *Guardian* in April 2004. In the piece he described his first recollection and personal brush with death, which happened when he was living in Adelaide in the mid–1970s, when he was "a gap-toothed, freckle-faced pommie migrant" ("Riddles"), who came face to face with the violent death of his friend's sister. Tania Kenny, "a sunburnt, wordly tomboy, strikingly beautiful and endlessly insouciant" ("Riddles"), had gone missing. It was not until the next summer that her remains were found. For Penhall it was shocking to see the bones of his bike-riding friend in the local newspaper. It came out at the trial (held later that year) that she had accepted a ride from two men, who killed and then buried her. She was one of seven local girls who fell victim to the two serial killers. The rest of his article revealed that the local history of Adelaide was filled with the serial killing of children. While Penhall's article did not overtly connect this brutal murder from his past to his motivation for writing the play, the darkness of *Pale Horse* echoes this same sense of brutality and oppressiveness he noted as an element of growing up in Adelaide.

Like many of Penhall's plays, *Pale Horse* is driven by an autobiographical incident, in this case his own crisis surrounding mourning. When Penhall was 21, he experienced the shocking death of "the first real love of my life" ("Re: E-mail"). His ex-girlfriend, Catherine Bey, died in a car crash. He remarked that her death "precipitated a long period of near unbearable mourning" ("Re: E-mail"). "I went on a binge for about six months. Other friends have gone on binges and never come back. Two has [*sic*] schizophrenia and I was seriously haunted by the notion that I could go that way" (Rees, "Bard"). In reaction to her death, Penhall also became much more reckless in regard to his own well-being, including being hospitalized for trying to prevent an assault. "A gang was 'gay bashing' one of my neighbours outside my house. There was talk they'd killed somebody some weeks before so I went for them" ("Re: E-mail").[1]

Bey's death was an additional catalyst in his decision to drop out of art school. In addition, his continuing difficulty in dealing with her death provided an impetus for his decision to leave Australia all together and fly to England. Eventually, Penhall came to the realization that if he wrote a play about his reaction to Bey's death, then "it would save me going to a psychiatrist or the wall" (Little and McLaughlin 318). The play was also driven by his inability to turn to religion after her death: "The premise for *Pale Horse* came to me during a particularly dark and arduous night of the soul in my Shepherd's Bush studio, when it had occurred to me that it was only the truly religious who could deal with death. A bereaved atheist doesn't have the full picture when it comes to mourning" ("Introduction" x-xi). Penhall confessed in a later interview with Ruth Little and Emily McLaughlin to some more of the autobiographical elements that inspired the work, including the fact that his grandfather was a vicar, but "my family had no religious beliefs whatsoever" (318). In addition, the work allowed him to "explore the self-destructiveness, rage and confusion I still felt, and document some of the more unsavoury ways in which I had attempted to assuage my demons ... hassling clergymen, one-night stands, bad company, booze and the odd smack in the head with a baseball bat" (318–21). He explained further, echoing what the thanatologists had noted in the changing shape of mourning in the latter half of the twentieth century and the sense of alienation that accompanies grief: "Charles finds that there is no solace in any of the belief systems you are brought up with, not amongst his friends and associates" (Klein 79). As Gorer and others noted, the community has failed the individual when it comes to mourning. For Penhall his play became "about a lawless, godless, loveless, self-regarding solipsistic community" (Klein 79).

The critical praise for *Pale Horse*, which premiered in October 1995, was similar to *Some Voices*. Carole Woddis called the play "exceptional" because "you can practically feel the veins stand out on the head" and "as a portrait of contemporary urban dissolution, the importance of love for one's identity and, above all the handling of grief, it's an emotional knockout." Michael Coveney of *The Observer* thought it as "compelling and extraordinary" as *Some Voices*. In addition, he deemed *Pale Horse* "as taut, tight and atmospheric as *Macbeth*." Dominic Dromgoole's assessment of the play was that Penhall "creates some unapologetically symbolist moments, and lets himself off the leash of naturalism a little more. Since the fabric of his world is so secure, the freedom is riveting" (222). Matt Wolf in *Variety* wrote that Penhall "is already staking out distinctive terrain as a chronicler of life's sufferers whose readjustments seem destined to go awry." And in becoming such a chronicler Wolf notes: "There's something commendable about the bleakness of Penhall's vision." On the topic of bleakness Dan Reballato noted this issue as he compared *Some Voices* with *Pale Horse*. "*Pale Horse* is, in my view, a much more interesting play. It's also much bleaker. It's a play about the nature of our ethical commitments—can we really face the idea that there is no God? I found that a very exciting, haunting experience" (Aragay and Zozaya 168–9).

However, there was also more criticism (but of the thoughtful variety rather than the demeaning) for his second full-length play. Jeremy Kingston of *The Times* noted that there was a problem with the dramatic expectancy that the play produces. "Penhall writes short scenes in which the dialogue usually closes on an unexpectedly simple, everyday remark. Following an outburst of insults, aggression or weird self-disclosure, it carries into the next scene a feeling that further danger is imminent.... But it all becomes tenuous and slips away." John Peter, who had been effusive in his praise of *Some Voices*, was clearly disappointed in the sophomore effort and found fault specifically with the same issue that Kingston noted in his review. Peter, though, focused on the effect of the play's conclusion on the audience. He felt that the end of the play leaves the audience member "jolted and short-changed, muttering to yourself: 'This is the end then, is it?'... What this tells you is either that the playwright has imagined a situation but not how it would grow and change, or that he has things to say about his characters but does not quite know why." Peter suggested that *Pale Horse* was still in the stage of being a workshopped play rather than a full-fledged play worthy of a production. Along the same lines Nick Curtis observed the potential, but not yet the final pay-off, of Penhall's writing ability. "His mastery of mood and of piteously amusing dialogue in *Pale Horse* show that Penhall is still promising, but not quite delivering." Lyn Gardner wrote that the play's grander ambitions doom it from being successful: "It wants to be deeply meaningful and won't settle for being a small but brilliantly effective portrait of ordinary blighted lives." This same observation was made by Paul Taylor who noted that once Lucy and Charles bury the body of her ex-boyfriend and then become lovers, the audience believes they will be seeing "a rerun of *Shallow Grave* intertwined with Last Tango in South London. [However,] Charlie's despair takes a rather more apocalyptic turn, with the play taking a turn for the worse and never quite persuading you that the beautifully observed initial material can bear the pumping up and belatedly swollen significance." A clearly bifurcated response to Penhall's sophomore effort, though it would not be the last time he would receive such diverse reaction to his work.

The first scene of the play perfectly exemplifies Penhall's economical ability to establish character and theme for the work as a whole. With only a few words Penhall immediately defines the nature of Charles' character before he comes face to face with his crisis of mourning. The scene opens with Charles on the phone in his bar and his first four sentences are: "I know. I know. I know. I know." (93), and with each utterance he informs the caller (and the audience as well) about his sense of surety and confidence in his knowledge of the world around him. In so doing, Penhall introduces his main character at his greatest sense of self-assurance about himself and the way the world works. All of which, though, is a facade as the next two lines begin the undermining process that will continue throughout the play. The caller then informs Charles of new information to which he responds: "I didn't know that. *Pause.* I didn't know that either" (93).[2]

Charles, a business owner, considers himself to be a success and wants to be perceived as someone in charge and control of his professional world.

However, just like with his assurance being undermined, his professional decision-making skills are equally suspect and destabilized throughout the duration of the phone call. When the person on the other end of the receiver inquires as to why Charles hired a certain unnamed employee, Charles responds, "Because I believe in giving people a chance" (93). However, he then remarks shortly thereafter that he fired him because "he was a wanker" (93), revealing that while he might want to give someone a chance, he really is not that successful in judging the character of his employees. This same fault is echoed later in the play through his selection of Lucy as the replacement employee for the previously fired one as she violently attacks two of his customers during the course of her employment. This disparity and discordance between the manner in which he wants to be perceived and the reality of his situation is emphasized when it comes to his wife, who is, as he tells the caller, "the very oxygen I breathe," but then he reveals that she hates his bar, calling it a "den of iniquity" (94). After he hangs up, the phone rings again and he coincidentally receives information about his wife, "What about her?... When? Where? No, I didn't know..." (94). Penhall repeats the phrase "I didn't know" from the first phone conversation, but now instead of being a bit of comedic business undercutting the attitude of Charles, the sentence is a harbinger of tragically fatal information and the bar owner's immediate immersion into the dark circumstances of the rest of the play.

In such a brief scene (only a little over a page long) Penhall provides enough information about Charles to set him on the path of his journey, which will be the difficulty of mourning in our contemporary society. And Penhall, in terms of Charles' condition, captures the angst and uncertainty that goes into such a situation. In a later scene when Charles visits his wife's grave he engages in a conversation with another mourner.

> WOMAN: They say it takes three months before you finish mourning properly.... Mind you, if you can bring yourself to be positive about it, the world's your oyster.
> CHARLES: Absolutely.
> *Pause.*
> What if you can't? [119].

Charles' question captures the essence of his dilemma as he hopes to find a solution to his suffering and difficulties, even though he doubts whether he will ever emerge from his grief. As with *Some Voices*, Penhall focuses on the psychological state of his main character. However, instead of depicting a psychological state that the majority of his audience members have not experienced or encountered as he did with Ray's schizophrenia, Penhall turns his attention to the nature of mourning and the difficulties inherent in such an act in contemporary society, which *is* something almost all of his audience members have experienced at some point in their lives. However, Penhall complicates the situation of Charles' grief through the abrupt manner of his wife's death. Her death is unexpected, adding an extra layer of complexity for the bereaved, in comparison to an anticipated death (like a long illness) where the grieving party has advanced notice. Therese A. Rando describes the characteristics that occur when dealing with the surprising death of a loved one.

> The sequelae of sudden, unanticipated loss of a loved one tend to leave the mourner stunned, feeling out of control and confused, unable to grasp the full implications of a loss that is perceived as inexplicable, unbelievable, and incomprehensible. The mourner becomes bewildered, anxious, insecure, self-reproachful, depressed, and despairing. He or she is in shock emotionally and physiologically, and it persists for an extended time [145].

Adding to the condition of Charles' grief is the violent manner of his wife being struck and killed by a bus. The nature of such a violent incident also has a more powerful impact on the mourner than a forewarned death. Rando writes that the mourner will feel "terror, shock, helplessness and powerlessness, vulnerability, threat, anxiety, fear, violation, hyperarousal, and victimization. Ultimately, they typically lead to significant anger, guilt, self-blame, and shattered assumptions" (147). Kai Erikson discusses the additional traumatic psychological effects that such a death can have on the mourner: "By *individual trauma* I mean a blow to the psyche that breaks through one's defenses so suddenly and with such brutal force that one cannot react to it effectively.... [One suffers] deep shock as a result of ... exposure to death and to devastation.... [People] withdraw into themselves, feeling numbed, afraid, vulnerable, and very alone" (qtd. in Homans 28). While Penhall admits that his own questions about his lack of religion and a need for catharsis over Dey's death drew him to write the play, the nature of the tragedy surrounding Charles' wife's death creates a personal crisis for Charles that requires more comfort and assistance than merely can be provided by the institution of religion. The thanatologists' descriptions above of a mourner's emotional and psychological response to such a shocking death is perfectly captured by Penhall in the nature of Charles' behavior as he demonstrates all of these characteristics in reaction to his wife's death.

After the news of her shocking demise, Charles begins his journey to find an answer to her death and a means to mourn. Charles first visits the established institutions trained to deal with death and the survivors left behind (a mortuary, the church, and the medical field). Not finding any sustenance from these usually solid supporters of grieving, he then turns to individuals in his life (friends and family) and the community of his regulars at the bar. In none of these places does he find succor, supporting the findings of Gorer, Ariés and others who argue that in our contemporary society mourning and death are not consider significantly important community issues anymore. Instead, Penhall's play, through Charles' struggle, indicates that everyone is on his own with his grief. Unlike his two previous plays which end with some form of communal connection at the play's end, *Pale Horse* refuses to offer any sense of comfort or support to those dealing with grief and mourning. The vicar who conducts the ceremony for Charles' wife's funeral exactly expresses the contemporary difficulty (as created by Darwin and Freud) involved with mourning: "You are of a generation which searched for self knowledge and identity through science. And it's no surprise when something happens, a fundamental sorrow alights, you find it perplexing" (100). Even the vicar's remarks indicate the church itself has lost a contributing say in the communal and societal nature of the process of grief. No longer are the tenets offered through doctrine enough. Instead, everyone is left to follow their own individual path.

After the death of his wife, Charles visits the mortuary and talks to the undertaker while his wife's body is being prepped for burial. While the undertaker is uncomfortable with the grieving husband's presence, Charles expresses an uneasy sense of distance as he looks at his wife's body. He presses the undertaker to explain how the corpse is prepared, including what happens to the blood and how the body is made ready for internment. On the surface it is a cold, harsh scene as Charles tries to distance the body on the table from the woman he married and looks for an explanation about death from someone surrounded by it every day. Their conversation though quickly turns to suicide as the undertaker lists the type of person more likely to kill him or herself: "People with families.... And people without families. Lonely people. Single people" (97). Essentially, what originally starts out with a specific situation of those who kill themselves as being limited to "people with families" quickly turns into a blanket statement covering everyone, especially lonely, single people, which is what Charles becomes more and more over the course of the play. The conversation with Charles, not surprisingly, is not welcomed by the undertaker, especially when it turns to the disposition of the corpse on the table between them. Charles justifies his inappropriate questions through the culturally dictated response that a mourner needs to talk to someone and in talking to the undertaker about the nature of his profession, he is actually discussing science and as Charles argues, "science isn't ... emotional" (96). According to Terry Martin and Kenneth J. Doka, Charles's behavior demonstrates a perfect pattern for masculine grief. And, not surprisingly, his self-proclaimed absence of emotion is an important characteristic of masculine grief. Martin and Doka explain that for this type of grief "feelings are limited or toned down" (167). In addition, "thinking precedes and often dominates feeling," as in this scene where Charles subsumes his feelings for his wife through his questions about the scientific nature of the undertaker's profession. The male mourner focuses "on problem-solving rather than expression of feelings" (167). What especially becomes apparent over the course of the play are the feelings of anger and guilt that Charles will express and feel, both of which are also primary characteristics of masculine grief. Charles' choice to start with the undertaker is a perfect representation of his looking for answers from the most basic element of the death process. He sees the job the undertaker does as a science, but in one sense the undertaker's position harkens to his own profession as bartender. While the undertaker does prepare the body for burial and handles the impersonal arrangement of the process, he represents the economic and necessary bodily preparatory steps in processing the deceased. The undertaker, while usually polite about the nature of death, cannot provide the professionally institutionalized guidance one pursues for help with the psychological battles of coping with mourning. Like Charles' own job as a bartender, the undertaker hears a great deal of stories about the deceased from the grieving families, but he really cannot provide any assistance on the journey. He is merely there to provide a listening ear and a comforting pat on the hand before moving onto the next body in his back room. For the undertaker, death is about the ritualized and scientific preparation of the body for burial for a substantial fee, not about providing guidance to the grief-stricken.

Charles' next conversation occurs with the vicar after his wife's funeral. In seeking guidance Charles admits his agnosticism, and the man of cloth offers him a Bible for comfort. It is a prop which Charles will carry around with him throughout the play, and he even will open it upon occasion, looking for solace and sustenance, which he never finds. Instead, the words of the Lord are merely a hollow totem for him as are the words from the vicar. Like the undertaker, the vicar too fails him, offering homilies and biblical quotations, which Charles is unable to appreciate because he misses the religious references that the man of the cloth makes.

> VICAR: Have you not heard "how good and how pleasant it is for brethren to dwell together in unity"?
> CHARLES: I keep myself to myself [101].

The emptiness of the exchange between the two men echoes an early scene of Tony Kushner's *Angels in America* (1991) where Louis looks for some answers from the rabbi about the death of his grandmother and the guilt he feels about his feelings of wanting to leave Prior. He fails to receive any clarity about either issue, mainly because the rabbi wants to get on the road since he has a long drive home to the Bronx. Whereas Kushner's play looks to challenge the larger concept of Judeo-Christian principles (after all, in his play God has left), Penhall's play is not crafted to condemn the church. Instead, the church's failure to provide comfort is merely a part of a much larger failure of the institutional structure that aids those who mourn. These two men do not communicate on an even playing field. Due to his agnosticism, Charles cannot find comfort in the biblical allusions and the vicar is unable to find a sympathetic link with Charles to help ameliorate the pain he feels. Instead, he turns the requests back on the requestor and provides general words of support. Charles asks, after the funeral is over,

> CHARLES: Should I say some more prayers or something?
> VICAR: Would you like to?

CHARLES: Which ones?
VICAR: Any ones you like.
CHARLES: I don't know any.
VICAR: Perhaps you have a prayer of your own.
CHARLES: Make one up, you mean? [98–99].

For Charles the comfort for his mourning cannot come from the church because he does not share the common language or belief system, just like he cannot find comfort from the undertaker because of the corporeal nature of his actions. In addition, the vicar's words fail to provide comfort to Charles at all. To each one of his requests the vicar responds with generalities and evasions—"Everybody deals with the passing on of a loved one differently" and "I can't advise you.... I listen" (100). According to Homans, these kind of evasions provided for "the erosion of tradition-informed institutions [and] forced more and more responsibility for living upon individuals. Answers to moral questions once taken for granted now required more self-awareness and more reliance upon one's own resourcefulness" (6). It is here where the failure occurs for Charles as his own sense of self-awareness and resourcefulness has become strained. His value system has been skewed as he has placed his bar business at the center of all of his needs, even making it more important than his wife, which he admits to the doctor in the next scene. He has disrupted his priorities. Religion, then, has not failed him. In fact, at the end of the play he returns to the church for help, the only place he visits twice. Instead, the problem Charles faces is much broader due to the changed communal structure of mourning. Society no longer has room for death and, in turn, no longer offers a ritualized comforting response.

After being unable to find a scientific or soulful solution to his malaise, he seeks medical guidance from his general practitioner, who also fails to placate Charles. Unlike the previous two meetings, this exchange becomes much more heated. As with the vicar, he fails to receive a straight answer. When he describes his physical and mental state since the death of his spouse, his general practitioner first states that he is not experiencing depression, but then upon hearing further symptoms, she changes her mind and proceeds to diagnose him as suffering from depression. When he asks whether his dreams have any meanings in relation to his wife's death, she distances herself, like the vicar and the undertaker, from any comforting words: "I'm not a psychiatrist.... It's more than my job's worth to attempt the work of a specialist" (103). Charles requests medications, but she refuses. All he gains from her is frustration. In this scene Charles, for the first time, discloses information about his wife, as he admits his spiritual struggle over and feelings of guilt about her death, both of which stem from having to decide between his profession and marriage. Just like Stu and Pete before him, Charles faces the question of what is more important to him: business or relationships. Like Stu opting for the burger bar over his friendship with Danny, Charles favored his business over his wife.

He admits: "I cared about her with every drop of life in my body. I cared about her and I adored her more than life itself.... But I had a business to run" (104–5). By choosing money over his wife, Charles now, because of her loss, questions his value system: the gain of what he actively pursued at his bar versus the loss of what he could have had waiting for him at home. Charles will not open up again about his wife until later in the second act when he tells Lucy about their honeymoon: "I remember her sitting on the bed in the hotel, with the sun and the sea-air streaming in and her skin and her wet hair all golden in the lights, gulls cawing in the distance.... Fuck work. I'm a cunt" (145). Driving part of Charles' guilt then is his abandonment of his wife, the frozen in time, idyllic nature of that honeymoon snapshot of her and his failure to hold true to his commitment to "fuck work." He must reconcile himself to the fact that he betrayed what she meant to him.

And yet, despite the protestations he makes about his failures with his wife and the ensuing guilt he feels, there is still something slightly disingenuous about Charles' linguistic choices. Throughout the entire play Charles never once uses his wife's name, and neither does any other character. In fact, the only other character in the play with a name is Lucy. (Everyone else receives generalized descriptors.) Charles' inability to name her may be another sign of the guilt he feels about his treatment of her. In addition, one of the bar customers reveals to Lucy that Charles and his wife fought constantly and sometimes Charles hit her. The violent nature of their relationship indicates the stark contrast of their married existence to Charles' honeymoon memory. To name her is then to even more acknowledge his failure to fulfill his promise to her, but in terms of the process of mourning his failure to name her makes his grief all that more difficult to assuage. William Watkin addressed the significance as well as difficulty inherent in acknowledging and speaking the name of the deceased: "The aim of such acts of repetition and verbal superfluity at the graveside was to give brief extra presence to those in absence.... During the period that the name is spoken, sung or moaned, the dead live on a little while longer with the mystical power of naming. Nevertheless, once the song stops, the dead are truly dead and buried" (5). His refusal to name his wife by using pronouns to fill in for her linguistic presence keeps her at a distance and allows her to remain alive. By refusing to name her, he cannot finalize the process of grieving because she has not yet died for him, even though he has seen her in the preparation room of the undertaker. Instead, she still stays in a state of limbo because he cannot confront that final mental image of her that plagues him throughout the weeks after her death. In addition, by refusing to name her, he does not have to confront his disastrous treatment of her when she was alive, but at the same time he also cannot mentally overcome those same actions. So even though his wife is "truly dead and buried" physically in the play, Charles cannot see her as "truly dead and buried" until he finally confronts his sense of her, his naming of her, which is something he is unable and unwilling to do.

The simple nature of Charles' linguistic patterns and his inability to express himself except through anger and later violence only highlights his struggle to mourn because "the poetics of mourning is still marked by language's magical powers of saving, preserving, honouring, prolonging and having" (Watkin 10). Instead, Charles finds himself investing in violence instead of language as a means of expression, demonstrated by his teaching Lucy to direct a baseball bat at a potential problem customer's chest. "'Cause you want to break his ribs. Get to his vital organs. Teach the fucker a lesson! Go on!...'" (122). In his consultation with his GP, he admits his irrational propensity for anger and violence, citing his violent reactions to the driving techniques of bus drivers. "Always stopping too late or stopping too early, slamming the brakes on, they drive like they got a club-foot some of them. It just makes me want to hit somebody" (102). The GP clinically responds that there are rules governing society and everyone shares the same sense of anger and frustration that Charles describes.

And yet, the comment that rules govern the behavior of society is important in Penhall's plays. In *Some Voices* Pete professes about the importance of rules but then learns that the institutional body that creates rules for his brother's treatment does not concern itself with ensuring that the rules are put to protective use of him. Here, the GP indicates that there are rules governing our behavior, but as we have already seen, when it comes to mourning, the previous rules that governed how one mourned have been revoked. As the vicar indicates, everyone makes their own rules as to how to make it through the grief. Later Charles admits: "If a man can't play by the rules then he deserves every dark fucking day that befalls him" (129), and while he is talking about the man that Lucy kills in an act of self-defense, it equally applies to him, as he has failed to follow his own rule of staying true to his wife. His grief, as well, influences his struggle with the rules that govern normal behavior. For example, he decides to aid Lucy in dispatching the dead body of her ex-boyfriend. He helps her dig the grave and bury the body, not reporting the death to the police. He later sleeps with Lucy, his employee, and then beats up a customer, offering him money to forget the whole encounter even happened. Finally, at the end of the play, he roughs up the vicar who conducted his wife's funeral service. For Charles all the rules that govern and define proper behavior have disappeared.

After failing to find comfort from established institutions, Charles turns to a friend for aid and succor. At first it appears that Charles has finally found someone to listen to him, but his friend admits his own inability to provide any help to assuage the pain. He says, "I'm so sorry, Charles. If I knew what to say, I'd say it" (109). However, similar to Charles' own admission about favoring his business over his wife, his unnamed friend also believes his business to be more important than Charles' personal struggles. While Charles pours out his failure with the doctor, his friend, who is only identified as the maître d', trains his new waitress and current girlfriend, Lucy. His divided attention shifts between the complaints of Charles and the inability of Lucy to correctly play her role for the club's customers, who expect their waitress to engage in S&M antics. As Lucy explains to Charles later, after she has quit the club and been hired to work in his bar, her job was to hit the customers and "the more you smacked 'em the more they misbehaved, the dirty old sods" (117). According to the maître d', the behavior of the customers and the business's plan that caters to them have become all the rage. Penhall then provides us once again with another incongruent scene. Charles aims for comfort and sympathy from a friend, who is in the midst of training Lucy to endure the abuse from the customers as well as to confer it right back, even being explicitly trained in the manner in which she should be hitting them. The popularity of such a business reflects directly on the nature of the world in which Charles seeks a salvation to his grief. How can he be expected to ameliorate the pain of his wife's death in the midst of a community where its members are more interested in the pain that they can have inflected upon themselves and others? This individualized societal focus, which thanatologists have commented upon, has taken a dramatic and violent narcissistic turn. According to J. Todd Dubose, one of the most crucial components in the process of mourning is the "rebuilding of a new self-in-a-life-world. This process focuses less on the personal reactions of someone to loss and more on the readjustment to the social arena: mourning is the most public expression of loss" (368). Just as with the minister, doctor and undertaker, Charles once again fails to find succor in sharing his feelings of loss with a person he identifies as someone who can and should support him. Instead, in such a situation then, Charles' comment to his friend—"Well, I'm glad you're around.... I can come here, any time of the day or night and you always listen" (110)—takes on a rich irony. If Charles fails to see the larger, societally bankrupt nature of the maître d's endeavors, then his own quest for salvation from his grief is also doomed. After all, Dubose writes that "mourning takes place inside the body as it reacts to the outside world" (369). If the outside world, as represented by the vicar, general practitioner and now the maître d's club, is bereft of compassion, understanding and guidance, then Charles' grief cannot even begin to be assuaged.

Later he and Lucy discuss their personal encounters with death, and Lucy's comments reinforce not only the community's lackadaisical, easy acceptance of death but also suggest that generational differences play a significant role in how one reacts to sudden death. She tells Charles: "I've known a lot of people who've died suddenly.... Then there's suicides. Everybody I know knows somebody who's either thought about it or actually tried it or actually done it.... Live life while you can, when you can, as fast as you can. Within reason. That's my motto" (130). Lucy's laconic observations—they have this conversation after she has killed her boyfriend the maître d' with a baseball bat in Charles' bar — proffer a far different perspective than Charles'. Nothing represents this better than when Charles comes upon the body of the maître d' in his bar. Charles stresses that they should call the police, but Lucy manages to convince him to embrace her plan, which is to bury him in a spot where no one ever goes. She argues, matter of factly, that no one will miss him, so why should they report his murder? This second sudden death in Charles' life adds yet another level of stress upon his already fragile handling of the death of his wife. Highlighting this difficulty is his inability to provide closure over the murder of the maître d'. As they both stand over the grave, Charles pulls out the Bible that the vicar handed him and tries to say a blessing over the corpse. However, he fails at finding anything appropriate to read over the makeshift grave. This opportunity to provide linguistic, spiritual and moral closure over the death of his friend is impossible, not surprising since he is unable to find any resolution in his wife's passing.

Whereas the undertaker, vicar and doctor represent Charles' institutional support, the maître d' and Lucy represent Charles' immediate supportive community of friends. In the early part of Act 2, his extended community of customers has the chance to aid in his grieving process. As noted before, the extended community's participation in the ritual of mourning was a crucial component to the closure of the experience for the individual and community itself.

> The community was gathered around the bed where he lay.... The community was weakened by the loss of one of its members. It expressed the danger it felt; it had to recover its strength and unity by means of ceremonies the last of which always had the quality of a holiday, even a joyous one [Ariés 603].

However, as already seen, that time has passed and the extended community, just like Charles' immediate community, fails in offering solace. The community (in this case represented by the characters Woman, Customer 1 and Customer 2) visit his bar and as the scene opens they drunkenly sing the following lyrics from "The Wonder of You."

> When no one else can understand me
> When everything I do is wrong
> You give me hope and consolation
> You give me the strength to carry on [136].

Penhall's choice of the song is incredibly apt and rich as the lyrics ironically refer not only to the strained relationship he had with his wife but also his own struggle after her death, as the "you" references the persons with whom he has come into contact. None of these attributes ("understand[ing]," "hope," "consolation" and "strength") have happened for him (and in turn the words have their own aching absence for the rest of the customers in the bar who reveal their own personal struggles), but it is only the non-singing Charles who recognizes the emptiness of the words being sung. Penhall makes it clear that Charles wants nothing to do with the customers. Instead, for much of the scene he broods around the bar cleaning up rather than engaging with his patrons and their own stories about death and mourning, especially that of Customer 2, who only reifies the darkness that Charles feels as he describes the rain-soaked funeral for his own wife and his epiphany about the oncoming boredom that was to be his life. A frustrated Charles ends up throwing all of them out of his bar.

At the start of the second act Penhall presents us with the same scenic setup as the beginning of the first act: Charles on the phone. This time, though, he has called home to talk to his parents and for Charles it is his perhaps his best chance to find some solace and comfort to deal with the loss of his wife because he is seeking help from the people who love him, but like with his other attempts, he finds failure once again. While Penhall does not provide much backstory to Charles' history with his parents, it is clear from the short, one-sided dialogue of his phone call that a rich complexity exists in his connection with them.[3] The reason for Charles' call is to talk to his father and engage him in a conversation about his wife's death. His parents, though, failed to attend the funeral and his father only wants to talk about how the weather was during the ceremony and how the weather is now. Like in the first scene, where Charles tries to control the conversation through his knowing *I know*'s, he once again wants to direct the conversation with his parents, but is unable to do so. Like at the grave of his dead friend, he cannot express what it is that he wants to say to them, especially his father. However, it is clear from Charles' side of the conversation that his father really does not want to talk, has nothing really substantial to say and would much rather put his wife on the phone rather than continue the conversation with his son. The ensuing conversation with his mother bogs down into small talk about the weather and when he will get a new girlfriend (his wife has been dead only a few weeks). Clearly, his mother's social ineptitude is not what Charles desires to hear and he cuts the conversation short and begins drinking in reaction to his futile call.

However, his mother's comment about a new love in his life is not far off the mark, as Charles' final attempt to find solace occurs shortly thereafter as he and Lucy have dinner together, which results in them making love. For Charles, he feels that perhaps he has begun to make a connection. True, the two of them have shared in covering up the crime of her former boyfriend, but their lovemaking is the first time he has had any kind of positive reinforcement in regard to himself and his suffering. Through the physical contact he can find a grounding that has been absent in his other pursuits. And yet, like with all his other attempts to find answers, Lucy dispels any sense of commitment to their relationship by admitting it was merely a "quick fuck to keep our spirits up.... It doesn't mean anything" (145). Noting Charles' dismay at her dismissal of the meaning of their sexual dalliance, she proceeds to brutally dismiss him as a potential partner and mate. "Big fat belly, hairy arse, toenails need cutting, you stink, boozer's breath, hungover again, big hairy bollocks like a gorilla, big ugly cock.... You haven't got a pot to piss in, no future, you're moody, ugly, bad tempered, old..." (146). The generational differences in their perspective toward death has now recurred in the bedroom, and in both situations Charles comes to see that he and Lucy do not and will not share the same perspectives.

By the end of the play Charles has descended into a miasma of depression concerning his lot in life. He has, in effect, given up the pursuit of his business and the reasons to live. He has completely lost his feelings and connections. And despite Lucy's attempts to chide him out of his perspective, his experiences since his wife's death have led him to see that failure completely surrounds him. He tells Lucy: "Everybody knows, we're just taught not to think it.... We've had it. We're doomed" (155–6). Among the many monikers placed upon Penhall and his peers was the New Nihilists, and clearly the philosophy of nihilism perfectly encapsulates the mindset that has overtaken Charles not only as he talks to Lucy in the scene above but in the play's penultimate scene when he returns to the vicar to seek some guidance and answers after he badly beats up a customer who was harassing Lucy. His confession of "I'm lost.... I don't know who I am" to the vicar highlights the short cycle of depression and loss that Charles has experienced during his attempt to mourn for the death of his wife (160). The confident Charles at the play's beginning who repeatedly stressed to the caller, "I know," has now fully admitted that he does not know the most important thing: who he is. This crisis of self-identity and assurance reveals finally to him that there are no answers, no matter where he looks. He truly has descended from his pinnacle of certainty to a state of loss of identity, morality and self-assurance. As he is taken off by the police, he is a completely broken man, representing our own uncertainty in the face of death and our inability to mourn over those whom we lose.

4

Love and Understanding *and* the Demise of Relationships

David Mamet's *Sexual Perversity in Chicago*, which detailed in explicit emotional, sexual and linguistic terms the battle between the sexes and the harsh dynamics of heterosexual relationships by focusing on the arc of one couple's relationship, premiered in London in 1977 at the Regent Theatre, which at the time had a reputation for randy farces. The advertising for the play proved problematic and controversial. The poster for the London production suggested that the racy venue of the Regent Theatre was aptly chosen, as it was even more suggestive than the highly suggestive cover of the American Grove Press version of the play, which featured two stockinged, high heel-wearing legs languorously entwining the Sears Tower. The London poster and program featured the nude back and bottom half of a woman with her buttocks on prominent display. Like her American counterpart, she sported high heels and stockings, but this time she seductively straddled the Sears Tower, preparing to have the building sexually penetrate her. *The Sunday Times* reviewer found the poster not only pornographic but also an incredibly irresponsible advertising gimmick because it misled punters about the true content of the play. Ned Chaillet tut-tutted in his review that "it does not do to sell [plays] with naked bottoms." *The Daily Mail*, *The Daily Telegraph* and *The Sunday Telegraph* refused to accept advertising because of the play's title. Despite or perhaps in spite of these minor controversies, the play received mixed reviews from the critics, ranging from Michael Billington's observation that the play featured the "funniest dialogue to come out of America in quite some time" to Milton Shulman's *Evening Standard* tetchy comment: "I cannot say that all this explicit talk about sexual daydreams was relieved by much wit or perception." A number of reviewers, though, did note the strength of this new young American's voice and ear for dialogue and within just a few years of *Sexual Perversity*'s premiere, Mamet became the darling of London theatre and eventually received the distinct moniker of being the American Pinter.[1]

While Mamet's stylized theatrical vernacular emulated Pinter's own reliance on the importance of language, it was his thematic interests, especially in *Sexual Perversity*, that had lingering influences on the plays of the new writers of the 1990s. Anne Dean's description of the "desensitized" world of Mamet's play could describe many of the plays written by In-Yer-Face dramatists like Penhall, Ravenhill and Kane: "The characters inhabit a cheap and fraudulent world.... Human relationships have become attenuated to the point at which men and women view each other as little more than media-created stereotypes" (51). In addition, C.W.E. Bigsby noted Mamet, the social critic, on display in the play as he "exposes the alienations generated by urban life, deplores the substitution of artificial for real values, the erosion of human relationships and the decay of a language expressive of genuine human needs" (49). Numerous commentators have also noted how rooted Mamet's play is in the 1970s mentality of sex, pick-ups, bar scenes and the heavy-handed saturation of media images of male/female relations. Mamet has expressed his own frustration about the expectations he had about sex, all of which stemmed from the media's representations. He said: "My sex life was ruined by the popular media.... The myths surround us, destroying our lives.... You have to sleep with every woman that you see, ... utter nonsense" (qtd. in Dean 55). These same pressures surrounding expectation of male/female relationships echo in the plays of the 1990s. Even more importantly, Dean, like other critics, noted the telling cultural backdrop to the world of *Sexual Perversity*, which found a mirror image with the plays that emerged in the 1990s in Britain. Dean wrote that "erotica flourished, pornography boomed, and sex could be found in the unlikeliest places.... Such an emphasis upon the nonemotional aspects of sexuality was bound, sooner or later, to result in a deleterious blunting of the nation's consciousness" (51). Like Mamet, the writers of the 1990s responded to the previous decade's cultural, sexual and gender changes and in the process their plays traveled over remarkably similar territory. During the seven-year period from 1994 through 2001, one could find on the British stage a number of In-Yer-Face dramatists presenting their own interpretations of the themes found in Mamet's play. Like the response generated by the London premiere of Mamet's play, many of these In-Yer-Face playwrights provoked, as we have already seen, initial eye-brow-raising stares from critics and audience members.

In addition, as discussed in relation to *Wild Turkey*, by the mid–1990s a previously silenced voice from the 1980s was now reappearing nightly on the stages around London. The "lad" had made a marked return, as the theatrical programming had shifted to all male, all the time. In fact, these works returned males to their stereotypical predatory, violent, misogynistic characteristics so closely associated with the plays and characters of Mamet, with the first poster child for Mamet's misogynistic males being Bernie Litko in *Sexual Perversity*. In a sense these mid–1990s playwrights stripped away the more equal footing British female characters had obtained on the stage, starting with the feminist movement and the emergence of numerous female playwrights in the 1980s. These new playwrights returned female characters to mere peripheral items as they once again were relegated to the position of being pursued, manipulated and conquered. No other play better epitomized the reduced status of the theatrical female character than Nick Grosso's *Real Classy Affair*, whose only female character Louise irons clothing throughout both of her scenes, clearly an homage to Osborne's *Look Back in Anger*, where in the first scene of the play Alison irons throughout the course of Jimmy and Cliff's bickering and at the start of the third act Helena performs the same domestic chore. Seemingly, Grosso's work heralded that a return to the world of the 1950s was in order. And again, in *Sexual Perversity* a similarity can be seen in the male reaction to the perceived threat from the growing power of females, as Bernie Litko provides a short commentary on the push for the Equal Rights Amendment in the United States punctuated with: "I mean, I'm a big fan of *society* ... but this bites the big one. I'm sorry" (50).

Sexual Perversity in Chicago clearly articulates the inability of men and women to communicate at even the most basic level — made clear through the angry conversations that Danny and Deborah have:

> DANNY: Don't give me that look, Missy.
> DEBORAH: Or you're gonna what?
> DANNY: I don't mind physical violence. I just can't stand emotional violence. (*Pause*.) I'm sorry. I'm sorry, Deb. (*Pause*.) I forget who I am talking to. I'm sorry. You're very good for me. Come here. (*Pause*.) Come here.
> DEBORAH: No. You come here, for Christ's fucking sake. You want comfort, come get comfort. What am I, your toaster?
> DANNY: Cunt [57].

Their relationship ultimately cycles simply around sex, highlighting the enhanced difficulty of simple communication between them. The artistic ability of Mamet to place profanity is an oft remarked upon and admired part of Mamet's *oeuvre*, as demonstrated by the Danny's shocking and seemingly out of context use of the word "cunt." That same reliance on the pejorative is also a feature in the plays of these new writers.

Grosso again perfectly exemplifies the new writers' use of language, especially profanity, being as equally as important to the characters as they are in Mamet's plays. Grosso's second play *Sweetheart* ran into a problem with the overabundance of this same profane term. His first play *Peaches* featured, according to Grosso, "only one 'cunt' ... and, when it was said, there used to be a sharp intake of breath in the audience. But in *Sweetheart* there were over fifty 'cunts.' One theatre on the national tour wrote a letter saying: 'We can't possibly put on a play which has more than fifty cunts in it.' They'd actually counted them" (Sierz 184). The male characters that dot Grosso's two plays *Peaches* and *Sweetheart* are similar to the male characters in *Sexual Perversity in Chicago*, as they struggle with their insecurity in understanding the opposite sex, the uncertainty of communication, the difficulty in relating to one another, the struggle to hold a solid conversation and the uncomfortableness of the male's own expectation and peer pressure versus the reality of an actual, intimate relationship with a woman. Sierz wrote that in Grosso's plays "the sex war is scary not because it is violent but because it is confusing—these hip youngsters only have good intentions and words, and the words often fail them. In both plays, there is a sex war but very little sex. Instead, there is a void that is filled not so much with damage as with hurt" (185–6). Even though Sierz describes Grosso's characters, the same description can be attributed to the males and females of Mamet's world.

While Grosso captured the linguistic nature of Mamet's play, Ravenhill's controversially titled *Shopping and Fucking* created a similar controversy like Mamet's play, provoking a public relations bonanza for the Royal Court Theatre, which became the first West End theatre to produce a play featuring "fucking" in its title. Editors of London papers found themselves debating in house and then later publishing articles about their debate of whether they should carry advertising for the play and if so, how to list the play's title. Box office workers at the Royal Court were forbidden from saying the word "fucking" when mentioning the title to possible patrons. In addition, the cover of the Royal Court's playscript had the word "fuck" obscured by a fork breaking up the offending letters. At the Festival of British Plays in London in February 1998, the politician Neil Kinnock, former leader of the Labour party, had the distinction of introducing the play and before doing so he noted his discomfort not only with the word "fucking" but also surprisingly with "shopping," as he proposed new titles for the play, asking if he could introduce Ravenhill's work as either "Retailing and Fornicating" or "Consuming and Coitus" (Norman). Despite the controversy surrounding the play's title or perhaps because of it, *Shopping and Fucking* became a major hit for Ravenhill and the Royal Court, who produced it twice at their West End Ambassador's location during the renovation of their Sloane Square signature space.[2]

Mamet's play features Bernie graphically and hilariously describing a sexual encounter with a woman, who, in the midst of their intimacy, dons a Flak Suit, has a friend on the phone making battle noises and demands that he sets fire to her hotel room. His story opens up the play and sets the tone for remainder of the piece. Ravenhill offers his own take on an over-the-top sexual encounter. In fact, the story told by Mark, like Bernie's, is one of the play's most memorable set pieces, as he describes an encounter in a bathroom stall with a familiar-looking woman dressed in uniform.

> And as I walk past I take a cool glance to my left, cool look into the cubicle, cubicle with the door ajar and—wow.... The skirt is up around the waist. The skirt is up and the knickers are off or maybe she never had knickers—who knows?—but the skirt is up and she is like displaying this beautiful, come and get it snatch to die for, OK?... So I'm in there. I'm in and I kneel. I pay worship. My tongue is

worshipping that pussy like it's God. And that's when she speaks. Speaks and I know who she is.... She says, 'Oh yah. Chocks away.'... Yup. Fergie [75–6].[3]

While his play featured a cornucopia of sexual behaviors, like the one above as well as onstage blow, hand and rim jobs, Ravenhill admitted that the economic materialism of the 1980s and early 1990s had a fundamental influence on the sexual mores of his characters. His characters' "whole vocabulary had been defined by the market [and] had been brought up in a decade when all that mattered was buying and selling.... The market had filtered into every aspect of their lives. Sex, which should have been private, had become a public transaction" (Sierz 123). Despite the controversy over the play's name and its sexual explicitness, Ravenhill's piece was, at its heart, a statement against the policies of Margaret Thatcher and John Major, driven by an intense desire to politicize the economic changes in Britain, while at the same time redrawing, as his like-minded peers were doing, the kind of characters being depicted on the stage. Even though it was politically intentioned, his play, partly because of the title, partly because of the strong directorial sense of Max Stafford Clark, partly because of the location of the theatre in the heart of the theatre district and mere blocks from Soho, turned into a cultural phenomenon. However, Ravenhill felt that, because of its success, the play was becoming bigger than its parts.[4] Ravenhill remarked: "There was a slight worry that with *S & F* that it had become an event, something to be crossed off a list, that it was really more important to be there than to engage with what was being said, which was to look at what is happening to young people after 17 years of this Government" (McAuley 72). For a time it became the height of cool to attend a performance, with its rock concert feel — a pounding techno soundtrack blasted between scenes — and when it played at Ambassador's, the Royal Court instituted an open rush policy for the best seats. Before the house opened, a crush of under-25 bodies packed into the small lobby of the theatre, hoping to snag seats in the first couple of rows. As well, Ravenhill's play tapped into a popular established market of the early 1990s that addressed homosexual relationships. Just as the new writers began emerging in the mid–1990s, the British stage was undergoing a rash of what London reviewers called "pink plays," which focused on homosexuality, including Kushner's *Angels in America*, Jonathan Harvey's *Beautiful Things* (1993), Kevin Elyot's *My Night with Reg* (1994) and Nagy's *Butterfly Kiss*. Mark Ravenhill astutely argued that this new dramatic movement was a result of the creative impasse between males and females when he remarked:

> So deep are the suspicions and tensions between heterosexual men and women that it is almost impossible to stage their relationships. The male and female part of our psyches are pushing further and further apart and to bring them together on stage can only result in a huge conflict, a conflict that only David Mamet in *Oleanna* has dared to stage ["Plays about Men" 50].

Shortly after Ravenhill made the above statement, Patrick Marber's play *Closer* opened at the Cottesloe Theatre, completely encapsulating the cruelty and nastiness that Mamet had shown twenty years before with *Sexual Perversity in Chicago* and, in effect, breaking upon the impasse that Ravenhill mentioned above.

If Mamet is the American Pinter, then Marber is the British Mamet. Not only did Marber star in a revival of *Speed-the-Plow* (1988) and direct the Royal Court production of *The Old Neighborhood* (1997), but also his first two plays, *Dealer's Choice* and *Closer*, shadow the worlds of Mamet. *Dealer's Choice* details an all-male poker game that takes place in the back room of a restaurant, while *Closer* is, essentially, an English 1990s version of *Sexual Perversity in Chicago*, as Marber explores the sexual, emotional and psychological relationships between two men and two women. Like Mamet's play, *Closer* features graphic language, a hysterically funny sex story, in this case, a cybersex scene, and a brutal scene highlighting the dissolving of the relationships because of communication and mistrust between the sexes.

Marber, a member of Gambler's Anonymous, used a card game metaphor to explain the play as being about "the poker game of love, sex, desire, as it were — the series of manipulations and counter-manipulations we all seem to get into, the mess we make of our love lives" (Hanks 14). Like Mamet in the 1970s and the new writers of the 1990s, Marber was driven to write about the sexual politics issue at stake in relationships:

> One of the starting points for the play was that I hadn't, since the film *sex, lies and videotape*, seen anything that put my generation's romantic concerns in any kind of perspective.... I just wanted to see something that expressed the conversations I was having — that my friends were having — that people in their thirties were all exploring [Shone 17].

Like *Shopping and Fucking*, *Closer* garnered a great deal of publicity, much of it positive because of it being the first piece commissioned of a new writer by the Royal National Theatre. However, the publicity hoopla surrounding the play produced some slap back as audience members did not find the theatrical nirvana that reviews had promised. Clearly, a play entitled *Shopping and Fucking* will filter out and, in turn, filter in a specific audience, mostly one that skews toward the younger demographic. However, the average audience member for the National was not necessarily the same at the Royal Court and, more specifically, for a play called *Shopping and Fucking*.[5] One upset audience member for *Closer* told Lesley Garner of *The Sunday Times*, "I hated it. I thought it was coarse and pretended to break barriers of theatre that it wasn't close to breaking. It was trying to shock, but in such an old-fashioned sensationalistic way.... None of us felt shocked; we were simply embarrassed at the obviousness of the attempts at audience manipulation" (Garner 15). Writer Shane Watson told Garner: "Men and women don't talk to each other like that. I was just aware all the time that a man had written it" (15). However, Marber acknowledged that despite the detractors many audience members made a personal connection with the biting romantic relationships within the play. He told Charles Spencer: "To some members of the audience it's a horrible reminder of what they've been through. To others, who are going through this stuff as the same time as they are watching the play, there is a strong element of recognition. I've had letters from people saying, 'You've written my life, how did you know?'" ("Patrick Marber"). Like Mamet and Ravenhill, Marber saw his piece as political—"it's about a city in permanent decline, evolving, gone mad. It's certainly involved in sexual politics. I don't know how far men have evolved, and the women are just managing to brush off some of the slime" (Lezard 32). Marber's acerbic, but also humorous, take on the contemporary nature of London relationships was undoubtedly one of the most successful of all the new plays produced during the 1990s, as it had an extended run on the West End, a transfer to Broadway, productions around the world and a film version written by Marber and directed by Mike Nichols, who also directed the film version of Albee's scathing commentary on marital relationships in *Whose Afraid of Virginia Woolf?* (1966).

Clearly, male playwrights looking at the battle of the sexes in the middle part of the decade was all the rage. And like his peers, Penhall entered the fray of depicting the battle. However, unlike Grosso, Ravenhill, Marber and the other male playwrights writing on the same topic, Penhall did not channel Mamet's *Sexual Perversity in Chicago* as an influence. Instead, as he had done with *Some Voices* and *Pale Horse*, he once again went against the tide of his contemporaries.

Love and Understanding features the couple Neal and Rachel, both 100-hours-a-week working doctors, who share a mortgage on a flat, which rests beneath the flight plan of Heathrow. As the play opens, they are struggling to maintain their relationship due to the stress work has placed on them individually and as a couple. Unable to find time to talk with one another, they communicate through voice mail messages and Post-it notes. Entering into this domestic arrangement is Neal's childhood friend, Richie, who has just arrived back in the country after having broken up with his girlfriend in Mexico. Richie, "a one man cyclone of dysfunction" ("Re: The Final"), manages to finagle his way into their household, taking up residence on their couch and, in the process, adding additional tension to Neal and Rachel's already frayed relationship with his drinking, drug dependency and mendaciousness. He also manages to squeeze into the arms of Rachel, first on a drunken afternoon when she skips work, and later after Rachel and Neal have a fight. However, Richie, because of too much drink and/or guilt, is unable to perform, when they go to bed together. Neal, having quit his job, comes home early to discover his best friend and girlfriend dressing in the bedroom and breaks off the relationship with Rachel. Richie, despondent over what he did, overdoses and slips into a coma. Upon his recovery he leaves London to wreck his havoc upon the citizenry of Wales. Neal and Rachel, despite splitting up, remain friends and as the play ends they share a drink at a pub, discussing the uncertainty of them becoming a couple in the future.

As with Sierz's take on Penhall's early plays fitting into the In-Yer-Face movement, critics attempted to group *Love and Understanding*, *Shopping and Fucking* and *Closer* together, creating a triumvirate of relationship plays. An article by Matt Wolf in *American Theatre* declared a brotherhood of nihilism between the three pieces. And while the piece, like the others, is a relationship play, its focus and interests are far different. The reliance on detailed sexual escapades (the Diana speech and hand, blow and rim jobs in *Shopping and Fucking*, the explicit cybersex and stripper scene in *Closer*) featured in both plays makes the flaccid attempt of Richie to have intercourse with Rachel in *Love and Understanding* feel quaint (and unlike the other two plays, his attempt occurs before the scene begins). The media blitz in Britain on Ravenhill's and Marber's work escaped Penhall's. When all three plays ended up transferring to New York City, Penhall's piece received the smallest amount of coverage from the New York press because of the lack of controversy inherent in the piece. Perhaps the most telling difference between the three is the depiction of the relationship itself in the plays. *Shopping and Fucking* begins with the break-up of the threesome Mark, Lulu and Robbie, and their subsequent journeys in the sex trades (Mark's hiring of the rent boy Gary and Lulu and Robbie entering into the phone sex trade) before they all are finally reunited in the violent and fatal fulfillment of Gary's fantasy. With his death and the lucre of his payment the threesome are reunited, but only through the murder of Gary. Throughout *Closer*, relationships start, deconstruct, restart and break apart again between the four characters, with Marber's narrative focus being on the moments when the characters are at their most cruel, as they verbally hurt and romantically betray one another. The last scene of the play reveals the death of Alice (the youngest member of the foursome), the lie surrounding her identity and the separation of the remaining three from one another's lives. In *Love and Understanding* the relationship between Neal and Rachel is a well-established one as the play begins, even though they are struggling to keep their situation intact. What truly delineates the play from the others, though, is that Penhall embeds their relationship within the reality of an everyday life to which the audience can relate. Bernie Litko's description of the World War II fetishist, the dark corners of Ravenhill's sub-cultural London and the various levels of celebrity of Marber's characters exist beyond the experiences of average audience members. Instead, the physical and mental exhaustion from work, the details of the niggling, little annoyances that fester into provocative recriminations among couples and the drudgery of everyday life play out believably and uncomfortably in Penhall's play. While his contemporaries expanded the subject matter and theatricalization of their characters for the focus of their plays, Penhall turned inward. In *Shopping and Fucking* and *Closer* the audience merely spectate on the ever-surprising, emotional, out-of-control moments of the lives of those characters, who are authors, world-recognized photographers, strippers, drug dealers, rent boys and gangsters. In *Love and Understanding* the audience sees itself reflected back in the everyday nature of the characters.

In the early stages of the writing process Penhall found himself gravitating more toward Richie and his dysfunctional behavior, inspired by Penhall's own actions of turning up at his brother's home unexpectedly and "pouring vodka down like crazy and scaring away all his friends" (Morgan 13). Penhall admitted that what drove his early plays was his fascination with those characters that just did not fit in with their surroundings, prompting them to become loners. In reflecting on those plays, Penhall explained: "In a very adolescent way I thought that's what being a real person was. I just didn't trust anybody who had any kind of purchase on reality, jobs and relationships. Then I grew up a bit" (Rees, "Bard"). That self-awareness of growing up is reflected in the direction of the play and its attention to the smaller details that make and break relationships. His increasingly upwardly mobile economic situation, due to his success as a playwright, also influenced his writing. "I got my own flat, started making quite a bit of money out of theatre and got a lovely girlfriend. It was my friends who were still struggling musicians and dolies who would come around and drink me out of house and home and hit on my girlfriend" (Morgan 13). The previously immature Penhall who had crashed in on his brother now found himself on the receiving end of this disruptive behavior. The view from this new perspective offered him an epiphany as to the direction of his play, shifting his focus from Richie to Neal. In making this change, the play's tone shifted dramatically. Citing the fact that so many films and plays were featuring "extraordinarily brutal criminals" or characters "extraordinarily rapacious in their sexual appetites," Penhall admitted that he "just wanted to write about someone who was, to all intents and purposes, boring" (Rees, "Bard"). At a National Theatre Platform, which was chaired by Aleks Sierz, Penhall revealed that Neal was based on a friend who was a good doctor but actually quite boring. This type of middle ground character, according to Penhall, was missing from the stage and especially absent in the work of his contemporaries. The characteristics of this type of character, who was "cool ... funny ... charismatic ... hard-working and moral" (Kingston), stemmed from the attributes of his own friends and peers. And the play then became for Penhall an homage to the middle-class, middle-way person who is not a theatrical staple, unlike the problem-creating, Richie-type character.[6] Penhall noted the attractiveness of Richie for the audience "because he's funny and he's charming" (Kingston). However, he also made a case for the theatrical viability of a character like Neal. "If you work hard all your life and subscribe to a set of ideals, which this doctor does, it shouldn't be laughed at" (Kingston). Penhall posited a nobility in Neal's commitment to his profession. Penhall explained this position in more detail to the Platform audience by offering the following scenario: if you were going to have surgery, who would you prefer doing the work? A doctor who does drugs, drinks and stays up all night long or a doctor who was a bit more sedate, boring and spent time doing course work instead of partying?

It is also noteworthy that *Love and Understanding* is especially striking when put in context with Penhall's earlier work, as its structure and characterization demonstrate Penhall's development as a playwright. His first three plays, as has been noted, focus on men too heavily invested in lower- to middle-class business pursuits in the restaurant/bar industry. The worlds they inhabit are dark and forboding, filled with smashed windows, crime, escaped mental patients, violence, threats, attempted suicides and murders. *Love and Understanding* moves away from the troubled streets of London to the flat, workplace, and pubs frequented by a middle-class, professional couple. Penhall deliberately wanted a change from characters with psychological issues surrounded by a depressingly dark world. In addition, he saw the big media and theatrical fuss being made over the In-Yer-Face plays and found the current theatre system to be a bit disaffecting. "Theatre gets very pretentious, particularly in London. It needs to be demystified" (Williams). So, he intentionally set out to write something in a different vein, as he felt a change of tenor was due on the scene.

> Everyone identifies with the wild cards at the moment. It's sexy, it's cool, it gets the headlines.... So this new play turns on a sixpence. Little things, which don't have to be boring things. Style things, questions of sensibility.... But to write drama about a new shower curtain is more challenging [Kingston].

He also acknowledged that writing the piece itself was challenging. He found it easy to write "monosyllabic Scorsese-type dialogue" (Williams) about lower-class characters involved in nefarious deeds. A far more challenging activity was "to write about ordinary people who go to work and squabble over Post-it notes on the fridge" (Williams). Penhall then responded in not only a macro way to the larger nature of what his plays had been about but also a micro way in regard to his use of language. Finally, Penhall rotated his dramatic lens, focusing on the doctors themselves rather than the patients in need of assistance.[7]

While the play features a new type of character for Penhall, it also showed off a previously untapped aspect of Penhall's writing: comedy, which he would continue to mine in *Blue/Orange*, *Dumb Show* and *Landscape with Weapon*. According to Penhall, because the play was much lighter than his previous two plays, the Royal Court Theatre did not produce it. Instead, the piece ended up at the Bush Theatre, which had been one of the many theatres to turn down *Some Voices*. Like at the Royal Court, the Bush was also undergoing a renaissance of new writing on their small pub stage in Shepherd's Bush.

The critical reaction to Penhall's third main stage production, which premiered in April 1997, was mixed. James Christopher of *The Times* was direct in his attack on the play, writing "this is anything but an elaborate piece of self-advertising by a skilled copywriter. It beats selling insurance, sure, but maybe Penhall will write a piece of theatre next time rather than an episodic soap." John Peter, writing for *The Sunday Times*, disagreed with his colleague, and like with his enthusiasm for *Some Voices*, he once again praised Penhall's work, calling it a "tough, eloquent, bruising play," and declaring that this Bush Theatre production was "one of the best plays I've seen, ever, at this powerhouse of new writing." Michael Billington shared Peter's enthusiasm for the play and pronounced that with *Love and Understanding* Penhall had definitely succeeded in separating himself from the group of young playwrights, like Grosso, Ravenhill and Marber, who had emerged over the past two or three years. He called Penhall a "more warm-hearted writer than many of his late-twentyish contemporaries" and declared him "a romantic realist with an unbudgeable belief in human goodness." In addition, he noted that in the midst of all the violently tough plays being produced, Penhall "says some unfashionable things: that friendship carries with it unspoken obligations and that a loving heart, even when badly fractured, can still heal." Carole Woddis of *The Herald* thought *Love and Understanding* was "a funny, devastating, typically compassionate exploration of modern day personal relationships that also asks awkward questions about attraction and expectations." In addition, she remarked that humor "is used to maximum subversive effect." Matt Wolf, who was not fond of Penhall's two previous works, identified Richie as a crucial component of the play's success because "you know you shouldn't like [him] and yet you do. This complicated response is crucial to a play some will dismiss as one more houseguest-from-hell scenario, though that is to sell short the real cunning and stagecraft" of Penhall. Unlike Wolf, Paul Taylor of *The Independent* saw the play as a step backward for Penhall, mainly because the "artificiality" of the play was completely unbelievable, remarking that "neither Neal's professional disenchantment nor Rachel's romantic nostalgia for carefree student days can adequately explain why they allow a walking anti-advertisement for hedonism to lure them into a temporary hell of half-hearted unfaithfulness, ditched careers and whisky-slurping regression." On the topic of Richie, Carol Woddis agreed with Matt Wolf as her review announced that Richie is "one of the stage villains of the year," while others agreed with Taylor, like Andrew Billen of *The Observer*: "The play doesn't work because, while it is always hard making niceness interesting, Penhall has also fallen down on the easier job of making evil appealing." In addition, Robert Hanks of *The Independent* remarked that the play has a "major plausibility gap: Richie is so transparently obnoxious that you can't believe they don't call the police on him within about 10 minutes of his arrival, let alone lend him money and tell him their most intimate secrets."

The critical dustup over Richie provided an opportunity for Mike Bradwell, the production's director; Paul Bettany, who played Richie; and Penhall to weigh in on the character and his motivations. All three noted their own experiences with Richie-like acquaintances and friends. Bradwell relayed that he had had two Richie-like friends, both actors and alcoholics, stay with him at different times: "You know it's going to be horrible and dangerous and they're going to burn a hole in your carpet and steal money from you and try to screw your girlfriend. And yet you do it" (Rizzo). Paul Bettany admitted: "I met someone like Richie who was an absolute hedonist and whom you knew was on every [drug], yet you wanted the excitement of being around him" (Rizzo). Penhall too weighed in on the consequences of Richie's visit to Neal and Rachel's home: "It's ambiguous whether Richie coming into their lives has been a good or a bad thing in their relationship. In a sense it's been good because they've had to face the reality that they bore each other. But it's a bad thing because they were really happy" (Klein 81). In an article for the *Guardian* he addressed the critical dustup among London reviewers about Richie's character by placing it within an international context. He wrote that in one production done in a foreign country, whose name he refused to reveal, the critics "wanted the other two squares thrown out" ("Who Wrote"), rather than the problematic Richie.

Like in his previous play *Pale Horse*, Penhall's opening immediately establishes the nature of his main character. As the play begins, Neal and Richie stand in the middle of the flat as the sound of a plane drowns out their conversation. As soon as the disturbance ends, Neal explains that he and Rachel live directly under the flight path of Heathrow airport. The constant sounds of the planes remind him and Rachel every day about the exciting trips others are making, while they are stuck in London, always working. Richie, who has just returned from Central and North America, reinforces their lack of travel experience by describing the scenes of exotic beaches he visited. All Neal can offer in telling travelling stories is that he and Rachel went to Richmond and punted on the river, all for the cost of a fiver. Work, though, is not the only thing keeping the couple from breaking out of their static life and travelling. While Rachel desires for them to travel, it is Neal who is not so readily interested. When they revisit the topic of them going away, their dialogue resembles the pattern of a previously well traveled conversation, as Rachel finishes Neal's sentences.

> NEAL: You know that holidays make me nervous. It's the leaving that's the worst part...
> RACHEL: And the coming home...
> NEAL: Airports make me nervous...
> RACHEL: And all that time in between...
> NEAL: I can't stop thinking about work [199].

He is, in the parlance of the times, a homebody, one who is more comfortable at home and within the confines of the world in which he exists. Richie comments on this exact nature of Neal to Rachel, calling his best friend boring.

RACHEL: He isn't boring. He's just ... quieter than you.
RICHIE: A little shy and retiring. Absolutely.
RACHEL: Unpretentious.
RICHIE: Unpretentious and a little unadventurous sometimes....
Earnest even. Humourless [188].

Despite her open defense of her partner, she later admits her dissatisfaction with him. She wants their situation to change from the ritual of work and sleep, which has taken over their lives, back to the way things used to be. Work, responsibility and adulthood, though, have changed everything: "I want Neal to come away with me. Ditch the mortgage and the job and vanish. No work, no responsibilities, just us and the backpacks" (209). However, Rachel is attached to a man embedded in the comfort of ritual and routine. He lives by rigid preconceived expectations about how things are supposed to work and fears any and all of those elements that might disrupt his mindset, which is why Richie's visit is so incredibly disruptive, as he represents all the unpredictability that Neal fears.

RICHIE: You shouldn't get so wrapped up in it. Who cares?
NEAL: I have to be wrapped up in it. I have to care. I do care. More and more. I don't want to. But there you go... [194].

Anything out of the ordinary makes him nervous and concerned; the act of Richie going through his work refrigerator and handling the various vials of drugs and specimens therein makes him jumpy and edgy. In addition, he cannot help but compare himself with his best friend whose take on life is so carefree that it simply bewilders Neal, making him feel inferior to his problem-causing friend precisely because he cannot see the world in the exact same manner. He bemoans to Rachel: "I'm thinking people like him are having all the fun. Even when he's not having fun he does it better than me. I've wasted my entire life!" (227).

While both members of the couple are stressed about their situation, Rachel admits that she has grown tired of work and looks to escape from its drudgery, pursuing a new route with her life. In fact, she exhorts Neal to stop complaining about his situation because it only exacerbates her own disgruntlement with her own disappointing experiences at work. However, Neal, who is too invested in the work world, finds separation from it impossible to contemplate. His perception is so narrowly focused on and consumed by the components of work that make up his world that he cannot (at least at first) consider the possibility of quitting. And yet, despite his adherence to this mindset, Neal is increasingly jumpy and concerned because he feels that he is not qualified to be in charge of the intensive care unit of the hospital. Whereas before in *Some Voices*, Ray was caught in a no man's land of red tape surrounding medical care, in *Love and Understanding* Neal is now a cog of the bureaucratic nightmare of the National Health Service, caught with a level of responsibility that he does not want and distanced from being able to aid patients anymore. He additionally bemoans the fact that he is not situated in a posh location like Chelsea or Westminster, where he would be treating patients whose most serious medical issues would be tennis elbows and tripping at a barbecue.

Richie's presence also exacerbates the already strained relationship Neal has with Rachel. When the play opens, Rachel and Neal have been struggling with finding the time to spend with one another to work on their relationship, which has been fraught with long work hours, inconsistent sleeping schedules and illnesses, caused by Rachel's various residencies. And, in turn, precisely because of work, their relationship suffers. Because of their work hours, they are unable to communicate properly with one another, relying instead on Post-it notes to make their intentions known to one another about possible events they can do together. Inevitably, the notes become lost, misplaced or inadvertently covered over with other papers, prompting the note leaver to believe the note recipient ignored the request to get together. What began as an attempt to set up an evening together manifests itself into a fight, as they leave each other testily written and dictated answer phone messages, exacerbating their relationship woes. The end result being that they end up fighting about the lack of communication between them, when the whole intention behind the incident that prompted the fight was an attempt for them to be able to communicate and spend time with one another. Ironically, the result of the fight is that neither one now wants to spend any time with the other one. *Love and Understanding* then stands in stark contrast to *Some Voices* and *Pale Horse*, which featured characters who were desperately longing to find the connection that Neal and Rachel are having such a difficult time maintaining.

The miscommunication problems between Neal and Rachel are highlighted and manipulated by Richie, who seeks his own form of attention. No longer having a girlfriend whose attention he can command as she broke up with him, he now wants to be the center of attention for Neal and Rachel. He manipulates them to cause that focus to occur. On his first night staying with them, Rachel and Neal, for the first time in weeks, have the same night off and plan to go to dinner. Richie butts into their evening, at first promising only to have drinks with them at a local pub before dinner and then go on his way. Throughout the various combinations of characters going to get drinks, checking on reservations at the restaurant and getting a taxi, Richie manages to disrupt their romantic evening by critiquing the absent member of the couple to the other and misstating the comments made by one about the other when they were away from the table, including restating to Rachel what Neal had shared with him about their problems communicating with one another. What was a true concern about their faltering relationship by Neal becomes in the mouth of Richie a seemingly callous statement by Neal about Rachel. He tells her: "He just said that there wasn't any … communication at the moment. If you know what I mean.... He could've been a bit more discreet I suppose but ... what could I do?" (188). In a sense, the confusion of the Post-it notes and answer phone messages have now been physically embodied by the presence of Richie, who uses his chicanery to cause issues for the couple, and, similar to their reliance on indirect communication as their sole means of communication, they rely on Richie to provide the communicating link between them rather than talking directly to one another. Interestingly, a reluctance exists on the part of Neal and Rachel to actually talk with one another. They are instead much more comfortable with a barrier present, whether it be a piece of paper, an answering machine tape, or Richie himself, who steers the direction of their relationship. Richie's presence highlights the state of their relationship, mired in its woeful miscommunication and even more disturbingly their relative ease in accepting the truth of Richie's puckish comments, which skewer their trust of one another and highlight their ever-growing, underlying uncertainty about the other. Richie becomes the tangible manifestation of their attitude and difficulties with one another. If their relationship was built upon trust and understanding, then none of the personal issues that Richie brings into their relationship would be a problem, but because they struggle, they are in a weaker position in relation to one another. With *Love and Understanding*, then, Penhall continues to highlight the tenuous nature of relationships when one places a priority upon the world of work over the loved ones. In his three previous plays he demonstrated work's effect on friendships, sibling relationships and marriage. Here he once again demonstrates it through Richie's ability to manipulate a relationship damaged because of work. While he wants attention, Richie's behavior is also driven by a base desire of needing a place to stay while in London, and so he behaves this way at the pub with the expressed purpose of gaining entry into their household, so he can not only stay with them but also have some company for the evening. He succeeds on both counts. In disrupting the dinner date, Rachel, angry over Neal's comments, storms home, and, in turn, Richie acquires an anchoring position on their sofa.

While Richie poses a threat in disrupting the already fragile nature of their communication with one another, he offers an even greater disruption to the success of their relationship because of his lack of any type of ethical conceit. His drive is purely impulsive and egoistical, prompting him to lie and steal to attain whatever he feels as important at the moment he feels it. His actions, though, highlight the distance growing between Neal and Rachel. While they have drinks on that first night, he tells Rachel a story of Neal's constant desire to play doctors and nurses with a girl friend when they were younger. When Rachel later reveals what Richie told her, Neal angrily comments that Richie has been lying about Neal's preoccupation with the opposite sex for as long as they have been friends. While the story only provokes more ire for Neal, Rachel finds it appealingly cute.

NEAL: It's nonsense. It's a lie.
RACHEL: It's a rather charming one.
NEAL: I hate it when he does that. He's so ... mendacious.
RACHEL: Well, I dare say it's fairly harmless [198].

While Neal calls out his friend's lies, Rachel reveals that she has no problem with his fable. This differing mindset about Richie's behavior, though, will end up having graver aspects on their relationship. The most startling example of Richie's ethics occurs at Neal's office, when a call comes in about a death that occurred when a power failure hit the hospital. It was Neal's responsibility to restart the generator to bring the halls back up to power. Neal, though, was not at the hospital and he was the only one who knew who to restart it. During the downtime, a patient died. A public relations officer from the hospital calls Neal to discover the truth about the matter. Richie quickly grabs the phone away from his friend and spins a free-flowing litany of lies about the incident, saying the death was coincidental as it happened during the power outage but in a different part of the hospital unaffected by the lack of electricity. The stark contrast between the two men becomes apparent in their exchange after the phone call. Neal protests Richie's behavior, saying that such behavior is unethical.

RICHIE: It's standard practice.... There's no point in your sticking your neck out.
NEAL: A man died. The least we can do is tell the truth.
RICHIE: Don't be ridiculous [195].

When Neal shares the event with Rachel, she admits that she does not see anything wrong with Richie's lie because it not only saved Neal from getting into trouble but also more than likely prevented him from losing his job. Her mindset parallels the philosophy of Richie which says that lying for one's own benefit or for a little bit of fun is perfectly acceptable. No one really gets hurt and others are protected. Neal, though, being the incredibly buttoned-up person that he is, cannot fathom the concept of lying for any reason whatsoever, but at the same time his refusal to take the blame also suggests Neal's own complicity in the lie. While he might not believe in lying to cover his tracks, he does not feel enough impetus to correct the misunderstanding with the hospital.

Despite their struggles and Richie's interference, Penhall does provide an important scene, which allows the audience to view Neal and Rachel one on one without Richie's undue influence. Its inclusion is significant when one compares Penhall's piece with Ravenhill's and Marber's. In their plays no scene is present that allows for the couples to share a romantic moment with one another, where they profess their true feelings. Penhall, though, breaks away from the housemate-from-hell scenario to provide a brief glimpse of what Neal and Rachel's relationship could be if they were able to escape from the downward spiral into which they have recently fallen. After the mix-up over dinner with Richie and his lies about the generator, they find time to be alone and they share their thoughts and dreams about the possibility of where they might go as a couple, as they both profess to wanting the other one to rub off on them as they grow older, seeing the positive characteristics each embodies and wanting to emulate them.

> NEAL: Maybe that's how marriage works. You become more like each other. Given the right proximity and exposure, people rub off on each other. And I want you to rub off on me.
> RACHEL: I want you to rub off on me, too [200–01].

It is worth noting, though, that this scene is the only time that they share such a personal and private moment with one another as a couple. It will not be until the end of the play after they have broken up that they will again have an opportunity to have an honest talk about their futures, but in the last scene it is about a future without the other one in it. And yet, despite their claims to want to rub off on one another, there is an awkwardness present in their conversation. A distancing effect takes place as they talk about potentially marrying one another, but they never fully articulate the words of commitment.

> NEAL: I mean, I'd love to be married to you. I'd get a big bang out of that.
> RACHEL: Me too. You know. One day...
> NEAL: Have we just proposed to each other? [201].

Their language choice keeps them at a safe distance from actually committing to a marital future with one another. Neal's wishful statement of "I'd love to be married to you" is far different than a direct proposal of marriage and Rachel's simplistic return of "me too" followed by a conditional situation of "one day..." highlights that this is a couple that is not yet ready to make the commitment necessary to one another, especially when the current status of their relationship is still fraught with tension and uncertainty. Their exchange is reminiscent of a comment made by Jerry to Emma in Harold Pinter's adultery play *Betrayal* (1978), where Jerry, who is having an affair with Emma, tells her cryptically: "I don't think we don't love each other" (55). He actually is saying they love one another, but the double negative embedded in his statement obscures the message of affection. The ultimate inability of Rachel and Neal to commit parallels *Shopping and Fucking* where Mark leaves Lulu and Robbie, unable to commit to their home life, and *Closer*, where all four permutations of couple pairings eventually break up. Aiding the difficulty between Neal and Rachel is that as soon as Neal has asked whether they have actually proposed to one another, Richie enters the room and disrupts their romantic reverie, which they never regain.

After this momentary period of communication, their relationship begins its precipitous fall, starting with Rachel surprising Neal by taking a sick day and spending it with Richie. During the course of their outing, they have too much to drink and take a walk by the river. Her conversation with Richie is revealing about the difference in opinion about Neal's view of the world and hers, which is closer to Richie's view. As Rachel tells him, "What's wrong with the occasional sickie? What's wrong with the occasional ... lie?" (209). The philosophy here correlates with the *laissez faire* attitude of Richie rather than the rule-bound philosophy of Neal, who, like many of Penhall's protagonists, finds it difficult to believe that others do not follow the rules set down by society. Rules are there for a reason, and when they are broken, bad things can occur. Rachel demonstrates, as she suggested earlier with her support of Richie's lies about the deceased patient, that she too does not have a problem with lying, eschewing the same rules that Neal adheres to in his staid, structured way. During their walk on the river, Richie makes a pass at her, and she rebuffs him. Richie, undaunted, professes his attraction to her in a multifaceted display of his smooth and easy linguistic glibness, finely honed through years of prevaricating. He tells her: "When I'm not with you I walk about lost, staring, talking to myself, my shirt is on back-to-front, my fly's undone, my trousers falling down, hollow, completely hollow. I want to preach the gospel according to Us. Yell it from the rooftops. From a multi-storey car park.... I think you're lovely" (215). Once again similarities can be seen between Richie and Jerry from Pinter's *Betrayal*, as Jerry also has a moment of professing his feelings for Emma as he drunkenly accosts her. "You're lovely. I'm crazy about you. All these words I'm using, don't you see, they've never been said before. Can't you see? I'm crazy about you. It's a whirlwind.... Listen to me. It's true. Listen. You overwhelm me. You're so lovely" (135–6). Both men share empty platitudes filled with romantic clichés. Pinter saves Jerry's speech to Emma until the last scene of the play, which is the play's earliest scene chronologically, to show that the supposedly great love affair between Jerry and Emma that they had for seven years actually emerged from a drunken clinch and rambling romantic comments from Jerry. It was not romantic, merely seedy. Richie's comments provide a comparison between Neal's earlier assertion of love and marriage with Richie's exuberant need to share his feelings with the world. Despite Richie's questionable character, his comments about love are forceful and direct. He does not distance himself but instead is fully invested in his feelings for Rachel. Neal, though, can barely articulate his perspective on love. After Rachel has taken the sick day, Neal tries to reconnect with her and explain to her his concept of love, which involves a metaphor of a tall building, its elevators and how love manifests itself when the doors to those elevators open. He explains to her that when the doors open we share our love with the other person: "Our souls hold hands and romp naked together.... No ... we're the lifts and our hearts are.... No ... there's all these buttons, see ... and we press them..." (219). Neal's inarticulate explanation about his concept of love to Rachel only reinforces the distance that is growing between them due to Richie's influence. She cannot help but make comparisons and feel flattered when she compares Richie's romantic assertions with her partner's stumbling, bumbling ineffective description of his love for her. While Richie wants to

Love and Understanding *and the Demise of Relationships* 95

proclaim his feelings and share them with the one to whom he is attracted and to all those around him, Neal sees the experience as being intensely private, tucked away within ever shrinking spaces, first a building, then its corridors and, finally, the elevator itself.

It is not surprising then, in comparing the two men's comments, that her initial reluctance to get involved with Richie does not last long, as a few days later she takes another sick day and ends up in bed with Richie, although, interestingly enough, for all of his talk, he is unable to perform. Neal, suspicious of Rachel's recent Richie-like behavior, walks in on them, and it is in this dramatic moment that *Love and Understanding* does share the same theatrical moment as *Shopping and Fucking* and *Closer*, as all three plays feature the discovery scene of a partner having slept with someone else. In Ravenhill's play it occurs when Mark brings the rent boy Gary to the flat he shares with Lulu and Robbie. In that meeting Robbie becomes furious that Mark abandoned them and then took up with Gary. In a fit of pique he attacks Gary, choking him, while Mark tries to pull him off. Robbie, though, is unable to control his anger at the betrayal of Mark and later, in trying to fulfill Gary's fantasy of being murdered during sex, Robbie ends up brutally attacking Gary, slamming his head against a tabletop and exercising his anger toward his boyfriend Mark and the rent boy. Once again he is pulled away by Mark, who eventually does fulfill Gary's request. In *Closer* the confrontation is not as violent, but much more powerful and emotionally devastating as Marber reveals two discoveries of adultery concurrently, in a technique that borrows from Kushner's *Angels in America*, which also features a double discovery of adultery. As Larry and Anna engage in a loud, vituperative argument over her year-long affair with Dan, Dan and Alice are engaged in their own fight as Dan confesses to his affair with Anna. Alice's response differs from Larry's as she is quieter, but equally effective as she gathers up her things and leaves him, while he continues to talk to her from off-stage. In contrast, Larry is angrily obsessive in his need to know every explicit detail of Anna's relationship with Dan.

LARRY: You enjoy sucking him off?
ANNA: *Yes.*
LARRY: You like his cock.
ANNA: I love it.
LARRY: You like him coming in your face?
ANNA: Yes.
LARRY: What does it taste like?
ANNA: It tastes like you but *sweeter.*
LARRY: *THAT'S* the *spirit.* Thank you. Thank you for your *honesty.*
  Now fuck off and die. You fucked-up slag [Marber 61].

His powerful attack dominates the scene, as he demands an answer to all of his questions, prompting the two into a devastating argument that ends the first act of Marber's play and sends the audience reeling toward their interval drinks. Marber's play, especially through the writing of this scene, completely captures how quickly and painfully relationships can self-implode. In addition, the absolute honesty and anger of Marber's scene demonstrated how quickly love turns to hate between couples.

While both Marber and Ravenhill depict the powerful and violent emotions that stem from betrayal in relationships, Penhall offers an opposite approach from his contemporaries, who follow the confrontation through to its bitter end. In *Love and Understanding*, as in the other two plays, Neal enters and learns of the betrayal of Rachel. He asks: "Was it good? ... Was it a laugh? Did you laugh? Did you giggle? Did you scream? Did you gasp and say 'fuck' at the point of no return? Did you cry out his name as he held you down? Did you kiss his eyes and whisper to him? Did you see something in his eyes? Did he see something in yours? ... Why?" (236). What is interesting is that rather than pursuing the emotional invective that would come from such a discovery, Penhall ends the scene quickly, closing off the ensuing conversation between Rachel and Neal. In stark contrast to his contemporaries, the cheater, Rachel, is not provided an opportunity to respond. The victim merely asks questions and waits for a response which the audience never sees or hears him receive. In one sense, it is a powerful way to end the scene, as it echoes his desire to write like Chekhov, who refused to show the large dramatic moments of his characters' lives, but instead the smaller moments. Penhall takes us to the precipice of this defining moment for the two of them and then allows it all to happen off-stage, just as Chekhov does with the selling of the cherry orchard or the duel that ends *The Three Sisters* (1901). However, by ending the scene where he does, Rachel never has an opportunity to answer the question of why, which is a prominent question that hangs over her character, as her attraction to Richie and her decision to completely jettison her relationship with Neal is never fully explained. True, Richie may provide a jolt to the tedium of her life and is more articulate than Neal, but she really has no emotional connection or investment with him. In removing her explanation, Penhall maintains the cipher-like quality of Rachel's character, which may be deliberate on Penhall's part since he has admitted that the driving elements of the play were the boring doctor Neal and the houseguest from hell Richie. Rachel's presence merely allows their battle between each other to have a greater consequence.

From this point on, though, their relationship is irrevocably broken. Even though Rachel hopes that they will once again become a couple, Neal excludes that possibility from happening. In the midst of their relationship's demise Richie, after a drinking binge, falls into a coma. After recovering, he opts to leave for Wales to begin his life anew. The play ends with Rachel and Neal once again alone without Richie's presence coming between them, as they have coffee and talk about their futures. While they will not be a couple again, the final scene suggests that they will still be friends. There is a sense of healed feelings between them, especially because of Rachel's endeavors to make amends and profusely apologize for her transgression with Richie. Penhall's ending contrasts starkly with *Shopping and Fucking* and *Closer*, where the closing scenes of reconciliation occur over a death. In the latter Alice's death in New York City brings the three characters together for a final time at Postman Park for a summing up of their relationships, as Emma now finds solace with a stray dog, Larry begins a new relationship with a nurse, and Dan lives alone. In *Shopping and Fucking* Lulu, Robbie and Mark reconnect with one another, but only because their murder of Gary has allowed them to come together again, solving not only Mark's emotional woes with relationships but also the financial debt they owe to the drug dealer Brian because of Robbie's giving away of 300 ecstasy pills at a club. No deaths occur in *Love and Understanding* as Penhall's play ends with a sense of certainty that Rachel and Neal will never be a couple. Just as Marber's title *Closer* is ironic considering the separation that ends the play, Penhall's *Love and Understanding* contradicts its title in the final moments of the play, which ends without any love; Neal's tortured attempt to describe what love is indicates the complex and almost indescribable and indefinable nature of love, or understanding; none of the characters have ever really understood one another, ranging from the bizarre unpredictable behavior of Richie, Rachel's sudden decision to completely uproot the relationship she had built with Neal, and Neal's inflexible ability to understand and accept the behavior of others who are different from him. Love and understanding for these characters has been impossible to find.

However, the play ends with a sense of possibility, especially for Neal, who finally seems to be emerging from his controlling, narrow view of the world around him. As he sits with Rachel and drinks coffee, he admits: "For the first time in my life I feel free.... I've never been single and unemployed before. These are exciting times for me" (250). Despite his travails with Richie and the failure of his relationship, Neal can still see the positive possibilities in what lies ahead of him. His struggles with work and the ensuing problems it caused in his relationship have been stripped away and he is free to make his choices and begin all over again, which is an option that few people have. While Penhall's previous plays ended with an edge of uncertainty and unhappiness, which for many of his characters was created by their world of work, here Penhall allows one of his characters to look forward to the possibilities that are out there. For in *Love and Understanding* it is actually the freedom from work and its expectations as well as from a relationship and its expectations that provides an awareness of the freeing nature and wonder of life.

5

The Bullet *and the Stigma of Redundancy*

Joe Penhall's fifth play, *The Bullet*, opens with a nighttime tableau of a young couple, Robbie and Carla, standing in the doorway of a middle-class, south London household, holding their luggage. Lying on the sofa is the patriarch of the family, Charles, passed out, an empty glass in one hand, a bottle of liquor leaning against the sofa, while the light from the television set casts upon his inebriated body. The image of the couple in the doorway harkens back to Harold Pinter's masterpiece *The Homecoming* (1965), as Ruth and Teddy stand, with their luggage in the middle of the night, on the precipice of the doorway of Teddy's embattled South London childhood home. Thirteen years after Pinter's play a similar theatrical image of a couple standing in the doorway with a passed-out, television-lit patriarch on the living room sofa appeared in *The Homecoming*-influenced, Pulitzer Prize–winning Sam Shepard play *Buried Child* (1978), as Vince and Shelly at the start of the play's second act stand, early in the morning, in the doorway of Vince's grandparents' home as Dodge, the cantankerous and sickly patriarch of the family, is passed out on the sofa with his whiskey bottle.

Adding to the similarity between the three plays and their analogous homecoming scenarios is the female visitor, who is the familial outsider and stands hesitantly in the doorway, reluctant to enter. In *The Homecoming* Ruth is at first diffident about their arrival at the house asking Teddy, "Shouldn't you wake someone up? Tell them you're here?" (36) and then a few minutes later admitting,

> I think ... the children ... might be missing us.
> TEDDY: Don't be silly.
> RUTH: They might.
> TEDDY: Look, we'll be back in a few days, won't we? [38].

Ruth's reticence, however, does not last long, as she spirits the key to his family's home away from Teddy, so she can go for a walk. Upon her return she meets Lenny, Teddy's pimp brother, since her husband retired to bed during her absence. After Lenny regales her with stories about two different times when he beat up women, Ruth disarms him completely by simply addressing him as "Leonard," which only his mother used to call him, and holding a glass of water, which she offers to pour down his throat before archly consuming it herself. While Ruth may have been briefly hesitant about entering the home, Pinter makes it clear before she heads upstairs to join her husband that in this unfamiliar, male-dominated household she will have no problem achieving a dominant position. In contrast, in *Buried Child*, Shepard at first has Shelly giggling out of control on the front porch of the house, as she facilely connects the Midwestern façade of the house to a Norman Rockwell painting. The whole look of the homestead is far too Americana for her to keep a straight face. However, once they enter the household and Vince goes upstairs to see if his grandmother Halie is home, Shelly meets an angry and hungover Dodge, and the previous humor she found in the situation changes to uncertainty and fear. She calls upstairs: "Vince, maybe we oughta' go. I don't like this. I mean, this isn't my idea of a good time.... Vince, why don't we spend the night in a motel and come back in the morning? We could have breakfast. Maybe everything would be different" (88). Eventually, Shelly overcomes her wariness and while Vince leaves to acquire liquor for Dodge, she manages to draw out from Tilden, Vince's father, the secret that the family has been hiding for so many years, namely that Dodge killed the incestuous love child of his wife Halie and Tilden. Penhall echoes this same format of uncertainty and reluctance on the part of Carla, who, like Ruth and Shelly, visits Robbie's family home for the first time. As she eyes the sleeping Charles, she asks: "Do you think we should wake him up?... Are you sure they're expecting us?" (258). When Robbie announces he is going upstairs to see if his mother is awake, Carla immediately jumps at the chance to leave the sleeping Charles.

> CARLA: I'll come with you.
> ROBBIE: He won't wake up.
> CARLA: He doesn't know who I am. He'll get the fright of his life.
> ROBBIE: He won't eat you.
> CARLA: I'll get embarrassed [258].

Robbie, like Teddy and Vince, goes upstairs alone. Contrary to Robbie's pronouncement, Charles does indeed wake up while he is gone, and Carla finds herself having to introduce herself to her boyfriend's father and engage in awkward small talk, just as Ruth and Shelly before her had to do with Lenny and Dodge, respectively.

Despite the visual and situational similarities between *The Bullet*, *The Homecoming* and *Buried Child*, Penhall quickly indicates that while the opening moments of his play pay homage to the two dramatic giants that came before him, his ensuing action will not follow in either shadow cast by Pinter or Shepard. This distinction becomes immediately noticeable when looking at the significance of the roles that the two visiting female characters play within the narrative. In effect, Penhall reverses the format used by Pinter and Shepard. Unlike Ruth and Shelly, Penhall's Carla does not factor significantly within the action of the piece, while Robbie, unlike Teddy and Vince, plays a significant role in the play's development. Teddy merely watches what transpires between his wife and family, and when he informs her that he wants to return to the States, Ruth refuses to go with him, instead negotiating a business proposition with Lenny to stay in London. As many critics have noted, the play's title actually refers to Ruth's homecoming, not Teddy's. Similarly, in *Buried Child* no sooner does Vince arrive at his grandparents' home than he disappears on a liquor run for his grandfather. His absence allows Shelly to ferret out the dark secret of the household and in turn prompts the magical growth of the crops outside and the discovery of the buried child by Tilden. In both plays the female visitor becomes the prominent player in the plot. Penhall, though, does not exile Robbie from the action. He becomes, along with his father, Charles, the play's major focus as Penhall examines, in part, the strained dynamic between this father and son pairing. Carla, in turn, moves to the background, where she sits silently on the stage observing the family for many stretches of time. Her role instead is to provide the professional and clinical socio-psychological analysis of the mental state of Charles and how his behavior about his redundancy is only natural considering the current nature of the British economy. The homecoming, in the scenario that Penhall presents, is completely Robbie's. While the first few minutes of the play reminds the audience of the tradition of the homecoming play in contemporary drama, Penhall quickly guides his work in a different direction.

The Bullet covers a twenty-four-hour period in the life of a London family hit hard by its patriarch's redundancy. Robbie has been abroad for a number of years doing informational technology work in numerous Far East countries for a myriad of companies. He has reluctantly returned home with his girlfriend Carla to see his parents, especially his father, who has been made redundant by the newspaper where he works as a chief sub.[1] Despite receiving his notice, Charles reveals to his surprised family that he does not intend to leave his newspaper position. Instead, he searches out as many things as possible wrong with their treatment of him, including the flawed syntax of his notice letter, the misspelling of his last name and the personal questions they raise in conversations with him. Bearing the brunt of his cantankerous, boisterous and unpredictable behavior is his long-suffering wife, Billie, who encourages her husband just to accept the offered severance package, so they can pay off their home or, perhaps, move to Italy. He harshly dismisses the latter option as entirely unfeasible. The final member of the family is the elusive Mike, who, like Robbie, has been missing from the family for a number of years. Unlike Robbie, who has been out of the country, Mike lives on the street in the surrounding London boroughs and periodically comes by when his parents are asleep and takes food from their refrigerator. Mike's nightly prowl is discovered by Robbie and then the rest of the family. As in most family dramas, lies are told, but eventually the truth will come out. In this case, Robbie admits that he has been lying about the importance of his position in the Far East and, like his father, he has been made redundant and grapples to define himself and who it is he wants to be. As Robbie and Charles labor to confront the reality of their shrinking economic identity, they drive Carla and Billie away from them. Charles then gets into a physical altercation with Mike, driving him out of the house as well. The play ends with the closing image of Robbie and Charles left alone in the kitchen, now reliant on one another to face their uncertain futures.

Penhall wrote that *The Bullet* is about "the pathological need to go home" ("Introduction" xiv), but he noted that once one arrives, one immediately wants to leave as quickly as possible, which is Robbie's attitude after being home for a few hours. While the plays prior to *The Bullet* were inspired by Penhall's real-life experiences and observations, this play is his most autobiographical as he drew inspiration from his own family experiences. In his introduction to the first volume of his collected plays, Penhall recalled a memory of his home life growing up: "My brother and I played with Scalextrix and Meccano and re-enacted bits from James Bond films in the sandpit" (xiv). At one point in *The Bullet* Robbie and Mike relay the exact same memory. In addition they share other happy moments from Penhall's own childhood, including his mother cooking fondue and his father playing jazz records. However, a darker memory from his childhood also drove the autobiographical elements of the play: his father's redundancy. "When my dad was twice laid off.... I was infuriated by the pain and injustice — and that anger it had engendered in him. I was glad he was angry, but we were all conscious that the family was becoming a different family and that the innocent, playful idyll would only ever return momentarily" ("Introduction" xiv). Admittedly, the sense of injustice and pain at shocking institutional and societal failures motivated Penhall's earlier plays, most notably his outrage at the Care in the Community policy in *Some Voices*. *The Bullet*, though, became personal for him. He revealed: "When someone is made redundant, I want people to feel viscerally the impact that has on an individual" (Fanshawe 11). For this play he drew upon a lifetime of experiences with his father and the difficulties his family faced. Penhall, having seen and lived through all of the struggles firsthand, wanted to convey that same sense of helplessness and turmoil.[2] A few years after the production though Penhall admitted his own sense of dissatisfaction with the final version of the play: "It was an incredibly personal play and it came out half-arsed" (Maxwell), and he admitted to Samantha Ellis of the *Guardian* that he felt guilty writing the piece. No doubt, part of that discomfort came from Penhall's awareness that he shared his father's and entire family's private experiences for a paycheck, as finances played a significant role in his reason for dredging up such a personal and eventual uncomfortable situation within his own family. When *Some Voices* and *Pale Horse* were produced at the Royal Court Theatre, he was paid three thousand pounds for each play. The Donmar Warehouse, under the leadership of eventual Oscar winner Sam Mendes, who was seeking a new play to allow for his theatre to participate in the explosion of new plays occurring all over London, offered him thirteen thousand pounds for the script. Penhall admitted: "I felt terrible when it went on. So I kind of do know what it's like to exploit somebody, and I'll never do it again" (Ellis). He later assessed himself even more harshly: "I sold out, I sold my soul" (Maxwell). He vowed that in the future he would only write a play if it needed to be written, implying that money would not be an influence in his future theatre endeavors. To this point of his career, it has been a vow that he has kept.

The London critics shared Penhall's own uncomfortableness and disappointment, and of Penhall's eight plays *The Bullet*, which premiered in April 1998, received the worst set of reviews. Charles Spencer noted some of the strengths of the work, namely that Penhall "tackles tricky, interesting themes ... with a spare, laconic style that puts you in mind of a young Pinter." In addition, moments in his writing highlight a talent for "unshowy poetic richness." However, even though Spencer praised the writing, he found the play's depiction of the "sad family in decline ... deeply depressing" and difficult to like because "Penhall observes his characters with a cool detachment rather than becoming fully engaged with them." Penhall's writing, though, did not impress Renata Rubnikowicz of *The Observer*, who noted that the piece featured "some indigestible speeches," namely those heavy on authorial agenda making in the guise of Carla. David Benedict noted that the piece reeked of an "aura of a Fifties drama" and therefore covered "well-trodden territory." Playing upon the title of Luigi Pirandello's seminal work, he announced that the piece featured "five characters in search of a play" and that the play "fatally lacks momentum."

Michael Coveney saw the influence of Eugene O'Neill in the familial nature of the play: "This is a short day's journey into night with exact plot and character details to O'Neill's lacerating family drama." Benedict Nightingale was equally dismissive, especially about the main character Charles, quipping: "since [he] spends most of the play whizzing about his ugly living room like dumdum in search of a target, the title is doubly apt." Nicholas de Jongh wrote perhaps the most scathing review, suggesting the play should have "been subjected to a lethal shot and not been allowed to reach the stage in its present, inept form" because Penhall crafted "a preposterous melodrama," lacking "any coherent dramatic shape." He finished by noting: "The technique and the form is very old-fashioned and contrived — reminiscent of a Radio 4 family drama in the 1970s." One strong positive voice to counter de Jongh's biting comments came from John Peter of *The Sunday Times* who called it a "harrowing new play" as "Penhall writes about emotional bankruptcy, psychological inadequacy and inherited misery with a searing sense of truth." In addition, Robert Potts, writing for *The Times Literary Supplement*, found the play successful, writing that Penhall "has made an individual and highly effective piece about masculinity in a changing world, and has done so with an impressive mixture of comedy and bleak revelations."

Alastair Macaulay was also direct in his assessment of the play: "This is a too neat play with a too heavy pulse about too unsympathetic people." In addition, he noted the detachment of Penhall's writing from his characters, creating a reaction in the audience of "dislike father, dislike sons. Don't much care for their womenfolk either." Macaulay, though, revealed his own theatrical prejudices with his summation: "Penhall writes, in short, as if he wished to be the English Arthur Miller: not a fate I would wish on anyone." Michael Billington also noticed the Miller influences on the text, remarking that Penhall's writing "has something of Miller's decency and compassion, but without his poetry and mythical resonance." The play is "honest and humane without ever achieving the status of dramatic metaphor." He did admit, though, that he "liked Penhall's exasperated affection for his angry hero." Nevertheless, Billington made it clear that even though *The Bullet* was Penhall's fifth play, he had yet to establish himself within the theatre, suggesting that he "is a promising writer who still has to find his own private language."

Billington and Macaulay aptly identified the influence of Arthur Miller behind *The Bullet*. While the influence of Pinter and Shepard is fleeting, Miller's *Death of a Salesman* (1949) plays a significant part in the DNA of the work. Miller's seminal work introduced the world to Willy Loman's failed acquisition of the American Dream. Almost fifty years after Miller's play, Joe Penhall's play premiered at the Donmar Warehouse. In an interview with Harriet Devine Penhall revealed that the first play he ever saw was Arthur Miller's *Death of a Salesman*, which he attended as a teen when he lived in Adelaide. A teacher, with a predilection for Led Zeppelin, took Penhall and his classmates to see a performance of the play, his teacher's favorite, at a fringe theatre. As a British emigrant living in Australia, the prevalent theme of the bankruptcy of the American Dream was not significant for the young Penhall. Instead the play impressed upon him its theme about the inherent difficulties of fathers and sons and, more specifically, that it was "about the naughty brother and the good brother, and the parent who let them down" (Devine 241). Penhall's play clearly resonates with Miller's play as both examine the failed expectations and troubled familial relationships surrounding an economically challenged household as its patriarch nears the end of his career. "[T]he past sixty years of age" (Miller 12) salesman, struggling to earn a living and keep up the façade of his perfect American life, was transformed into Penhall's fifty something, newspaper man faced with redundancy and the fear of what his future holds professionally, personally and familially.

Death of a Salesman is about Willy Loman at the end of a career that never attained the level of notoriety or respect that he had always desired and the subsequent effect of his professional failure on his family. His career featured lost opportunities, especially in relation to the possibilities of going off with Ben to make money in Alaska, and imaginary wages, as each time he returned home from the road his initial bravado about his selling prowess dissolved under the excited calculations of Linda over the sudden windfall of Willy's changing fortune. Two hundred dollars would quickly melt to seventy-five dollars under Linda's excited calculations and Willy's ensuing backtracking on his sales. By the time the play begins, Willy has failed to sell anything for weeks, having to rely on his neighbor next door to give him fifty dollars a week to cover his expenses. Miller's play details a man who saw opportunity, growth and fortune all around him: the open expanse of land around their home when they first moved outside the city; Dave Singleman, the green-velvet, slipper-wearing salesman, who never had to leave his home to make a sale; the collegiate sport prospect of Biff, as the All-American Hero; and an America that was immersed in the pursuit and the promise of success and prosperity, no matter an individual's abilities, skills and likeability. Willy believed in it all, influencing the way he way he lived his life, pursued his career and raised his sons. But while he believed the propaganda surrounding America's easily acquired capitalistic success, he lived a daily life on the American underside of mediocrity, finding himself constantly bifurcated between positive and negative emotions and energies toward success. At one moment he would expound the importance of one characteristic (always start with a joke, he tells Biff as the son prepares for an important meeting) only to immediately contradict it in the next moment (make sure a client takes you seriously, never joke with them). Ultimately, the only place Willy seemed to find success was with the opposite sex when he was on the road, but even then the other woman's main interest in Willy was for the silk stockings he could provide her rather than anything else. In Willy Loman, Miller crafted a complicated and dense portrait of not only a man but also a philosophy of a country.

 In contrast, Penhall's play is not as densely plotted or crafted in terms of characters. Miller makes the history of the Loman family, the discovery of Willy's adultery by Biff and his subsequent failure to go play football at the University of Virginia, an intrinsic element in terms of their present economic position. The personal and public coincide in the collapse of the family's fortunes. Penhall, though, is not as interested in depicting those components of his play and characters. While the past is discussed and memories are shared, no one significant moment from the past has determined the family's current situation. The betrayal of the family is not tied to the philandering ways of Charles, unlike Willy's adulterous dealings on the road. In fact, no one single moment defines their family, unlike the Lomans. Instead, the family's problems stem from Charles' maddening propensity for getting into trouble and becoming too emotional. Penhall's piece, then, is much more rooted in the personal aspects of this family's existence rather than in providing a commentary on the larger issues of a country's expectation of economic betterment and fulfillment for its citizens. After all, his family resides in England, which does not have the same history of expectation surrounding the ability of one man to pull himself and his family up the economic ladder through his fortitude and business savvy. The complexities of the American system of capitalism's success and failure does not exist as readily for the contemporary English family (although one can argue that the capitalistic philosophy of the country has leaned more toward American-like over the past 30 years), and whereas Willy is prominently at the end of his career, Charles is at least a decade younger and still has time in order to search and find a new job. Penhall's admitted focus is much narrower, much more precise than Miller's in terms of what his play examines: the effect of redundancy upon a middle-aged man and the resulting ripple effect of his behavior upon his family. Penhall does not blame any larger institution or image of British society and government. Instead, all the failures that occur for Charles are of his own making.

However, there are identifiable moments in *The Bullet* where Penhall appears to be updating and corralling moments from Miller's play into a contemporary British setting. Perhaps the strongest example of his updating technique can be found with his use of a tape recorder. In *Death of a Salesman* the newfangled device is Willy's undoing. Miller relies on the new technology of the tape recorder to show that the world is moving far too fast for Willy's comfort level. After having received a demonstration of how the device works by his boss Howard, Willy is left alone in the office with the recorder, and he accidentally turns it on. In response to the voices of Howard's family coming out of the device and disrupting the silence of the office space, Willy panics, as he does not know how to stop it from playing. This scene begins the downward spiral that will culminate in Willy's suicide at the end of the day. The tape recorder returns in Penhall's play as Robbie gives Charles a Dictaphone as a present. Charles decides to use the device as a means of catching out his bosses in their various subterfuges concerning his job. After taping the device to his body, he heads off to work. Penhall creatively uses the tape recorder to take us outside of the household (the only set for the play) and into Charles' work space, so we can hear his interactions with, first, his boss and then, later, a counselor. He dissects all the recorded dialogue back at home to the ever-growing disgust of Billie. However, most importantly, the tape recorder also shows, like in Miller's play, how out of touch Charles really is. His paranoid use of the Dictaphone highlights his lack of understanding of his situation, demonstrating his growing irrationality and refusal to acknowledge the changing business world around him. Unlike during Willy Loman's time, there no longer is an obligation of a lifetime career to the employee as businesses have a different template for success— more profit over personal. Charles, because of his attitude as well as his age, no longer is a valuable or wanted member of the staff.

While Miller's use of the tape recorder indicates the growing economic success of post-war America as citizens now have discretionary income to spend on an advanced piece of technology for the living room (Howard plans to have his maid record radio programs that he will miss), Penhall's play presents a dark view of our increasing reliance upon technology. Carla reveals to Billie that Robbie's temp job of aiding little old ladies in using their computer to make shopping lists for their visits to the grocery store was eliminated because a computer program was invented that served the same purpose, making him non-essential. Similarly, Charles learns he and some of his colleagues are being replaced by younger workers who understand how to use the emerging computer programs much better than the older generation does. As Carla notes, technology has become the driving force of business: "You know this ... it's just that ... computers for instance, and computer courses are everywhere. And money ... money is the sole criteria for personal success etcetera and the use of computers to make money, and the use of robots to make the computers that ... make the money" (300). The rise of the technology that begins to appear in Miller's play blossoms into a full-throated omnipresence in Penhall's work, so much so that the dynamics of work are completely redefined and redirected for both Robbie and Charles.

In addition to the updating of technology found in *Death of a Salesman*, Penhall also creates a familiar unhappy familial situation of two sons' difficult relationship with their father. Robbie and Mike echo Biff and Happy as Penhall's brothers are equally dissatisfied with their life, lack of success in the work world and the strained relationship they have with Charles.[3] In addition, Robbie, like Biff, is peripatetic in his continual and intentional wanderings away from home. However, the difference is that Willy built up Biff in terms of who he could and should be due to his sports success and the future professional life awaiting him. All those pretenses shatter when Biff discovers his father's affair and realizes that the man he idolized is not the man who he thought he was. The entire foundation of the Loman family precariously rests on the secret that is kept between father and son and underpins any and all conversations that take place between Biff, Willy and the unknowing Linda. In contrast to Biff, Happy is the forgotten son, who attempts to gain the attention of his folks but disappears from their attention with his brother's return home. In Penhall's play Robbie and Mike fulfill similar roles as Biff and Happy. Robbie, like Biff, has fled his home, works varying temp jobs and lies to his parents about the importance of the positions he holds. He shares the same brooding intensity of Biff's unhappiness and dissatisfaction with the world around him, as he too constantly moves from one place to another, seeking an unlocatable sustenance in every new location and temp position. Robbie also possesses a bit of Happy's need to please, as both sons try to placate the worries of their mother by falsely promising to marry within the year. Mike is similar to Happy as well in that he is the son who remained nearby. However, unlike Happy, he does not maintain contact with his parents; instead he floats through various London neighborhoods like a shadow, and on occasion he sneaks back into his childhood home to steal food. Penhall's play, though, offers no dramatic moment of recognition on the part of the son about the façade of the father, which, in turn, drives the two apart. Instead, the sons have long known their father's weaknesses: drink, hubris and anger. Whereas Biff's whole life changed in an instant with the discovery of his father's adultery, the discontented fate of Mike and Robbie have been crafted through their daily experiences with their father, until they eventually are able to live on their own away from their parents' care. Perhaps the most striking difference is in the presentation of the confrontation between father and son. The harrowing, emotionally soaring final confrontation between Willy and Biff, which provides closure to all the years of animosity, is absent in *The Bullet*, which ends in the uncomfortable and silent pairing of Robbie and Charles, left alone in the kitchen after everyone else has abandoned the household. While Miller's conclusion is intrinsically connected to Biff's showdown with his father, Penhall's ending does not feature the same interconnectedness between father and son, meaning there is no moment of epiphany possible between the two, thus leading to the final, inconclusive and ambiguous moments of the play.

Work has been a defining element of Penhall's plays up to this point. In *Wild Turkey* the world is righted by Stu and Ben's closing mantra about the importance of work as they restore the burger place back to normal so they can open for business. Pete from *Some Voices* and Charles from *Pale Horse* have chosen, as each play opens, to define themselves through their role as restaurant and bar owner, respectively. *Love and Understanding* stresses the incredible demand and deadening influence work is for the two doctors, as it precludes them from having a life together. In contrast, *The Bullet* presents a scenario where the absence of work is just as detrimental to finding happiness in one's life. As the play opens, none of the characters are working—Robbie and Charles have lost their jobs, Carla is a medical student, Billie gave up her job ten years prior when Charles received a promotion and Mike exists day to day on the periphery of society. Of the five characters, Penhall is most interested in examining the state of Charles, who wallows in his inability to succeed. He embodies a sense of helplessness in falling behind others as well as an inability to achieve a status of recognition due to his age. In facing a future without work, he yells at his supervisor: "I don't want to just stop my life ... grind to a halt ... I want something ... better ... I want what everybody else wants" (315). His cry is not an unfamiliar one. Willy Loman expresses a similar idea to Howard, when he begs to keep his job, "You can't eat the orange and throw the peel away—a man is not a piece of fruit!" (Miller 82). One can trace the same sentiment even further back to the turn of the century and Anton Chekhov's *The Three Sisters* and *Uncle Vanya* (1899), in which his characters also declaim the importance of work and its essential connection to one's sense of self and survival. At the end of *Uncle Vanya* Sonya exhorts Vanya that "we have to go on living. We'll go on living day after day.... We'll work selflessly, with respite, now and when we are old" (Chekhov 156).[4] Charles refuses to accept his employer's dismissal of him because he feels they owe him respect and professional courtesy: "It's hardly professional. It's one thing to get the boot but to be booted out by amateurs takes the biscuit" (278). His accusations of amateur leadership continue throughout the play and he seeks out every mistake they make. Later he complains about the misspelling of his name on a letter, demanding: "I want my dignity! And I want an apology! I want a fucking apology!" (315). While Charles' rejection of their firing is ultimately a losing gambit on his part, his anger about their brusque treatment of him has validity. The problem is that his rabid behavior at work and ensuing inconsiderate treatment of his family undermine any credibility he may foster with not only his employers but also the audience.

In Penhall's desire to make the audience understand the anguish of Charles and other men in his position, he embeds in the play contemporary research data about the effect of redundancy on the work force. In his previous plays, Penhall relayed the important contextual sociological/psychological/economic information smoothly within the believable conversations of his characters and the situational components of the play. A perfect example can be found in the Chapter 2 discussion of Pete and Laura about the ineptitude of the National Health Services' bureaucracy in *Some Voices*.[5] Unfortunately, in *The Bullet* the relevant information is not so easily transferred to the audience, as Penhall relies on the expertise of the medical student Carla. While she sports the educational background to provide the framework and context for the audience about the stifling nature of redundancy, her sharing of this knowledge does not have a believable dramatic motivation. Her characterization is a rare misstep for Penhall as the words of Carla, while factual and truly informative, simply draw attention to their awkward inclusion in the text and point to the purely political posturing of the play rather than being an intrinsic extension and narrative element of character. She essentially becomes the editorial voice of the play, providing a passionate and biased commentary about the nature of the work world in contemporary Britain. In this example the ability to capture the realistic language and tone for which Penhall is known vanishes as Carla explains to Robbie why his father responds so strongly to being made redundant.

> Psychologically what aggravates it for somebody of your dad's age is that he's of a generation who a) believe that employment is everything and b) paradoxically was weaned on the notion that as long as you have your health, you should be happy — which of course is anathema to contemporary capitalism. I mean, it's quite Darwinian and really a lot more complex and subtle than you imagine [270–1].

Toward the end of the play, Penhall, perhaps expressing his own dissatisfaction with Carla's role in the play and acknowledging his misstep, has Robbie draw attention to Carla's annoying manner of speech by mimicking her clipped, detached professional style when they have their final argument, including her tendency to highlight various points of her argument via alphabetical designations.

While Carla offers a clinical, dispassionate assessment of the current workings of capitalism, Charles offers his own passionate and personal reasons as to why he lost his job. At first he surmises that it is about a story he wrote condemning the building push in a local neighborhood, despite all the good that others had professed would come from the construction. He tells Carla and Robbie that the collusion between the builders and the local government is "undemocratic. It's unprincipled. And apart from anything else, it's a fucking nuisance. The noise, the traffic, streets full of lorries, skips etcetera. It's untidy" (263). Because of expressing this contrary opinion, he is being let go. He later opines that he is being fired because new ownership is sacking all the older employees in order to hire younger employees, who have the wherewithal to master the computer programs dominating the profession. At no time, though, does Charles acknowledge a sense of his own weaknesses and difficult behavior. He never turns an eye upon himself. Instead, he always casts an outward view upon the weakness and foibles of others and the injustices that have been done to him. His lack of self-awareness is precisely the reason why he struggles with the news of his firing. He has no real sense of self, and without it he does not understand how to go forward in seeking new employment. Instead, he is an angry man, trying to find his way. Contributing to his anger is his realization that his career has not been a stellar one. He has had only a modicum of success. At one point after Robbie complains about his father's behavior, Billie reminds her son about the struggles that Charles has had at the newspaper as he has always been a step behind and a step older than those around him. She tells her Robbie: "Charles didn't become a junior reporter until he was in his thirties. Imagine that. A man with a young family and he was a junior. All his colleagues were kids—younger than you" (313). Consequently finding himself constantly at the bottom of the ladder when compared with his peers has contributed to Charles' need to lash out at the inequity of his journalistic career.

Charles has completely defined himself by his work, and the impending absence of it from his life has provided a contradictory view on himself and his role in society. He tells Carla: "Everybody says to me, You're redundant now. But I don't feel it. I don't know where to put myself. It's like growing old. Everybody tells you you're getting old but I don't feel old" (274). In an effort to comfort him, Carla shares that her own father was made redundant from his teaching job, but managed to find a new happiness in becoming a potter. Breaking away from his usual self-centeredness, he acknowledges a connection with her father, saying, "When you see him ... you know ... tell him I know how he feels. Tell him ... he's not alone" (261). The anecdote about Carla's father, though, really does little to alleviate Charles' concern about his future. In essence, what Carla's father did is precisely what Charles refuses to do: he moved onto a new profession. He took control of his life, accepted the reality of his situation and pursued new avenues of economic stability and professional definition. Charles embraces a different option. He decides to fight the paper on his dismissal. In the process Charles does briefly find a new life and vigor. If he no longer has employment as the chief sub for the paper, then his new job will be trying to make the life of his bosses as uncomfortable as possible by refusing to accept their firing of him. He plans to continue going to work and positioning himself at his desk for as long as it takes. However, his facade of excitement over the possibilities of fighting his employers hides what he really is experiencing, as he reveals to Billie: "Feel that. My chest. It's like a pigeon caught inside my ribcage.... It's fear. I've never been afraid of anything in my life" (282). His blowhard exterior shields him from the true uncertainty of his future. The more fearful side of his character, though, is not developed much beyond this scene, as his angry exterior is the dominant one presented to the audience.

While the task energizes Charles, it drives Billie to distraction because of his refusal to accept his current situation and move forward. She wants them to begin their life of retirement, while her husband continues to be stuck in the past, a characteristic that he shares with Miller's main character. Like Willy's obsession with the lost opportunity to go to Alaska, Charles also returns to moments from his past when he could have had a different fate, if only others had not held him back from attaining a higher status in the work world. One of the most striking memories of failure for him was when he accidentally stumbled upon the Queen Mother at a building dedication. The subsequent story that he wrote about her, that she had had a face lift, was buried by his editors. If he had worked elsewhere, he argued, he could have controlled his destiny with the publication of such a revelatory piece. For Charles it was the story that got away. If he had been freelance and managed to sell the story, then he could have had his own newspaper and been in control. "I could have started my own weekly standing on my head. Free advertising for the first two issues, crank up the rate, float it on the stockmarket, I'd have my bum in butter by now" (280). While he stews over this lost opportunity, a much darker event from when he was a child still haunts him. As a boy Charles would play the piano in order to drown out the noise of his drunken male family members. He was successful "until they stopped me. Those men ... the men would gather around the piano and down would go that lid on my fingers.... They thought I was a poof. Because I was musical. I was ten years old and they ... they broke my fingers..." (325). The treatment he received as a child, just trying to calm a disruptive situation down, hampered him for life. His attitude turned from a placating nature to a combative one because of their violent reaction to his piano playing. Much to his detriment, he no longer trusts anyone except for himself to achieve his goals.

In addition to his refusal to vacate the past, Billie and Charles have relationship problems as well. This becomes apparent with Carla and Robbie's arrival. After Charles goes upstairs to bed, the couple begins to fool around on the sofa with Carla first massaging Robbie's back and then undoing his buckle in preparation for massaging another part of his body. Charles, on the landing, has watched the coupling between the two young lovers and interrupts them before it proceeds any further. After Carla and Robbie go upstairs to bed, Charles is left alone downstairs. Billie enters, asking Charles to come to bed. He then attempts to replicate the physical caresses of Robbie and Carla with Billie, even copying their dialogue, but she refuses to humor him as their emotional and sexual relationship has been strained for quite some time. They have not made love in a number of years. Unable to stand the rebuff to his sexual advances, he confronts Billie: "You know, the last time I felt another person's hands on me was when I had my fucking vasectomy. You don't touch me the way you used to. I haven't felt your skin in months" (283). Watching his son and his girlfriend engage in sexual activity reinforces his loss of worth and unattractiveness to his wife, echoing exactly the same response of rejection he has received from his employers. His value in both his public and private life is negligible.

While his situation with Billie is fraught with tension, at least she still interacts with him. Both sons left home, refusing to come back and see him for a number of years. Despite Robbie's attempt to distance himself from his father, Penhall indicates that the concept of generational recycling, where a son follows in the same footsteps as his father, is a prevalent component between Robbie and Charles. Even though Robbie tries to be a separate person, working in the Far East as an IT technician, he cannot escape the connection that exists between the two of them. Penhall uses a visual cue to show the inescapable link between the two men early on in the play. When Carla goes up to bed, after having been interrupted by Charles, Robbie remains alone on the stage, sitting on the family sofa as the scene goes to black. When the lights fade up, Charles is now in the exact same position as his son, directly linking the two.[6] Later the connection between father and son is even more prominent. Robbie reluctantly admits that he, too, like his father, has been made redundant, and then at the end of the play both men find themselves alone with one another, as both of their partners leave them. While Penhall reveals the generational recycling that occurs between Robbie and Charles, he also highlights the stark contrast between Charles and Mike, who has succeeded in avoiding the generational recycling of his father by refusing to embrace the capitalistic system of work and reward. This father and son pairing shares nothing in common and they are unable to communicate with one another.

Charles' behavior eventually drives away a tired and disheartened Billie, who had tried to entice Charles to take the severance pay from the company, so they could retire to Italy. Billie's departure is truly tragic for their relationship as demonstrated by a story that Billie shares from when she was a little girl of four years old. She was walking around the city market and someone gave her a tangerine to enjoy. After showing the fruit gift to her father, he picked her up, put her on the kitchen table and told her to jump. "And he held his arms out and I jumped off the table and I flew through the air and he took two steps back and I landed flat on my face.... And he said to me, 'Now you've learnt.' Learnt? I was four years old. I didn't know what he was up to. And he said, 'Never, my girl, ever trust anybody...'" (304). Like Charles' story about his family members crushing his fingers, Billie's story echoes the same hardscrabble, difficult life that both of them have led. While Charles was scarred by the event, leading to his anger and distrust, she reveals that she overcame her father's advice and learned to trust one person: Charles. Even though she tells the story about her childhood to defend Charles against the accusations of Robbie, it is clear throughout the course of the play that she now nurses her own doubts about her husband's commitment to them as a couple rather than just to himself. Once he returns home full of vim and vigor because he secretly taped his meetings with his boss and counselor, she confronts him a final time as his behavior threatens the stability of their household. He, though, only has thought of himself. She tells him that she has spent "thirty years of supporting you so you can throw that settlement to the floor and snarl in our faces while everything that I hold dear collapses around us ... and what have you done for me? Have you ever thought about what I want...?" (320). She then leaves him. Equally, he drives away Mike, who has just begun to make a reappearance in the life of his family, as the two of them argue and then end up in a wrestling match, highlighting the fact that their inability to verbally communicate with one another must eventually dissolve into a physicality of pushes and shoves in order for them to truly share their feelings of hostility and disappointment in one another. The sequential loss of his job, wife and son represent the complete and total breakdown of Charles being the guide and anchor of this family. The Men's Free Press Collective perfectly described the nature of this household in terms of men experiencing a crisis in masculinity due to job loss. "Our alienation from our job, from our communities, our isolation, unrecognized, creates expectations of the family that cannot be fulfilled. In fear, we punish others, often the closest to us, for our own powerlessness" (84). Charles has demonstrated this type of behavior to his family not only when he becomes redundant but also when he was employed precisely because he never achieved the success he craved. As the play ends, Robbie and Charles sit alone at the kitchen table, awaiting an uncertain future and finding that they are more alike than they thought.

The final image of the play offers a lack of closure, which is a first in a Penhall play. Whereas his other plays have provided a sense of connection, self-realization and a sense of finality for the characters (Stu rebuilding the burger bar; Ray finding a home in a hostel; Charles going to jail; Neal embracing his single, work-free life), *The Bullet* offers a vision of uncertainty. While Carla has left Robbie for good as their relationship was still in its nadir stage and based primarily on sex, the question remains as to whether Billie has left for good or will return to her husband. As Billie said, she invested thirty years in Charles. However, as Penhall's other plays indicate about the nature of relationships, everyone has their tipping point. Ray and Pete's dad left their mother, Charles' wife left him in *Pale Horse* and Neal leaves Rachel and does not return to her, no matter how hard she pushes for reconciliation. If one extrapolates from the relationships in the previous plays, then it seems Billie has left her husband for good. Penhall, therefore, ends *The Bullet*, like *Wild Turkey* and *Some Voices*, with two men alone, looking to restore their lives. While in the previous cases, the men dealt with serious blows to their livelihood (the attack on the restaurant, Ray's breakdown in the kitchen), the play ends with a restoration of some modicum of normalcy. However, for Robbie and Charles, that sense of comfort has been stripped away with the absence of a job and a partner. Instead, they must either rely upon one another, a difficult solution as Robbie has tried to avoid being alone with his father the entire play, or go it alone. The play leaves them in limbo, on the precipice of a potentially dramatic change in their life, but whether in a positive direction is unclear, but clearly the two men have a lot to learn before they can begin the path to a happier life.

The ambiguity of the ending is a change for Penhall (and something to which he will return with his later plays) and signals a larger change for his plays as a whole. In essence, *The Bullet* heralded the end of Penhall's domestic pieces, as *Wild Turkey, Some Voices, Pale Horse, Love and Understanding* and *The Bullet* focus on family, friendships, romantic relations and the domestic sphere of British life. With his next three plays Penhall's theatrical vision shifts from an almost exclusive look at the private world of his characters to a much more scathing eye at the public spheres of Britain, as his plays examine institutional racism within the National Health Service, the lack of ethics within the profession of tabloid journalism and the British government's desire to be a major player in the production of weapons for the conflict in the Middle East.

6

Blue/Orange *and Racism within the National Health Service*

For his next play, *Blue/Orange*, Penhall returned to a previously unsuccessful script which he had written while in the United States in 1994. The impetus for this initial attempt stemmed from an experience in San Francisco, California, when he visited an overworked friend who was a care worker for schizophrenics. As his friend was overwhelmed with his responsibilities, Penhall helped out during his visit. In working with the patients, one in particular stood out, a black man who fluctuated between believing that he was a woman and a white man. During that visit, Penhall's previous experience in London's Shepherd's Bush with the cavalier treatment by the Tory government of the mentally ill was now augmented through this first-hand experience of the United States' treatment of their mentally ill citizens. Penhall's friend was allocated little money to feed his patients, forcing him to buy the cheapest food possible, including food past its expiration date. Penhall later commented on the effect that the unacceptable treatment of the patients had on him: "I was already aware of it in England, it just took America to blow my circuits about it" (Hemming, "It's a Mad").

Based on this encounter Penhall wrote an early draft of what would eventually become *Blue/Orange*. When he was in Manhattan, he staged a reading of the play, which immediately highlighted the limitations of the script as Penhall realized he was in unfamiliar territory writing about not only American characters in San Francisco but also the American health system. Penhall later acknowledged that he did not feel as comfortable basing the play in the United States. However, he admitted that if he could transfer the essence of what he had written to a London situation, then it would "really cook" (Rees, "Vexed"). Over the ensuing years Penhall would return off and on to this stymied piece of writing, until finally finding the dam breaker when he directed a staged reading for the Royal National Theatre of David Mamet's *Speed-the-Plow*, a three-act and three-hander, which relies on a triangular relationship between two insiders (being professional Hollywood types) and an outsider (a temp).

The structure of Mamet's piece provided Penhall with the impetus to go back to his earlier draft. Embracing the three-character narrative, he retained two characters from his original script — Bruce, a young doctor, and Christopher, a black patient — and then crafted a new one, Robert, a senior doctor, which he wrote with the actor Bill Nighy in mind. Nighy originated the role in the original Cottesloe production at the Royal National Theatre as well as the transfer to the West End.

Blue/Orange focuses on Christopher, a twenty-four-year-old black man, who, because of an incident at a market, has been legally remanded to 28 days of mental observation and hospital incarceration. The play opens on the eve of his release. Bruce, a junior-level doctor only a few years older than his patient, believes Christopher might be schizophrenic and wants to keep him beyond the legislated time for more observation. Bruce brings in Robert, his mentor and a senior doctor in his fifties, for a consultation about the severity of Christopher's mental state. Robert, citing the lack of bed space, depleted resources and, surprisingly to Bruce, the patient's ethnicity, diagnoses Christopher, much to Bruce's chagrin, as healthy enough to be discharged. Neither doctor budges from his perspective about the patient, and in turn Christopher becomes a pawn in their arguments about the current state of health care in England. After much haranguing from Bruce, including getting Christopher to reveal that the oranges on the table in front of him are blue and that Idi Amin is his father, Robert agrees to a one-on-one consultation with Christopher, who he begins to view as the perfect case study for his unfinished manuscript on black psychosis, the publication of which will earn him his long-coveted promotion to professor. During their discussion, which is the center part of the play, Robert discovers supporting evidence for Christopher's adamant claims to be Idi Amin's son as well as incidences where Bruce may have broken Health Services protocol in his treatment of Christopher. The next morning charges are brought against Bruce by Christopher, in language crafted by Robert. The two doctors engage in a heated argument about Christopher's health and the politics of the hospital. Robert, pulling rank, releases Christopher and the play ends with Bruce threatening to bring his own charges against his mentor Robert for manipulating the system for his own professional benefit.

Blue/Orange, which premiered in April 2000, became Penhall's greatest theatrical success. Besides winning the Olivier Award for best new play, Penhall's play also received the *Evening Standard* and the Critic's Circle Theatre award and was eventually filmed, using a script adapted by Penhall, for British television. In addition, Brian Logan, writing in the *Guardian*, pronounced that Penhall was the first of the young, new, hip writers from Sierz's In-Yer-Face troupe to produce a mature work. Not surprisingly, the Olivier Award winner received stellar notices, garnering him his best set of reviews for all of his plays. Dominic Cavendish was one of many critics to focus on the play's racial element: "What distinguishes *Blue/Orange* from its predecessor (*Copenhagen*) by a long chalk, and indeed from everything else on the London stage at present, is the fact that.... Penhall broaches the complexities of multicultural Britain today."[1] Carole Woddis of *The Herald* also noted Penhall's look at race: "In this era of heightened racial sensitivities, it is particularly brave of Penhall to confront head-on the subject of schizophrenia in the black community." In addition, she praised the quality of his writing, remarking especially on his use of humor: "the comic brilliance with which he handles the current mental health issues of diagnosis, treatment, funding and professional antagonisms is devastating and brilliantly achieved." Benedict Nightingale also noted the comedy inherent in the eccentric behavior of his psychiatrists. "The very thought of shrinks makes people feel insecure, which is presumably why a National Theatre audience laughed so heartily to see their eccentricities and inadequacies exposed." Like Logan and Woddis, Michael Coveney noted that Penhall's "skills notch up a gear" with this play. Alastair Macaulay, like Cavendish, cited it as the best new play since Michael Frayn's *Copenhagen*, calling it "thrillingly original" and "a most moving, exciting play." Michael Billington noted that "Penhall has the gift ... of conveying moral indignation without preaching." As well, he highlighted Penhall's return to the debate about Care in the Community, but "Penhall is really making the wider Shavian point that all professions are a conspiracy against the laity and eventually becomes wrapped in hermetic self-regard."

One of the most vituperative and rare negative reviews of the play was by Charles Spencer, who called it "hysterical melodrama," "meretricious and implausible," and accused Penhall of "hitching a cheap theatrical ride" on the topic of schizophrenia because "there is something deeply offensive about watching such a sensitive and harrowing subject being hijacked in the name of entertainment." Penhall responded to Spencer's criticism in an interview a few years later with the *Guardian* saying: "I know that I'm honest, decent and true. I know that I'm not exploiting anybody" (Ellis).

While inspired by Mamet's *Speed-the-Plow*, Penhall eschewed the reliance on machismo in Mamet's play and instead inserted the issue of race to provoke his audience into facing the relationship between race and mental illness in Britain. Penhall's end of the 1990s play tapped into a decade-long growing concern about the National Health Service where finances and political necessity became far more important than patient health—for example, the already discussed policy of Care in the Community in Penhall's *Some Voices*. While *Blue/Orange* is not his first foray into questioning the medical profession's treatment of mental health, its success would not have been possible without his previous examinations of the health system from the patient and family perspective in *Some Voices* and the mental strain and professional pressure doctors face in *Love and Understanding*. *Blue/Orange* expands on both of these plays by delving into the intricacies surrounding the role of a doctor and his relationship with his patient. Because this was Penhall's third flirtation with mental illness and the medical profession in six plays, the London newspaper critics began calling him "Mr. Schizophrenia" and "the laureate of lithium" after *Blue/Orange* opened (Hoggard).

A British playwright politically challenging the decisions and actions of a large British institution like the NHS is hardly surprising. After all, a traditional component of post–1956 drama has been the steady questioning of British institutions as seen in the political works of Howard Brenton, David Hare, Trevor Griffiths, David Edgar, Stephen Poliakoff, and many others. However, a white British playwright looking at the issue of race and, more specifically, race in terms of a British institution *is* surprising precisely because mainstream twentieth-century British theatre has rarely ever confronted the multiracial dimensions of the country, even though the minority population currently comprises 10 to 15 percent of the country. True, there have been the occasionally recognized and produced black British playwrights, for example, Mustapha Matura and Michael Abbensetts in the 1970s, Caryl Phillips and Winsome Pinnock in the 1980s, and Tanika Gupta and Roy Williams in the 1990s; black British theatre groups, the best known being Talawa, but over the 1990s their numbers steadily diminished until by the time Penhall's play premiered in 2000 only two were receiving any kind of government funding; racially blind casting decisions, including Sonia Swaby as Nancy in a 1998 West End production of *Oliver!* and Adrian Lester's Olivier-winning turn as Bobby in the 1996 West End revival of Stephen Sondheim's *Company* as well as his performance in 2003 as Henry V; and theatres partial to black plays, such as the Tricycle and Theatre Royal, Stratford East. But all of these are the exceptions, rather than the rule. Writing in 1998 David Benedict addressed the dearth of black actors in plays, television and films, noting that when cast, a black male always plays a pimp, while a black female always plays a prostitute. The most sustainable way for black actors to work was through the television show *The Bill*. If the roles for black actors were limited, then subsequently the draw for black audiences was limited as well. *The Times* examined the issue of the absent black patron for the theatre and discovered that they were not coming because "There's nothing there for them. It doesn't have a vibe" (Alberge). Yashim Alibhai-Brown also addressed the concept of the black audience, remarking upon its composition:

> The irony is that our black and Asian youngsters are much less inclined to go to the Royal Shakespeare Company than are their middle-class parents, who, if they were educated under the imperial sun, have strong attachments to western drama. Even now, you always meet intellectuals from India or South Africa, but not from London, at the RSC [263].

In fact, the first British black written play to premiere on the West End did not occur until 2005 with Kwame Kwei-Armah's *Elmina's Kitchen*, which transferred from the Cottesloe at the National Theatre. Some London papers surmised that the reason it was chosen to transfer was because Kwei-Armah, a regular cast member on *Casualty*, also played the main character, a father struggling with his restaurant and his son's flirtation with joining a gang, and his noted celebrity would bring in the needed audience to make the transfer profitable. In the same year *The Big Life*, the first British black West End musical, also debuted.

Highlighting the absence of black productions was the prejudicial attitude within the theatrical community itself toward black audiences. Penhall remarked: "I've actually been told by people working in the theatre, 'Black people don't come to the theatre ... and if they do they're always late, always talk during the show, it's a real hassle'" (Interview, *Guardian*). A few months before Penhall's above comment was published, the *Guardian* queried if indeed the British theatre was racist and discovered that while the casting of actors of ethnicity had increased over the years, the hiring of backstage workers skewed almost entirely white. Most tellingly, their research also discovered another reason for the dearth of black audience members. The "absence of black marketing officers means theatre is rarely marketed effectively to black audiences" (Allen). The source for the *Guardian*'s article was an Arts Council commissioned study, called the Eclipse Report, which examined the role of race in theatre hires. Using Arts Council statistics from 1999/2000, the Eclipse Report noted only 80 positions out of 2,009 were held by black or Asian employees. In addition, out of 463 board member positions, only 16 were held by blacks or Asians. After the report's release, *The Observer* remarked that "it is worth noting there is not a single non-white artistic director in any theatre in the UK. What we have is an industry that is institutionally racist to its very core, yet congratulates itself on being super-liberal" (Phillips). Highly cognizant of this weakness of racial representation within his own profession, Penhall challenged his audience and in turn his theatrical community on the subject of race in a way that had not been done before in the British theatre. In writing *Blue/Orange* he hoped to provoke "people to have fist fights in the auditorium afterwards, squabbling about whether they're racist or not" (Hemming, "It's a Mad").

Penhall's reference to fist fights was not just a sensationalistic, publicity-inclined phrase to capture the attention of the British public. In fact, the set itself, designed by William Dudley, resembled a boxing ring, which Paul Taylor aptly noted in his review as he described the experience of watching the play "with the audience ... in a tight diamond-formation around an almost boxing ring-like stage, the scene is set for an acrimonious battle." Roger Michell, the play's director, explained that they "visited a 19th-century lecture theatre at Guy's Hospital and were struck by the intensity of focus that was created by the 'tiering' of the seats— hence our 'boxing ring'" (Leek). Ariel Watson, in her article on psychotherapy in contemporary drama, found the choice of a boxing ring an appropriate device for Penhall's intended consequences of challenging the audience's concept of race as the set predispositioned the audience to relate with and accept the opinions of the doctors rather than Christopher. "This is spectatorial condescension made literal, the audience's gaze fused with clinical observation, implicating the viewers in the feral, packing medical contests staged below" (200).

In order to provoke the battle of his audience by ensnaring them in the play's tangled web of racist sympathies and outrages, Penhall relies on the white, senior doctor Robert, a glib, enticing, funny, well-spoken character. In discussing Robert, Penhall explained that if someone comes across as quite smart, then their racist comments go unnoticed. "So I wanted to push the boundaries and see how racist Robert could be while still being tremendously literate and witty and charming. In England, the more articulate you are, the more you get away with" (Litson). As noted earlier, when Penhall rewrote the play, he created Robert with Bill Nighy in mind. Nighy has made a career of making utterly detestable scamps lovable, like Bernard Nightingale in Tom Stoppard's *Arcadia* (1993). Under Nighy's control Robert became the type of character who can pull off cringe-inducing statements like telling Christopher: "Go home and listen to some reggae music.... What is it in Africa, 'jungle'?" (115). As already seen, the British theatre itself had been a white bastion and, as we will soon see, racist rhetoric has been staunchly embedded into the British culture via the language of politicians and the British government since the mid–1950s. Robert, being in his fifties himself, would have been influenced by the racist attitude toward black Britons, and in addition, being around the average age of London theatre goers, he becomes a generational representative for and uncomfortable voice of the audience at a time when questions about race were being heavily debated in the media. The play's premiere and the ensuing discussion about race in the theatre via the Eclipse Report was auspiciously aided by a government report released in February 1999, which cited the London Metropolitan Police Force as being guilty of "institutional racism." When the play serendipitously opened in the Cottesloe Theatre, a little over thirteen months after the report was released to the public, the whole country was in the midst of undertaking an examination of just how racist it truly was.

In order to understand the cultural context surrounding not only Penhall's play and Robert's attitude but also the entire mindset of the country at the end of the 1990s, it is important to go back a little over 50 years before *Blue/Orange* premiered to 1948, when one of the defining moments for black Britons transpired with the arrival of the SS *Empire Windrush*, a boat filled with 492 Jamaican citizens who were migrating to Britain with the hope of economic betterment. Despite one London newspaper's front page headline exclaiming "Welcome Home" to the new transplants, the arrival of the *Windrush*'s passengers sent white Britain into a state of fear about their country, which was still struggling to recover in myriad ways from the devastation of World War II, suddenly being overrun by boatloads and boatloads of black colonialists from the Caribbean and other colonial outposts with large black populations, all of whom were seeking a new beginning. After the *Windrush* docked and the passengers flowed into land, some Labour Members of Parliament requested that Prime Minister Clement Atlee immediately set policy on prohibiting the future of more blacks coming to Britain. Both political parties saw the immigration issue as a threat to the country and responded differently in their attempts to attack the problem. The Conservative party was "far more interested in inflaming public opinion against black people rather than combating racism" (James 376), while Labour supported the prevention of "others of dark hue from entering the country" (James 377). Over the next forty years, the ensuing Tory and Labour governments worked to preclude non-white British citizens from migrating from their colonies. Some attempts were bureaucratically sly, as the processing of passport requests were intentionally delayed, while others were more overt, as various Immigrant Acts aimed at keeping non-white British citizens from migrating were passed. Historians, like Winston James, have noted the government's hypocrisy toward migration.[2] While the migration of legal black British citizens was deemed entirely unacceptable, hundreds of thousands of white Irish immigrants were permitted in. "By 1951 there were an estimated 15,000 Caribbean migrants in Britain compared to nearly 750,000 Irish immigrants" (James 372). The height of racist politicking in the country occurred in the 1960s and 1970s with the passing of three Commonwealth Immigration Acts (one in 1962, 1968 and 1971), with each one even more severely restricting the freedom of non-white citizens to migrate to England. In addition, in the early 1960s conservative Peter Griffiths campaigned and won with the slogan: "If you want a nigger neighbour, vote Labour." A few years later Enoch Powell made his infamous "rivers of blood" speech which warned against the growing numbers of black immigrants in the country and called for a fiscal policy to provide economic aid so black citizens would leave England. Margaret Thatcher's draconian policies in the late 1970s and 1980s continued the policy of her predecessors, having made her racist intentions clear before she became prime minister when she admitted that she shared the same fear as other Britons that "this country might be rather swamped by people with a different culture" (Alibhai-Brown 78). According to James, Thatcher's turn as prime minister "was the worst for black settlers and their children in Britain since the dark days of the early 1950s," as it included the British Nationality Act in 1981, which "deprived non-white overseas British nationals of the right of abode in Britain" (James 382).

With such governmental disregard for black Britons, it is not surprising that unchecked racial violence ensued, from the Teddy Boys in the 1950s to repeated police abuse over the years to unprovoked attacks by white groups on black citizens in the 1980s and 1990s. The defining racial flashpoint of the 1990s that roiled the nation and is connected with *Blue/Orange* was the unprovoked and fatal stabbing at a bus stop of Stephen Lawrence, an 18-year-old, black, A-level student, by five white youths. Due to the ineptitude of the investigation by the police, fueled in part by the race of the victim, none of the attackers were punished for the crime. After Tony Blair became prime minister, he asked Sir William MacPherson to conduct an independent inquiry into the crime itself, the Metropolitan Police Department's response to Lawrence's death, the ensuing investigation and eventual failed trial. In February 1999, the MacPherson report was released, stating that there was a blatant existence of "institutional racism" throughout the London Metropolitan police force.[3] The report's release started a discussion and ensuing self-investigation for the presence of racism across the country in all of its institutions, including the theatre, hence the Eclipse report noted earlier, and, in the case of Penhall's focus for *Blue/Orange*, the National Health Service.

Tapping into one of the most damning aspects of the MacPherson report's findings, Penhall's play argues that the racist tendencies of the police force are partially to blame for Christopher's initial incarceration. A few weeks before the release of the MacPherson report, *The Observer* reported that "the police are eight times as likely to stop and search young black men as their white counterparts" (Phillips). This pattern of belligerent police behavior is explicitly at stake in Christopher's situation, especially since the police have remanded him into the hospital for the 28 days of observation. When Robert asks Christopher if he has some place to go to when he is released, Christopher reveals that he has council accommodations in White City, but that he doesn't plan on going there because of the heavy police presence on the estate. He tells Robert: "I get stopped a *lot* in White City" (36). When Robert presses him on why the police deliberately persecute him, he answers: "Cos they're *fascists*. It's obvious" (36). Because of the stops and searches, Christopher has become paranoid and suspicious of the authorities. In fact, his experiences with the police have led him to be suspicious of any authority figure, which plays out through his distrust of Robert's statement that he will release him at the end of his 28 days.

Clearly, Christopher's distrust of the police is well founded based on the findings of the MacPherson report. His distrust of doctors is equally well founded. The production's program featured results from a telling study of 450 patients with mental health issues conducted in February 2000 by the National Schizophrenia Fellowship. African-Caribbean males were twelve times more likely to receive a schizophrenic diagnosis than white males. Under the Mental Health Act, "88% of black respondents were detained" in comparison to only 43% of whites surveyed (*Blue/Orange* program). Finally, "72% of black respondents had been forcibly restrained compared with 39% of white respondents" (*Blue/Orange* program). In a platform discussion during the play's run, Penhall argued that the racism of the police department's stop-and-search policy, which was greatly expanded under Thatcher, had a direct corollary effect on the mental condition of black victims. He explained that the statistics from the National Schizophrenia Fellowship study were not surprising when put within the context of one being stopped and searched on a daily basis. Arguably, if one were stopped enough times, one would begin to be suspicious of everyone and, in turn, one's behavior would reflect the resultant paranoia. Penhall told his Cottesloe audience that at that very moment there were black patients in Maudsley Hospital who were completely correct in being paranoid, as they believed that people were watching them because they developed such a mindset due to being stopped and searched up to seven times in one week. Their treatment by the police caused their paranoia to be real and not a symptom of mental illness. In a later interview he remarked: "If you're black, you can't have a bad day. You can't be caught pissing and ranting. People are not only suspicious, but scared. I've heard of people being picked up and sectioned, even with no history of mental illness" (Smith). Penhall also acknowledged the doctors' responsibility in the high rate of diagnosed schizophrenia in black mental patients. Medical institutions use race like "a football, mental health is stigmatized and mendaciousness is generally rewarded" (East). In addition, Penhall suggested "people from a culture a little different from the doctors' are often diagnosed as mentally ill, when in fact they are just a little different" (Klein 85). Ultimately, Penhall presents a picture of inescapable consequences for blacks in similar situations as Christopher. Working separately, the police and the doctors, with their racist policies and cultural biases, make it an almost inescapable fact that a black patient will be found to be schizophrenic, even though the National Schizophrenia Fellowship study "does not accept that any individual ethnic group has inherent susceptibility to severe mental illness than any other groups" (*Blue/Orange* program).

In crafting the play Penhall also was personally aware of the bias intrinsically at work in his audiences when it comes to preconceptions about cultural identity. He first saw this documented with his father, who during his lifetime was South African, British and finally Australian. And yet, Penhall asked, "Did people contextualize him in terms of the defining migration of his life? Fuck no!" ("Re: E-mail," August 31). Penhall's peripatetic childhood had crafted for him a multifaceted identity, similar to his father, of being an Aussie and a Brit as well as the son of a South African father. His make-up was incredibly diverse, complicated and enriching and yet the acknowledgement of his complex identity failed to materialize in how others viewed him. "I spent my life being told by people who I am and where I'm from. In Australia they tend to view me as English. Some people [in England] see me as an Aussie. Wherever I was living, people judged I was from somewhere else. My behaviour is repeatedly judged in a cultural context" ("Re: E-mail," August 31).[4] Because of this treatment, he became frustrated with the "perceptions and preoccupations of a mono-cultural society" ("Re: E-mail," August 31) and aimed to address this issue with *Blue/Orange*, by featuring a black character, who was African but also English, was Ugandan but also from Shepherd's Bush. Christopher's make-up defies easy categorization. However, as Penhall demonstrates, the characters, and in turn the audience, aim to limit his identity to one facet, and in doing so avoid the complicated nature of his true self, but instead define him through a stereotype. Penhall uses the example of Christopher's Ugandan background as an example, as "the implication is that Ugandans are intrinsically rowdy. Whether this is racism, cultural assumption, cultural specificity or just bollocks is one of the ensuing arguments" (Penhall, "Who Wrote"). The audience, then, is influenced not only by police and medical institutions' treatment of blacks, but also by their own preset, limiting definitions of the individual when it comes to Christopher's race, cultural background, citizenship and even neighborhood. In turn, Robert will be caught out as representing this perspective as he relies on these same limiting definitions of an individual to define his patient and his actions.

As the play opens Christopher, 24 hours away from being released from the hospital, sits with Bruce. In Christopher's mind his release is a certainty, as he believes he has proven to be a capable and sane member of society. Bruce, though, is not so sure. This construct of different interpretations about his condition is at the heart of Christopher's situation. He feels he is ready to return; Bruce says no. Unfortunately for Christopher, he is at the whim of his doctors and their decisions: he really has no power at all. Instead, all the power rests with two white doctors, each with disparate views on the treatment of mental illness, and they will determine his fate based on their own medical and cultural readings of Christopher's behavior. In *Discipline and Punish* Michel Foucault argued that in such a situation the body of the disempowered finds itself "directly involved in a political field; power relations have an immediate hold upon it; they invest it, mark it, train it, torture it, force it to carry out tasks, to perform ceremonies, to emit signs" (25). Christopher's position within the power dynamics of the play as a patient to the two doctors perfectly emulates Foucault's observations. Throughout, Robert and Bruce fight over their ability to control and dominate the body that is Christopher, as he represents for each one a philosophical victory in terms of their diagnosis and prescription for the treatment of schizophrenia. Everything about Christopher is refracted, dissected and understood through the lens of these two white doctors. In turn, Christopher becomes a tool of the larger dynamic of the professional squabble and philosophical discussion between the two medical practitioners about the political and economic decisions of the NHS and their own professional pride and ambitions.

In the first few minutes of the play, though, Christopher attempts to negotiate for power, asking for a number of items, but in all requests he is denied by Bruce, who refuses Christopher's calls for caffeine, Coke, coffee and cigarettes. The only thing he is allowed? Water. Throughout the exchange Christopher is treated like a child in terms of how his requests are received and the comments from Bruce about his behavior. When Robert arrives for the consultation, holding a cup of coffee, Christopher immediately protests the hypocrisy of doctors drinking coffee when patients cannot. When Robert offers to ameliorate Christopher's distress by offering him the coffee, Bruce intercedes, grabbing it and draining it all in one swallow. When Christopher admits to already having packed his belongings in preparation for departure, Bruce asks who said he could get his things together. Christopher responds shortly: "No one, man, I just did it. I just ... I put my pyjamas in a bag and my toothbrush in on top.... Took a whole five minutes" (18). Bruce aims to not only control all the items that Christopher might ingest during his stay in the medical facility but also all of his individual actions, not allowing the patient any control over his life within the walls of the hospital.

The linguistic byplay between the characters also indicates Christopher's limited situation. When he states that in a day he will be a free man, away from the hospital, Bruce responds haltingly, "Well ... aha ha ... OK" (5), refusing to confirm Christopher's statement of freedom, which Bruce will continue to do throughout the entire play. Christopher, though, does not pick up on Bruce's equivocation. In his mind because he said it, it is true. This self-stated mindset has larger implications for Christopher when he later claims Idi Amin to be his father. Like with who is allowed to drink coffee, there also exists a double bind of who has permission to use certain words and how they can be used. Christopher describes his fellow patients as "nuts" and Bruce responds:

...crazy people here ... yes—
CHRISTOPHER: Crazies, man! Radio Rental.
BRUCE: People with — well — we don't actually use the term "crazy"...
CHRISTOPHER: You just said it [12].

The language issue becomes exceedingly important in terms of not only who controls it but also how it is interpreted. Christopher never is given the chance to control the language of the play, except for when race is raised. Only Christopher can use the language and racial epithets about his ethnicity, calling himself an "uppity nigga" (19), and when Bruce tries to appropriate the same language, echoing the same phrase as a means to help an upset Christopher to see the way others would view his behavior — "They'll think you're a, a, an 'uppity nigga,' that's what they'll think. Kissing your teeth. It's not you" (20), it comes back to threaten him in terms of his professional position when Christopher makes charges against him for using the racial epithet. While the doctors can control most of the aspects of their patient's life, they are unable to limit his ability to speak of his racial identity. To name it gives him a brief power of self-identity in the face of the institutional control over him. In fact, at the end of the play, Christopher exerts the only power he can upon Bruce, who he feels, via Robert's coaching, has been manipulating him, placing thoughts in his head and lying to him over the previous 24 hours. He draws immediate attention to their difference and the hegemonic power structure that allows white doctors to diagnosis and mistreat black patients. "You'll never keep me locked up, white man. This is one nigga you don't get to keep, white man" (110). It is a brief moment of anger and strength by Christopher, but it is a fleeting moment and the power of the statement is only made manifest through the action of Robert granting Christopher's release. The patient really has no say in his own incarceration. As the play progresses, though, the language shifts from Christopher's racial descriptions of himself to the more complicated and alienating medical argot of the doctors. As they debate the nature of Christopher's condition, he is, for the most part, silenced as their power, embedded in the language that they use, is beyond his knowledge and comprehension. He merely becomes a pawn in the face of their discussions, much like a child stuck between two warring parents. During his National Theatre Platform discussion, Penhall addressed this linguistic power dynamic inherent in doctor/patient relationships. He indicted the members of the medical institution as constantly engaging in heady medical discussions and diagnoses while a patient silently sits there as if he is not even present. Penhall described the behavior as "a kind of arrogance" on the part of the doctors (Wolf, "Power Games"). The whole profession then becomes a complicated game of language control and is therefore "open to abuse by silver-tongued tricky Dickies" (Wolf, "Power Games"), like Robert.

Having played the game for a number of years within the National Health Service system, Robert best exemplifies the kind of doctor who uses language to achieve and maintain power, and in the triangular dynamic that Penhall has created, Robert is at the apex of power, which includes the ability to make the defining diagnosis of Christopher's condition. When Bruce questions this authority, Robert stresses his seniority as justification for who is better qualified to make decisions—"I am, as they say, an 'expert.' I am Senior Consultant and I am here to be 'consulted'" (50). When Bruce continues to question why his own viewpoint has no validity, Robert turns the response to a much more personal level in terms of Bruce's future ability to be promoted.

> ROBERT: Do you know what most young doctors would do to have me as Supervisor? I mean normal ones ... the smart ones ... what they'd do to know they have a future. To have a shot at becoming Consultant? They'd *lick my anus.*
> *Silence.*
> (But that's beside the point...) [52].

Such a telling statement indicates the amount of hubris that has accompanied Robert's ascension through the system. He later stresses that same sense of hubris when he explains to Christopher why his diagnosis is more accurate than Bruce's: "*I'm* the Head of Department. I'm the Boss. I'm the Big Cheese" (76). However, with his position within the hospital comes an adherence to the policies set out by the NHS, one of which is that it wants the mentally ill released into the community rather than being kept behind brick walls. Robert uses his facility with language to explain this policy, arguing that the old policy dictated that they keep people like Christopher locked up, but now the Service believes they should go home instead. The emphasis on the comfort of one's home, rather than the institutional medical establishment of a hospital, suggests a more comforting and loving environment of care, which Penhall has already shown to be a misnomer in *Some Voices*. In fact, what the National Health Service is doing has a long precedence in previous hospital models as documented by Michel Foucault in *The Birth of the Clinic*. He noted that nationalizing "hospital funds sometimes went so far as the confiscation of liquid capital, and many bursars had no other course but to turn out boarders whom they could no longer keep" (66). Foucault proceeded to document a case where a hospital displaced patients so that they could admit soldiers in their place. The reason? The government paid for the soldiers' care; the patients they evicted had no means to pay. Foucault termed such actions the "dehospitalization of illness" (66), which aptly captures the mindset of the National Health Service's treatment of the mental ill by adhering to its Care in the Community policy. The system off-loads the costly long-term care and attention needed by mental health patients, many of them schizophrenic, back onto family members. In turn, the action frees up beds for more readily handled cases with a higher rate of success in terms of treatment and that offer a better financial return on the investment of time and space. In addition, Robert's dehospitalization decisions are controlled by the dictates of the already overcrowded space in which they work. He stresses to Bruce that there are no beds available for Christopher, but Robert makes that point moot by stating emphatically that Christopher does not need a bed anyway because he is healthy enough to be on his own. Robert cunningly diverts the discussion from the anemic condition of the institution, like the shortage of beds, to the healthy condition of the patient, well enough that he does not need to be hospitalized any further. Bruce's issue is then solved, in Robert's mind, by declaring the patient competent enough to be released rather than confronting the more endemic problem of underfunding and cramped quarters. He, and the rest of the NHS, play this linguistic game around the dehospitalization of their patients in order to maintain the already perilous status quo. Bruce, though, with his idealistic fervor, refuses to participate.

One of the characteristics driving Robert's behavior is that he suffers from a sense of paternalism toward his patients. As we have seen, he feels, due to his position, that he is always right and whatever statement he makes should be followed without any questions. Not surprisingly, this type of attitude and behavior in pronouncing his diagnoses causes problems for a number of reasons. According to Eileen Flynn, in her study about medical ethics:

> A paternalistic physician acts on his own values; by not learning the values of his patient and striving to work out a treatment regimen which would be acceptable both to himself and to the patient, the doctor does the patient a disservice. In addition, ... dangers of abuse could flow from a legitimized paternalism because, if physicians were to be situated beyond anyone's scrutiny but their own and that

of their colleagues, incompetent, wrongheaded or dangerous actions might not come to be recognized [297].

Robert's treatment of Christopher mirrors these components of paternalism. Robert's diagnosis of Christopher dismisses many of his patient's concerns and observations. While Robert adheres to NHS policy and states that Christopher is fine, the more Christopher speaks the more the audience begins to see, unlike Robert, that Bruce's concerns are well founded that Christopher really does have serious mental health issues. Like Ray before him in *Some Voices*, Christopher, too, hears things. He admits: "Sometimes I hear machinery.... Whirring. Like a ... strange droning noise. And beeping. A strange beeping noise. Very loud" (60). Robert casually dismisses Christopher's auditory concerns by explaining that London is in the midst of a building boom and he hears construction workers. When Christopher refutes any new building going on around him on his estate, Robert then suggests, "It's the dustbin men" (60). Robert only looks for his preconceived cultural explanation for Christopher's state rather than acknowledging the person in front of him. His paternalistic attitude continues as he rationalizes the difference between himself and Bruce as it comes to their different diagnosis of Christopher. As Bruce continues to reject all the arguments that his superior makes, Robert makes the observation that Bruce is thinking too much about that patient, as he explains "sometimes one can care *too much*. One can have too much Empathy — Understanding — an *overweening* Compassion" (55). For Robert and the NHS, emotions are to be jettisoned when dealing with patients as the bottom line takes precedence.

Rather than talking to the patient and getting to know him, Robert talks about himself, sharing personal information that has no context for Christopher. In fact, the patient professes to not understand what Robert is talking about, and the doctor does not try to couch his comments in a manner that allows them to have a meaningful conversation with one another. In their one-on-one, Robert is much more interested in talking about his issues rather than diagnosing Christopher, revealing that he desires to be promoted to professor, so he too can join expensive golf clubs, be courted at expensive dinners by pharmaceutical companies and drive a new Jaguar. In order to do so he needs to finish his manuscript on the effect of cultural differences in the diagnosis of schizophrenia in black patients, and he sees Christopher as the potential missing piece in his research and an object that needs to be wrestled away from Bruce. Ariel Watson noted how quickly Christopher's predicament moved from an issue of diagnosis to an issue of gamesmanship between the two doctors, writing, "Christopher as an individual falls away from the central position of importance and becomes instead an intellectual and bureaucratic problem over which the two white doctors can battle" (202). Penhall makes it clear even from the early stages of the play that Christopher the individual is merely an afterthought for Robert. When he first enters the consulting room in Act 1, he completely disregards Christopher and talks directly to Bruce about the previous Saturday night's excursion to see cricket and then dinner at Bruce's home. In the original production at the National Theatre, Nighy's Robert makes initial eye contact with Christopher, but his discussion of Welsh rarebit and rugby all are directed at Bruce and has no frame of reference for the patient. It is only after a few minutes that Robert acknowledges the patient verbally. Christopher's position as patient then is ignored for a discussion between the doctors of weekend conviviality, foreshadowing the level of importance that Christopher the individual will hold for them the rest of the play.

Robert and Bruce's ongoing debate over who is correct in their diagnosis places Christopher the person secondary to Christopher the medical conundrum, which exactly models his existence in the world outside of the hospital, where Christopher the person is secondary to Christopher the black man. At one point he tells Bruce about all the looks he receives from people on the street, "like they never seen a Brother before except on fucking *Sesame Street!*" (21). In addition, he feels persecuted by the soccer hooligans who call him "Jungle Boy" and defile his home "with shit smeared through the letter box, not dog shit — real shit. Pissing through the letter box, fires, firestarting on the front step" (66). He equally struggles with making connections with the people around him. He reveals to Robert that "I don't have any friends. I try to make friends with people but it's not easy" (60). Part of Christopher's problem, then, becomes his inability to find a sense of his identity amidst all the situations in which he finds himself. He is merely a categorization and a stereotype rather than a real person. Early on, Bruce does attempt to help Christopher come to a realization about himself and his societal position in terms of how others perceive him by trying to get him to see himself through the eyes of others: "You're not a, a, a, some type of '*Yardie*'" (20). However, the work Bruce tries to do is undone by the disagreement and tension between the two doctors and the charges that are leveled against him. By the end of the play Bruce completely loses his composure and treats Christopher just like everyone in the outside world does by calling him a "mad bastard," "idiot," "stupid fool," "moron" and "retarded" (111).

Because of his lack of status, Christopher explicitly understands how things work for a black man in Britain. In his session with Robert he makes two statements that delineate his position in the world as a lower-class black man in comparison with the white doctor's place in Britain. He tells Robert: "You know the average life expectancy of the modern black male? Sixty-four years old. That's how long we got. What age do we get the pension? *Sixty-five!* It's a fucking *rip-off*, man!" (67). The vehemence of his statement underscores the perception about the black man's absence from sharing in the same type of quality of life and expectation that white Britons take for granted. Hence, his experience is something that the doctors do not understand and cannot appreciate. In other words, the rules for Christopher and other blacks in navigating British society *are* different precisely because of race. In another example, Robert offers advice about how to deal with the people who give him a wide berth on the street. While Bruce earlier told him not to stare in a confrontational way or kiss his teeth at people since those are not socially acceptable forms of English behavior, hence their thoughts of him as a "Yardie," Robert simply tells him to laugh it all off. When someone angers him or confronts him, then the best thing to do is just laugh and make light of it. If he does so, the problem will be eradicated. Christopher sees the suggestion as being completely ridiculous, telling Robert:

> Laugh. Really.
> HA HA HA HA HA. HA HA HA HA HA. "Laugh and the whole world laughs with you."
> AND THEN THEY LOCK YOU UP!
> What the fuck are you on about, man? [68].

Their discussion, though, does eventually gravitate toward the confession Christopher made earlier in the day, namely that Idi Amin is his father. In order to prove his contention, Christopher provides Robert with a newspaper article about Amin that corroborates his story. In claiming to be the son of such a (in)famous and powerful Ugandan official, Christopher establishes himself as an important patient as well as individual, and hence, because of his parentage, his life should be better than living on an awful estate, being oppressed by the police, having no one with whom he can connect and being targeted by football hooligans. His claim to be Amin's son is a cry to restore some semblance of recognition to his paltry existence. However, in the third act Bruce reveals to Robert, who is persuaded that Christopher could be Amin's illegitimate son, that Christopher's claim has no merit because the previous week he had claimed to be the illegitimate son of Muhammad Ali, conceived during the time period of the Rumble in the Jungle. Christopher's need to redefine his identity from being just another anonymous Ugandan exile living in London into someone more important is telling about his mindset to achieve recognition, but it also provides perhaps the only similarity between the patient and his doctors, as all three men want to be more than what and who they are. As demonstrated by Christopher's ever-rotating claims of parentage, he keeps seeking some method to alter his position in terms of his stature and the lack of respect he receives. However, his personal situation, living conditions and place in society limit his ability to change his fate. He lacks a supportive framework that will allow him to improve his condition. He sells oranges in the market and that is the extent of his economic contribution to and level in society. Unfortunately, he will continue to remain stuck in his economically disadvantaged position, no matter what false claims he makes for parentage.

Unlike Christopher's static position, Robert and Bruce have the ability to change their status, but in order to so they need to play the game required of them within the inner workings of the National Health Service. Robert's current title is senior consultant, but he desires to move up to professor, which is a cushier position, offering the aforementioned golf memberships and fancy dinners. The only way for Robert to attain the next rung in his ascension through the medical hierarchy is to finish his manuscript. Christopher is the case study, he believes, that will solve his stalled research. However, he needs Bruce to agree with him on his diagnosis and is willing, at first, to coddle his younger colleague to get his approval, but as the younger doctor continues to protest and then later insult Robert's research, he turns to threats to bring Bruce around to his position. For Robert, his promotion and its accompanying perks are far more important than Bruce's concern about his patient's well-being. Equally, Bruce, who is new in his job, already is eying a promotion. Before the play begins, he latches onto Robert as a possible mentor to help him with his move, and he and his wife hosted Robert to dinner in hopes of swaying Robert to be a mentor. Both men need one another in their quest to acquire their promotions and Christopher becomes the negotiation tool in their pursuit. Kritzer noted this component of the play, remarking: "The psychiatrists' interaction most clearly points to the tendency of institutions to serve the interests of those in charge of them rather than the needs of those served by them" (50). Robert makes it clear to Bruce that both of their promotions could be in jeopardy if Bruce pushes forward in asking to reclassify Christopher for an extended stay in the hospital, as it will disrupt established government policy and play havoc with budgets and bed space. As a result, both of them will be tarnished. Robert says: "I'll never make Professor. You'll never make your Specialist Registrar Training" (24). Unlike Robert though, Bruce still maintains a sense of scruples and refuses to compromise the health of his patients over the opportunity for promotion. He has not become jaded like his colleague and still believes idealistically in the power of the hospital to heal. Precisely because of his stubbornness Bruce and Robert are frozen in a stalemate at the end of the play over the fate of both men's careers, with Robert threatening to get Bruce fired and Bruce threatening to bring charges against Robert for his manipulation and treatment of Christopher. Ultimately, like Christopher, who is socially trapped in his position, Bruce and Robert face the possibility that neither one will be going any further in their medical career, and the real possibility that each one will be fired for the charges leveled against each other. All three men end up being trapped.

Bruce's refusal to support Robert's diagnosis stems not only from his naïve belief in the NHS' ability to heal Christopher but also because Robert's thesis is entirely predicated on the fact that Christopher is black. Robert works hard to avoid saying the term "black" in their conversation of his diagnosis and he tries a number of times to cut Bruce off from even saying it. However, Bruce will not be dissuaded and eventually is able to confront Robert over his apparently blatant racist diagnosis that Christopher shows schizophrenic characteristics because he is black. Robert defends himself from Bruce's recriminations.

ROBERT: He sees himself as African. And we don't say "black" any more—
BRUCE: Yes we do—
ROBERT: We say "Afro-Caribbean."
BRUCE: Where does the Caribbean come into it?
ROBERT: All right, he's "African."
BRUCE: From Shepherd's Bush [51].

Robert's inability to assign the proper ethnic identity to Christopher, calling him "African," presumptively and ignorantly assigns his home identity to an entire continent rather than a nationality of origin and allows him to dismiss Christopher's place in a British context entirely, echoing the same mindset of decades of politicians who refused to allow blacks the full right of their British citizenship. In addition, his lack of knowledge that the correct and preferred terminology is "black," which in Britain is used to describe all non-white citizens of the country, and calling him an Afro-Caribbean, when Christopher's family comes from Uganda, reinforces that, for all of Robert's glib and at times persuasive[5] arguments concerning cultural antecedents and ethnocentric diagnosis in terms of his research, he actually is not a compassionate figure but instead a racist. In releasing Christopher, he believes that Christopher will return to his black community, which in Robert's mind is an amorphous group of individuals into which all blacks are accepted and adapt equally. However, Bruce points out the problem with Robert's generalization about Christopher's situation in regard to the black communities of London. He lives on the White City Estate, which is a Jamaican community. Christopher, though, is Ugandan. With the exception of his skin color, he shares no common bond with the community and culture that has been created and sustained there. He is as much an outsider in the realm of White City as he is in Shepherd's Bush, the tourist-laden Trafalgar Square, the politician-dominated Westminster or any other area of London. Robert, and the NHS by extension, oversimplifies the ability of Christopher to succeed in returning to his community precisely because his very place of residence and community partly contribute to his problems. Robert reinforces his generalizing view of Christopher and blacks, in general, when he posits that his inappropriate behavior, which prompted his 28 days of observation, may be exactly "what you do where he comes from" (31). Bruce questions Robert, asking what he is suggesting—as Christopher "comes from" the Shepherd's Bush area. Is Robert stating that all people who live in Shepherd's Bush behave in that manner? Or is Robert making a much larger generalization about the behavior of blacks, whether they have lived in London all their life or not? Bruce's ability to recognize and understand the intricacies of a multicultural London runs counter to Robert's more authoritarian, rigid and rooted-in-the-past take on the patient and his distinguishing differences, which suggests that Christopher's behavior is attributable to race, national identity or neighborhood location.

Despite his own racist proclivities, Robert's awareness of the currently sensitive racial climate of the country in the aftermath of the MacPherson report heightens his awareness of the racial missteps of others, even though he cannot see his own mistakes. After Bruce has been accused by Christopher in the final act of using the epithet "uppity nigga," Robert chastises him for his language choice: "I'm sorry, Doctor. It's pejorative whichever way you say it and these days racial epithets just don't wash." Bruce immediately zeroes in on Robert's use of the term "these days" by pointedly asking, "Did they use to?" (89). Robert brushes off the accusation as he seeks out further racist undertones in Bruce's language, exploiting their double meaning, in order to take advantage of the younger doctor's unfiltered ways and manipulate Christopher's anger. To make his point, he reminds Bruce of past terms he has used, "'Guinea pigs'? Honestly, Bruce. 'Monkeys, guinea pigs, voodoo....' You've an entire menagerie of piccaninny slurs to unleash" (91). What is so telling is Robert's own easy use of the offensive term "piccaninny," which is an implicitly racist term, whereas Bruce's so-called offensive terms have to be placed within a certain contextual situation in order to draw out a racist implication, none of which were used pejoratively by him. Robert's use of such language as "piccaninny" only reinforces his racist mindset about black English citizens. Not surprisingly, Robert's vague and racist terminology in describing Christopher's ethnicity and his manipulation of language for his own prerogative concerns Bruce. In a profession where minute distinctions are important in diagnosing patients, Robert's seemingly cavalier attitude of lumping Christopher into inappropriate designations as well as his inability to use the proper terms of designating race indicate Robert's lack of knowledge on a topic about which he claims to be a specialist. When it comes to race, Penhall's play shows that the language of precision is necessary to navigate its intricacies, especially in the multicultural communities of London.

While the play addresses the specific nature of racism within the institution of the National Health Service, *Blue/Orange* also confronts the larger racial issue that Britain faces in dealing with its non-white citizens as actually being considered British. Robert's telling comment of segregation, suggesting that Christopher behaves a certain way because of "where he comes from," in contrast to "where we come from," suggests that he does not view Christopher as having the ability to share the same values and consideration as Robert and Bruce (31). Winston James noted: "The British ruling class saw black people as colonials, and as such inferiors.... In the colony, they could be British, but not in Britain.... In short, the Nigerians and Antiguans belonged *to* the Mother Country but not *in* the Mother Country" (378). This philosophy of distinctly racist and separatist rhetoric can be found in Robert's comments highlighting Christopher's geographic distinction ("African," "Afro-Caribbean") from himself and Bruce. Robert considers him an outsider with different values and beliefs. His attitude about those aspects that are not clearly English comes clear when he comes in speaking about the rugby game that he attended with

Bruce, where he watched the French, or in his terms "the Frogs" (14), beat the English team. He then states that at least they had not been beaten by Australia or New Zealand "or any of the other hairy colonial outposts" (15). Sport is a perfect place to find this mindset about the nature of race within the British colonies.[6] Yasmin Alibhai-Brown's book *Who Do We Think We Are?* explains this analogy in relation to sport, noting

> the true test of identity for a British person was which cricket team they supported. In July 1995, the Wisden Cricket Monthly published an article expanding this theory to the players, claiming that the desire to play for England was "instinctive, a matter of biology" and that "outsiders" were unlikely to put their hearts and souls into fighting for Britain... [151].

Despite all of Robert's claims to being aware of the ethnocentric possibilities in their medical profession, his language and means of categorizing Christopher indicates that at the most primary level of recognition he sees his patient in a separate category in terms of not only race but also colonial citizenship.

Penhall's portrait of racism in terms of the NHS diagnosing and treating of black psychosis is devastatingly powerful. Robert's decision to ignore Bruce's recommendation and release Christopher back into the community is fraught with uncertainty in regard to Christopher's fate. Just before he leaves the hospital, Christopher's hard façade of protecting himself from the poking and prodding of the two doctors finally shatters as he faces the prospect of going out and facing the world again. He breaks down, admitting that "it's not my voice when I talk.... I don't know who I am any more! I don't know who I am!" (104). The two doctors continue to respond with their differing positions. Bruce entreats Christopher to stay; Robert tells him that he is well enough to leave. Even though Christopher's condition has worsened from 24 hours previously, he departs the hospital, leaving Bruce and Robert alone in the consultation room. Bruce, trying to ameliorate the damage that has been done to their relationship and his career, offers to make things right with Robert, including aiding him with his research. However, Robert reveals that his battle with him over Christopher's diagnosis is embedded in something far more primal than just differing opinions about medical philosophies concerning treatment. Essentially, Robert tells him: "I don't like you, Bruce. You talk too much. You get in the way" (117). For Robert, ego is all, as he explains that sick patients come to the hospital in search of succor and they go home better "because of me" (117). Bruce's battle over Christopher has impeded Robert's God complex and he plans to exact his revenge. While the play opens up a new dialogue about the institutionalization of racism in treating black patients, Penhall's ultimate message is that the hubris of doctors in terms of their treatment of patients is an even more problematic danger facing the profession. The Roberts of the medical world are not only controlling patients like Christopher but also pushing out concerned, well-meaning practitioners like Bruce.

Ultimately, the egocentric, powerful, controlling doctors are harming the profession with their behavior as much as they are with their racist diagnoses.

Blue/Orange was a significant theatrical moment for Penhall, reaping recognition and international success. Based on this success as well as the strength of his writing, opportunities arose for him to focus more on writing for television and film. Because of the scope of the projects upon which he worked, including drafting much of *The Last King of Scotland* (2006) screenplay before asking to have his name removed when new writers were brought in; writing two television series for the BBC, *The Long Firm* (2004) and *Moses Jones*; and directing his own short film *The Undertaker* (2005), his theatrical output would only be limited to two plays. His previous focus on the National Health Service and struggling lower- to middle-class characters was no longer of interest as his next two plays focused on more successful upper-middle-class individuals, who have achieved the type of professional and economic success that his other characters have only dreamed about attaining. The "laureate of lithium" was to be no more.

7

Dumb Show
and Penhall's Women

The awards, financial windfall and international accolades for *Blue/Orange* rocketed Penhall into a completely different level of theatrical recognition, joining the international success achieved by his peers Martin McDonagh, Patrick Marber, Mark Ravenhill, Conor McPherson and the late Sarah Kane. Because of the play, Penhall became a wanted commodity to write original scripts and adaptations of novels for British television as well as for motion pictures. While the offers were numerous, he only chose those projects which were too good to let get away, including adapting two novels, one by Jake Arnott for the BBC and the other by Ian McEwan for the cinema. With the increased demand for his writing services, his previous tight focus on the theatre lessened and four years passed between *Blue/Orange* and the premiere of his newest work *Dumb Show* in 2004.

The playwright dubbed "Mr. Schizophrenia" because of his perspicacious depiction of the breakdown of his psychologically challenged characters and his critical scrutiny of the National Health Service was nowhere to be found in his latest piece. *Dumb Show* instead marked a departure from the more seriously focused, biting social criticism that had been a staple in Penhall's previous plays. In this shorter, but still full-length play, featuring a 90-minute running time with no intermission, Penhall turned his attention toward tabloid journalism and in so doing crafted a more comedic and freeing structure than his other plays.

The first third of the play involves a scam being enacted by Liz and Greg, both tabloid journalists, who pose as investment bankers, in order to catch the highly successful Barry, a comedian with a popular Saturday night television show, in a compromising position. Tipped off by one of his producers about his drinking and drug problems, Liz and Greg invite Barry to a fancy hotel, the setting for the entire play, and woo him with the prospect of too-good-to-be-true banking services. Once he agrees to their offer to handle his assets, they dangle an additional opportunity to give a talk to their fictional employees, with a generous fee for doing so, paid directly to him rather than his agent. All the while, Barry basks in the attention and compliments being paid to him. On the afternoon of his talk he is left alone with Liz as he prepares for his speech. During their time together, Barry riffs on the nature of fame, his fans, the elements of what makes something funny, while consuming a number of alcoholic drinks. As sexual tension develops between them (their conversation turns to Liz's admittance of liking pornography at one point), Barry offers to procure drugs and then makes an awkward pass at her. In the next scene, picking up a few minutes later, Greg and Liz reveal to the flummoxed Barry that they are reporters and have caught him in a tabloid sting. They plan to write a story detailing his inappropriate behavior during his time with Liz, but they will allow him to offer his side of the story in the article if he agrees to confess to his indiscretions. After much wrangling by Barry, the journalists ratchet up the angle on the story by questioning the reason for his wife's extended stay in the hospital. Was he, by chance, the cause of her hospital visits? Writhing with anger, Barry reveals that his wife has cancer and storms off to the bathroom to call his lawyer. Greg begins to get cold feet about the story and wants to kill it. Liz, though, wants to run it, acknowledging that the wife's cancer makes the story better. In the final scene Liz and Barry are alone again in the same hotel room. In the interval before this new meeting, the article about Barry's actions ran in the paper and his wife succumbed to cancer. Liz convinces him to meet with her because she wants to offer her condolences about his wife's death, but she then pitches another newspaper story to address how he has coped with the death of his wife. In other words, she offers to now write the redemption story to his previous fall-from-grace story. He is at first affronted by her offer, but when a fee is proffered, his mood changes and the play ends with Barry on the phone with Liz's editor negotiating his payment.

Penhall revealed to Harriet Devine the rationale behind his change of pace with *Dumb Show*. *Blue/Orange*'s success with its indictment of the National Health Service and its problematic treatment of schizophrenia and race took on a life of its own. Penhall called the ensuing reaction and publicization of the play "a huge machine" (Devine 245). Amidst all the hoopla, he felt he was being transformed into "a tool of the Left" (Devine 245). In addition, he felt that the sensation surrounding his Olivier Award–winning play placed an exceeding amount of expectation and pressure upon his follow-up to be another British issues play, reported "from the trenches of worthiness" (Devine 246). As he had done throughout his career, he refused to do what was expected of him and instead wrote a play focused in a completely different direction: a comedy, focusing on a comedian. He drew inspiration from an evening, which occurred years before he wrote the play, spent with Stephen Daldry and Ray Winstone. After having met the two at the Royal Court, "we all got in a chauffeur driven limo [and] drove down to Camberley where we were forced to endure the dated ravings of comedian Jimmy Jones and his attendant booze addled heavies" ("Re: E-mail," August 31). The motivation for the night out was Daldry hoping Penhall would write a play for Winstone based on the performance of Jones. Nothing immediately came of the evening; however, years later, the night with Daldry and Winstone at Jones' performance would provide inspiration for *Dumb Show*. In choosing this genre and this particular main character Penhall announced that he just wanted "to entertain the audience, to entertain" himself (Devine 249).

Despite his claim of writing for the sake of entertainment and entertainment only, Penhall did have a specific focus for his play and character. Having been a reporter, he understood the nature of the press and its professional responsibilities and ethics in acquiring and reporting a story. However, the explosive rise of tabloid journalism — "so openly, willfully, gleefully manipulative and destructive" (Ellis) — disturbed him, especially the movement within the regular London papers to lean toward tabloid tendencies. He likened the growth of tabloid journalism to a virus, stating, "The tabloid media is as corrosive now as any other social ill we've dealt with in the last thirty years" (McLaughlin 5). Penhall decided that his comedian would become the victim of tabloid journalism.

Penhall's perspective was not new among his peers in looking at the press. Doug Lucie's *The Shallow End* (1997) is a scathing portrait of the decimation of a liberal-leaning Sunday paper by a mega-media corporation, with an intentional likeness to Rupert Murdoch's media empire. Throughout the play, employees are fired, including the paper's award-winning foreign correspondent whose story about the civil war in Eastern Europe was spiked in order to run a story about Sarah Ferguson. In the midst of the firings, the new youngblood editor excitedly plans for the tabloidization of the paper in order to win back readers. Two years earlier than Lucie's play, *Blasted*'s indictment of tabloid journalism was lost amidst all the consternation of critics surrounding the violence of Kane's piece. As noted in Chapter 2, Ian, a journalist, writes stories about British victims of serial killers in Australia rather than about the ongoing civil war outside of his hotel room. A soldier bursts in on Ian, and once he finds out about Ian's profession, he confronts him about his and his paper's failure to tell the real stories of the civil war. The soldier chastises Ian, telling him it is his job as a journalist to document the atrocities of war. Ian defends his professional actions, saying "I write ... stories. That's all. Stories. This isn't a story anyone wants to hear" (48). Instead, it is his audience that determines what is written about, like "shootings and rapes and kids getting fiddled by queer priests and schoolteachers. Not soldiers screwing each other for a patch of land. It has to be ... personal" (48).

The prevalence of the tabloids became more apparent to Penhall after he began traveling abroad. When he would return to Britain, he was always immediately struck by the screaming sensationalism of the British tabloid headlines beckoning for his purchase. He described them as an "Orwellian placebo saying it's all right to speak in monosyllables, look at a pair of tits on page three and crow at other people's grotesque traumas" (Hemming, "'I Did'"). In *Dumb Show* Greg argues that Barry should reveal his secrets precisely because the reading public desires to know them: "Because a lot of people might be interested to know that behind all the clowning, there's a, you know, there's actually a bit of a, a, a '*dark side*'" (160).

Martin Conboy's study of tabloids in Britain echoed Penhall's observations about the clamoring of the public for the dirt on celebrities. Conboy noted that the rise of tabloid coverage contributed to playing "an even fuller part in the construction of an imaginary Britain for a national audience" (185), whereby the media deemed personalities who captured the zeitgeist of the nation were no longer cultural, sport and political figures, but instead the quasi-celebrities dotting television programs and reality shows, like *Big Brother* and *Pop Idol*. In doing so, the tabloids crafted and defined a new sense of Britain as a community of readers obsessed with these individuals. Conboy wrote that "it is the concentration on UK-based celebrities which reinforces an impression that these newspapers are representing a particularly British sense of community" (186). This larger sense of not just the newspapers themselves but also the newspaper-reading community clamoring for the scandalous information solidified the popularity of the tabloid perspective on people's lives. Penhall commented that the tabloid readers "just think it's a bit of fun in the nudge-nudge, wink-wink, Benny Hill-type way" (Horsburgh). Penhall rationalized that the lighthearted interest and joking attitude of the public was actually driven by their own dissatisfaction with life. He reasoned: "It comes down to human misery. People feel miserable so if they find out that someone has a couple of pound of cellulite or has a secret mustache it makes them feel better. It's just schadenfreude" (Horsburgh). However, he still held the purchasers of the papers equally culpable for the proliferation and success of this type of journalism as the publishers and the journalists producing it daily, because for the readers "the love of the grotesque and the sadistic thrill of other people's trauma and embarrassment are becoming legitimate entertainment" (Ellis).

In order to do research on this "nakedly mendacious" element of journalism (Horsburgh), he decided to interview the most successful and feared tabloid writer in the British press, Mazher Mahmood of *News of the World*. Mahmood was known in tabloid circles as the Fake Sheik because he would impersonate a sheik, luring celebrities to an expensive hotel room with promises of bestowing upon them a hefty cash payment just for an appearance at an event in Saudi Arabia. Once they were in the suite, he plied them with alcohol and then gained their confidence so that they would reveal their darker selves. Penhall called the newspaper asking for Mahmood, claiming that he had a tantalizingly good story for the famous reporter. Once the reporter came to the phone, Penhall partially revealed the truth for his call. He told Mahmood: "I'm a playwright and I'm fascinated by what you do. It's so inherently theatrical and very rich; I think that the tabloids have been vilified for too long and what I'd like to do is focus on the heroism and the risk and the skill involved" (Taylor, "Trust Me"). Mahmood subsequently made an appointment to meet with Penhall at a London hotel. In the meeting between the former and current journalist, Mahmood admitted that "the buzz and the adrenaline" of his role playing and ensuing manipulation of the celebrity were the best part of the job (Horsburgh). When their interview ended, Mahmood surprised Penhall by revealing that he had videotaped their entire conversation with a camera on his laptop computer, which he had perched perfectly on a piece of furniture to observe their dialogue. (Penhall ended up having his reporters use the same secretive recording device to capture Barry's indiscretions.) He took away some surprising bits of insight about Mahmood — "I was struck by how much he enjoyed his work; he didn't do it for money — he did it for the love of it" ("Playwright Joe") — and tabloid journalists, who "think they're the famous ones. They think they're in show business" (Horsburgh).

Penhall compared the behavior and attitude of tabloid journalists to some Hollywood producers with whom he had recently worked. While writing a screenplay, he discovered that his father was dying of cancer. As Penhall dealt with the emotional, physical and creative toll of dealing with his father's illness, the producers supported him. However, six months later, they turned on him, threatening a lawsuit "when I couldn't comply with their mindless rewrites" (Taylor, "Trust Me"). In considering his experience with those producers, Penhall made the observation that in his previous writings he was "fascinated by how normal, decent and humane people cope with a system that's inherently flawed and inoperable" (Taylor, "Trust Me"). However, after that experience and his in-depth examination of tabloid journalism, his perspective shifted, admitting that now his writing interest was in "people who have so little imagination that they can't begin to comprehend the pain that they are putting somebody through" (Taylor, "Trust Me"). Despite his anger at the ethics of the newspaper business and the juicy dish from Mahmood, Penhall found that the writing of the play did not come as easily as his other works. For example, once he had cracked the conundrum surrounding the play's structure, *Blue/Orange* only took him two weeks to write. With *Dumb Show* Penhall found himself scrapping a number of widely divergent versions of the premise, including drafts with a larger number of characters and varied locations. Part of the reason for his difficulty can be connected to the fact that his previous plays all had autobiographical elements upon which he drew to craft his story. In the case of *Dumb Show*, he was working completely from scratch and, in addition, dealing with characters that he found extremely problematic. He explained his tribulations by comparing the writing of *Dumb Show* with *Some Voices*, which "dealt with real people with real dilemmas whom I cared passionately about" and *Dumb Show* features "artificiality and banality, ... it's the first piece I've worked on with characters I don't particularly like" (Taylor "Trust Me"). In another interview he expanded on the difficulty of tackling the oxymoronic nature of tabloid morality, which he described as "a chocolate egg with nothing in the middle" (Hemming, "'I Did'"), and the fact that for half of the play two of his characters are not who they say they are. "Here the people aren't real because they're pretending to be someone else, the predicament isn't real because they've entrapped him and the emotions are not real either" (Hemming, "'I Did'").

The last time Penhall's work had been showcased by the Royal Court Theatre was a decade earlier with *Pale Horse. Dumb Show* returned him to the venue that started his career. As a testament to Penhall's critical stature, his new play opened on the main stage in September 2004. He explained to Harriet Devine that he ended up back at the Royal Court because *Dumb Show* did not fit the expectations of the National Theatre audience because it did not address "anything particularly radical" (Devine 245). Instead, it worked perfectly at the Royal Court "because it was intimate and fun" (Devine 245).

The London theatre reviewers' reaction to the production was mixed, which might be expected since Penhall's play took direct aim at the London dailies. Some of the reviewers acknowledged the difficulty of responding to the play considering their profession. Charles Spencer was one of the few critics to relay his personal discomfort with the play's focus of its attack: "There are moments in Joe Penhall's superb new play that had me squirming in my seat with a mixture of embarrassment, pain and guilty recognition.... I had to acknowledge, that I, too, have sometimes used some of their repulsive tactics while interviewing celebrities." Kate Kellaway, though, found issue with the way that Penhall crafted his journalists. "Penhall's drama is brilliantly written and shaped ... but it would have been even more interesting had he made the comedian and the journalists less polarised. If the journalists had been allowed more lapses into humanity (by my count, they had one each), the piece would have had a less crudely satirical dynamic."

Victoria Segal of *The Sunday Times* thought the play was "delivered with the punch of a good headline, a toxic vignette of modern life, hot off the presses of Penhall's indignation." She also noted that while the play's main focus may be the press, celebrities are also a direct target of Penhall's pen, as he "shows that celebrities are not so much gilded gods ... as lumbering beasts who can easily be felled with a quick blow to the knees, dinosaurs waiting for their personal meteorite — drink, drugs, scandal — to blast them into extinction." Michael Portillo also noted the role of celebrity: "The public figure cannot quite resist the perverse lure of being exposed — which is fame of a sort — the opportunity to experience, almost enjoy, 15 minutes of notoriety across the Sunday breakfast tables of Britain."

Benedict Nightingale thought that Penhall's "outrage somewhat unbalances" the work and in turn he "pushes his satire a step too far." Michael Billington found the focus of the play to be far too limiting—"it lacks the moral dilemmas that make for gripping drama"—in part because of its length. A year later in an article on the preponderance of 90-minute plays dotting the London stages, he returned to *Dumb Show* and posed a number of questions about what the play should have been asking but did not because of its abbreviated length. "Who creates the ethos that makes such entrapment possible? Is it an editorial vendetta? Is it a by-product of the circulation war? Or does it spring from some public need to see our secular idols mocked and humiliated? I ended up none the wiser" because the play was too short, condemning the focus of the play to merely "an examination of a sleazy journalistic device" instead of a larger indictment of the newspaper business ("Short").

Some reviewers saw other dramatic influences on the piece. John Gross of the *Sunday Telegraph* thought that even though the piece was "Kafkaesque," Penhall chose "too easy a target," and that the play "doesn't teach us anything very significant that we didn't already know." Nevertheless, Gross admitted at the same time that "we go to the theatre for experiences rather than lessons, and it is a thoroughly gripping play." While Charles Spencer made a connection between the play and Ben Jonson's *The Alchemist*, Sheridan Morley compared it with Ben Jonson's *Volpone*, but found that the play was "more a debate than a drama." Finally, Alastair Macaulay was surprised by the play, since it was so far afield of other Penhall plays, claiming "it sounds as if it is by an English David Mamet."

Despite the play's look at the profession of tabloid journalism and the lure of celebrity, one element of the play went remarkably unnoticed and that is Liz, perhaps Penhall's strongest and most interesting female character. While Penhall's plays have featured female characters, they have been, for the most part, overwhelmed by his focus on male relationships and their ensuing perspectives of the world around them. In looking at the cast lists of all of his plays there have been 23 male actors needed to perform his plays versus eight female actors. Two plays (*Wild Turkey* and *Blue/Orange*) do not feature a female character. However, in *Dumb Show* Penhall, through Liz, presents a powerful and strong female character that differs greatly from her predecessors. If one were to describe the typical female character in a Penhall play, one would have to define her specifically in relationship to a male character, and in all of these cases, the female is unhappy with her male counterpart because, invariably, she is with the wrong partner. In addition, in almost all of the situations the female is a victim of some type of abuse, albeit physical, verbal and/or psychological. When Penhall was questioned about his female characters, he answered by discussing them through the lens of the male characters, saying, "it's not so much that they are abused or beaten up, but that they are dealing with confused, screwed up men" (Klein 87). However, while the plays may begin with his female characters in a problematic relationship, by the end of the plays the women free themselves from their troubles. Despite sharing the same troubled relationship situation, his females share some other characteristics. They are all comfortable with their femininity and sexuality, and many of them during the course of the play engage in sexual relations. Almost all of the characters are young, in their twenties or early thirties, with the exception of Billie, Charles' wife, and Ross in the yet to be discussed *Landscape with Weapon*. Finally, they are all intelligent and defend themselves ably from physical and verbal threats. In order to better appreciate Liz's character in *Dumb Show*, it is important to return briefly to Penhall's previous plays and examine not only the recurring elements of his female characters, but also the changing dynamic of his female roles over the ensuing decade from the premiere of *Some Voices*.

The females in Penhall's first three full-length plays perfectly exemplify the qualities mentioned above. Each play features one primary female character and the rest are male.[1] In *Some Voices* Laura is the abused, victimized, pregnant girlfriend of Dave, a violent thief/wannabe gangster type. Penhall first introduces her as she cowers before an enraged Dave, who demands to know what she did with a ring that he gave her, which he now needs back. In his rage he also accuses her of having another lover. Not receiving acceptable answers to his questions about her fidelity and the location of the ring, he slams her pregnant body up against a wall and threatens to attack her with a brick. Her cowering presence indicates her lack of control in the relationship and her pregnancy throughout the play reinforces her soon-to-be maternal role. In this opening scene she is defined completely through her relationship to others, as girlfriend to Dave and mother-to-be to her unborn child. Ray tries to rescue her and receives a beating from Dave. In the next scene Laura plays nursemaid to his wounds. While Ray attempts to banter with her, she keeps her distance, unwilling to engage in any type of friendly conversation with him because of Dave's treatment of her. Ray later encounters her in a pub, where she drinks and smokes, and manages to befriend her, as she has now left Dave. When they later escape to the shore for a day away, Ray presses her on why she was even with Dave, and she admits that as a child she was blamed for everything that went wrong. Her relationship with Dave was merely an extension of her childhood, hence its violence and anger was familiarly consistent with all that she had previously experienced. She rationalizes that she stayed with him because the more he abused her, the more she came to believe she deserved it. If you only hear negative comments, she tells Ray, you eventually come to think all that is said about you is true. Her mindset, then, has been manipulated by Dave, and she endures his abuse because she really had no one else to trust or believe in, especially since she does not believe in herself. Ray's behavior toward her, though, strikes her as far different from her previous experiences with men. He is kind, caring, spontaneous and funny. Before she knows it, she has fallen for him. At the beach they make love in a field and later he moves in with her. Briefly, she thinks that she has found a capable and sturdy man after suffering through years of abuse, but her situation soon begins to repeat itself. Ray has kept secret from Laura his schizophrenic condition and his refusal to take his medication causes his moods and comments to become far more unpredictable and cruel. When she meets Pete for the first time, she learns the truth of Ray's condition. While talking to Pete and Ray, the baby kicks her, prompting Ray to tell her that when the baby does it again, she should kick it back and give herself an abortion. He then continues to disparage her unborn child. Horrified, she realizes that she has chosen incorrectly again. Ray will not be able to provide her with the supportive, loving relationship that she seeks. In addition, his words are doubly damning because they attack the one thing she does believe in — her child. Having nowhere else to turn, Laura ends up back with Dave. When Ray comes to find her, Dave ties her up in a jealous rage. Ray defends Laura by hitting Dave in the head with her hammer and then runs away. She then finishes him off with more blows when he starts to reawaken. Throughout the play Laura passively dealt with the world around her. In this scene, she finally takes an aggressive action, defending herself against her boyfriend. She uses that impetus to leave London to start her life anew elsewhere.

Some Voices is about Ray's schizophrenia, but it is also about the madness in general that surrounds this Shepherd's Bush neighborhood. In addition to Ray's condition, there is the institutionalized madness that has descended upon Ives, whose lengthy incarceration has pushed him beyond the point of recovery, the sociopathic behavior of Dave, and Laura's irrational need to place herself in abusive romantic relationships. Unlike the men in the play, Laura escapes her situation through her own devices. In contrast, Ives dies from neglect, Dave ends up in a coma with little chance for recovery and Ray needs willpower, the support of his brother and medications to control his behavior. By the end of the play Laura makes the active decision to change her life and leave behind the relationships which have been so damaging. In effect, she is the only character to escape from the confines of this oppressive society and the reason she opts to leave is her unborn child, who provides her with a relationship where she can right all of the wrongs that have been done to her. Her child will love her unconditionally and not have any preconceived judgments about her. While she is still defined by play's end through a maternal role, she escapes from being an abused victim of the men around her.

Similar to Laura in *Some Voices*, Lucy in *Pale Horse* is in a violent relationship. Penhall first introduces her while Charles commiserates with his friend the maître d', who is training her to work at his S&M establishment. Her job entails being groped — he pinches her bum, shoves his hand down her blouse and strokes her leg all the way to her crotch — and insulted by the customers. Lucy, a stronger character than Laura in terms of her self-esteem, finds the job demeaning, quits, leaves her boyfriend and joins Charles as a waitress at his bar. Unlike Laura, she does not return to her abusive partner. However, like Laura, in a scene not depicted on stage, Lucy's former boyfriend threatens her with a knife, and she, similar to Laura with the hammer, defends herself with a baseball bat, killing him. Lucy is a highly persuasive character, an element that will be important in considering Liz's ability to manipulate Barry, and she convinces Charles to help her bury the maitre d's body, rather than informing the authorities. Lucy exemplifies toughness and a survival instinct, providing a sharp contrast to the despair Charles feels due to his wife's death and his continuous personal downward spiral as the play progresses. As he becomes weaker, she becomes stronger. Her toughness re-emerges when an abusive, recently released-from-prison customer threatens her. She once again uses the baseball bat to protect herself. That same toughness and coldness occurs after she and Charles make love. Charles becomes a bit romantic and mushy about what just transpired between them. Lucy, though, describes it as just a "fuck" and states, in a masculine way, that that is all it was. If it meant anything more, then it would harm their friendship. She then denigrates Charles in his moment of vulnerability and melancholy by blisteringly dissecting his physical appearance. Unlike Laura, who has to experience the lows of Dave and Ray before becoming more content with herself, Lucy keeps herself emotionally distant from Charles. Just as Laura, by the end of the play, provided a contrast to the men around her, Lucy provides a foil to the struggles of Charles in his quest for an answer about his wife's death. While he spirals out of control, eventually being taken to jail for his attack on the vicar, she maintains her confidence and, like Laura, escapes from the abusive clutches of the men around her.

In *Love and Understanding* Rachel is involved in a committed relationship with Neal. The stark contrast between her and the women in the early two plays is that she is not in an abusive psychological and physical relationship, but she is in a relationship where she does not receive the respect that she should, as Neal is too self-centered. However, Rachel is not as successful or engaging a character as Laura and Lucy. She is underdeveloped, as her actions and motivations are not as well defined when compared against the dynamic between Richie and Neal and the strength of their friendship and characterization. Nevertheless, Rachel is Penhall's first female character to hold a successful, important professional position. (Laura lived off the dole; Lucy was a bartender.) And yet, her professional challenges are never developed beyond the level of her complaining about her day. In terms of her relationship with Neal, work has affected their ability to communicate and her main telling characteristic is that she wants to burst out of their cramped, ritualized, boring world and travel, while Neal has no desire to do so. Because of her unhappiness with the incompleteness of their relationship, Richie easily manipulates Rachel, who has been the object of his gaze throughout the play, to turn against Neal after only a few misleading words about Neal's attitude toward her. After only a few days she ends up betraying Neal by going to bed with Richie. Neal discovers them in the bedroom and, unlike the previous two plays, the male breaks up the relationship. In contrast to Laura and Lucy, who are much stronger by the play's end in their rejection of the men in their life, Rachel still holds out hope for reconciling with Neal. Even though she is supporting herself and succeeding at work, she still defines her happiness through a relationship with the opposite sex. Unlike Laura and Lucy, she has failed to attain the same sense of self-awareness when it comes to relationships.

In *The Bullet* Carla and Billie are also in unhappy relationships. Carla desperately wants Robbie to face his limitations and confess the truth to his parents about his professional situation in the Far East. Despite her desire for Robbie to change and the implications it has for the play's narrative, Carla is the most undeveloped of all of Penhall's female characters. As noted in Chapter 5, she mainly serves the narrative and social criticism of the play by providing professional critical commentary about the psychological effects of redundancy as well as the challenging economic landscape to provide context for the audience about the situation that the male characters face. Like the characters before her, she also provides a sexual purpose, as she begins to give Robbie a hand job before being interrupted by Charles. Robbie sexualizes her further in desiring to leave England and return to the Far East and re-engage in their previous sexual endeavors, including the insertion of frozen fruit into her vagina. His suggestion and definition of their relationship is only a sexual one; in addition, his disregard for her professional advice about his family and his ensuing mocking of the way she talks prompts her to leave him. In a sense, her presence only serves the purpose of the play's socio-political agenda and relationship conflict, adding nothing to the greater scheme of the play as a whole.

Billie is equally problematic. She is the first older female Penhall has written as well as the first mother and wife, and she is entirely defined through those roles and nothing more. Her character begins and ends within her familial relationships. Like many of the other male characters, Charles has no respect for her, constantly ignoring her comments and remarks. Much like the relationship between Neal and Rachel, Billie and Charles struggle to communicate and find a common ground. Whereas work hindered the former couple, Charles' inconsiderate behavior has been the impediment for the duration of their relationship. She has given up everything for him, including a job that she loved, and devoted her life to him, considering him the only trustworthy person in the world, and yet, he refuses to acknowledge her equal position within their household. When she attempts to interject into the conversation about their future, her opinion is disregarded and she is told to be quiet. The world of the play posits the powerful position of the men in the family, while the women are expected to accept their inferior status. However, as seen before with his female characters, this Penhall woman eventually grows tired of the boorish behavior of her male counterpart. Billie leaves Charles at the end of the play. Even though it takes longer than the other characters, she finally exercises her own authority and sense of self to have a say about her future and she departs her unhealthy marriage.[2]

As Penhall deliberately decided to change direction with the subject matter of *Dumb Show*, he also changed direction with the presentation of his female character. Liz is not in a romantic relationship. She is not defined through her relationships with men, even though Greg does try to do so by propositioning her a few times, but she refuses his advances. She is intelligent, like the previous Penhall women, as well as comfortable with her sexuality, since she uses it to ensnare Barry. Perhaps the most striking element in his presentation of Liz is that Penhall presents her only in a public mode. Unlike his other female characters, who are almost exclusively presented in private scenes, except for Lucy at work in the bar, Liz is always in a public mode because she is always shown working. In addition, for the first time in one of his plays a female is in control of the entire dynamic of the play, as the entire sting operation hinges on Liz's ability to get Barry to reveal his excesses, weaknesses and character flaws. If she fails, then she, Greg and their paper have no story.

Whereas the earlier plays highlight the weak position of the female characters, such as Laura cowering before Dave and the brick that he wields, Lucy in a French maid-like outfit being pawed by the maître d', and Rachel being manipulated by Richie, Penhall immediately establishes the powerful position of Liz in *Dumb Show*. Her strength begins in the first moments of the play as she shakes Barry's hand firmly, causing him to exclaim, "She's got a grip like a boa constrictor." Liz responds self-deprecatingly by saying, "Oh, I'm a weakling really..." (123). Her comment hides the truth of her real character and nature, as the boa constrictor comment by Barry is not accidental. Liz will become that exactly. A constrictor slowly winds around its victim, squeezing the life out of it. Her motivation in the hotel room is to do precisely that to Barry, use her personality and looks to subtly and slowly circle around him in order to capture him, ensuring no escape by the comedian from her wiles. Once she successfully has Barry within her tabloid coils she will refuse to let him go, even after Greg wants to back off their investigation and story. After consuming him with the article and perhaps hastening Barry's wife's death, she returns for a second helping in the play's last scene.

Her means of gaining such a level of control comes through the use of her pseudonym of Jane to Greg's John. As Jane, she plays the part of the concerned woman, who pays attention to the needs of Barry, while Greg plays his role of John as being an overexcited fanboy of Barry's. These two roles aid in convincing Barry to let down his guard.

LIZ: Give him a seat.
GREG: Give that man a cigar, as they say.

LIZ: You must be exhausted.
BARRY: Oh — you know —
LIZ: Exhausted.
BARRY: Used to it really ... you know... [124].

Liz mimics the role of the concerned female before a hardworking man. (Barry has just finished performing his television show.) She acts precisely in the way that a male would want, catering to his needs and desires. In order to snooker him, she allows him to see her as the one interested in the personal and private Barry, rather than the public persona and celebrity worship that Greg portrays. Her questions pursue various aspects of his private life, including the relationship with his wife, which is one of the areas that she wants to exploit for the article.

LIZ: What does Valerie do?
BARRY: She just looks blank and sort of lets it all wash over her.
GREG: Classic! (See...? He's just...)
LIZ: No, for a living. She still works, doesn't she? [126].

Her response is telling as she does not allow Barry's glib comments, like the one about his wife, serve as a suitable answer. She brushes off the insult to his wife, continuing her line of inquiry. While it seems to be an innocuous question about his married life, again from the concerned female asking the usual questions about family, it is an avenue of exploration important to the journalist Liz, and she, under the guise of Jane, will return to it.

The second part of her role as Jane hinges on her using her femininity and sexuality as a means to entice Barry. Liz wants to be objectified and uses the power in the objectification of her body to sway Barry. Her looks empower her advantage in controlling the conversation and Barry's attention. At one point during Liz and Greg's initial conversation with Barry, Penhall writes that "*Liz crosses her legs*" (125). Greg immediately draws Barry's (and the audience's) attention to her underwear and the lower half of her body.

GREG: Jane, will you please put your legs away please — what is she like — flashing her knickers all over the shop — she is so naughty...
LIZ: Don't look then, John...
GREG: If you put the goods in the window...
LIZ: Don't look then ... nobody noticed... [128].

The scene closely parallels a moment from Harold Pinter's *The Homecoming* where Ruth draws Teddy's family's attention to her moving legs and the reciprocal effect it has on her underwear. In that scene, Ruth, who has quietly been listening to the men talking about philosophy, manages to not only silence them but also send them uncomfortably scurrying away from her, overpowered by her sexuality. Liz's leg crossing also is reminiscent of the iconic interrogation scene of Catherine Trammell (Sharon Stone), where she crosses her legs in *Basic Instinct* (1992). With the crossing of her legs she completely flummoxes a room full of male police officers and ensures her sexual dominance over

Detective Nick Curran (Michael Douglas). Equally, Liz looks to manipulate and control Barry through not only through playing the role of the concerned female but also by using her body to make him notice and then desire her. Liz is Penhall's most intriguing female character precisely because he has never written a female role quite like this one. The unhappy, victimized female is absent here; instead, the victim in *Dumb Show* will be the male comedian Barry.

Her ability to control Barry also stems from her ability to use language to disturb and disrupt. Even though Barry is a glib character, who riffs easily on a number of different topics, she cripples his linguistic dexterity. One of Penhall's strengths as a playwright is his keen ear at capturing the patterns and repetitions present in real conversation. His characters speak in abbreviated sentences and incomplete thoughts, while relying on the verbal tic of repetition when confused.[3] A perfect example of Penhall's use of language to comment on character occurs in *Blue/Orange*, where Robert's fluid, controlling arguments about bed space, patient distress, cultural antecedents and Christopher's condition suddenly disintegrate into a mass of stammering uncertainty at the end of the play, perfectly indicating through his linguistic breakdown that he has been caught by Bruce in their gamesmanship over the fate of Christopher. Here Penhall relies on a similar technique, showing Liz's ability to completely disrupt Barry's discourse to the point where he cannot even finish pronouncing a word. In the second scene Liz and Barry are alone in the hotel room and she continues the role of the concerned female by noting that he does not seem happy and prompting him to talk about what is distressing him. Barry lapses into a long diatribe about life on the road and staying in hotels, which has the over-familiar feeling of material that he has done before audiences that he performs for Liz as a means to gain her interest. At the end of his litany of complaints he mentions missing his wife Valerie and children. Liz, as seen before, is not one to be taken by the public persona of Barry as a comedian. She ignores his routine about hotel rooms and instead hones in on the last admission of his family.

> LIZ: I can see they're very important to you. I can see Valerie's obviously very, you know, good for you...
> BARRY: W ... y ... n...
> LIZ: Oh ... she is ... I'm sure she is ... isn't she?
> BARRY: Well... [141].

Her ability to ignore the Barry he wants her to see and directly question the Barry below the surface startles him. He does not know how to respond and throughout their private conversation she constantly keeps him off balance with her comments and observations, as she fluctuates between acting maternally and sexually. Liz quickly turns the conversation from his family toward sex, when she brings up the fact that Greg has pornography on his computer. She tells him:

>   I don't mind a bit of porn, everybody likes porn...
> BARRY: Y ... in small doses...
> LIZ: I can look at, you know, I look at women's bodies sometimes....
> BARRY: I'm the same...
> LIZ: Everybody has, you know, fantasies... [143].

After engaging his fantasies about possible lesbian tendencies on her part, she then draws attention to the way that he uses language in addressing her.

> LIZ: I like how you call me, Janie.
>   *Pause.*
> BARRY: W...?
> LIZ (*crossing her legs*): Friendly ... "Janie" [147].

She reinforces her sexuality by once again crossing her legs, but now she no longer needs Greg's overtly direct commentary to draw Barry's attention to her body. She does so on her own. As Jane, she fulfills the role Barry expects of her and, simultaneously, provides Liz with the material she needs to make a successful story. After tempting him with the discussion of pornography and her potential lesbian liaisons, she constructs a new element to her fake identity, emphasizing that she is a loner, making herself appear to be the hard-charging, dedicated, hardworking woman who scares away male accompaniment. She heightens the illusion by telling him that she has not had a boyfriend for two years. She creates, thereby, a scenario where he can then insert himself as the sole man who can provide her with the type of respect and relationship that she desires and deserves.

> LIZ: It's not as if I have high expectations—I don't—I have really low expectations.... I just think men don't like me because I'm, you know, I'm quite hard work, I suppose...
> BARRY: I like you...
> LIZ: I talk too much, I know...
> BARRY: I like talking to you... [145].

Through these manipulative actions she entices Barry to offer her drugs and then subsequently make a pass at her. With all of his inappropriate behavior revealed before the hidden laptop camera, Jane can vanish and the real Liz can now emerge and continue her dominance over both men.

Not surprising, Barry is shocked and feels betrayed when Liz and Greg reveal that they are actually journalists and have recorded all of his transgressions. When he expresses his dismay, Liz reveals her true character, which is far removed from the role she played for him.

> BARRY: I confided in you.
> LIZ: Well, I think we all know what that was about...
> BARRY: I poured my heart out...
> LIZ: Well, I'm sorry about that...
> BARRY: We really connected...
> LIZ: I honestly didn't mean to "connect" with you, Barry...

BARRY: I thought you cared, you cow...
LIZ: Well, I don't, I'm sorry, I just don't... [157–8].

The feeling, caring Jane who so much wanted him to be comfortable and take it easy has now revealed herself to be the coldly calculating Liz. With this exchange Penhall has reversed the usual roles of his characters. His male character, who has usually done the victimizing and mistreating of the female, now finds himself the victim, and the cold, heartless male attitude has now been adopted by Liz. Her job is about getting the story, which trumps any type of perceived emotional connection her prey might make with her. Interestingly, she is not the only woman to betray him. His producer Ruth initiated the entire sting operation when she contacted the paper about his excesses and her fears about the show not being renewed due to his behavior. In a telling moment, Barry reveals that he too can be as cold as Liz in terms of assessing the people around him: "Ruth is a vicious, venal, scheming bitch who would work with the Nazis if the price was right..." (156). Equally disappointing for him has been his wife's decision to leave him and live with a better behaved, less famous man. As a result, his time with his children has been taken away from him, leaving him only with family time at McDonald's. While Liz's behavior may have provoked him, his own telling revelations about his behavior indicate that he is not free of guilt in terms of his behavior and treatment of others. The women in Barry's life behave very much in the Penhall tradition as they have no interest in remaining in a relationship, be it professional or romantic, if the male partner is flawed and problematic.

As Jane, Liz was highly attuned to the power of her body in capturing Barry's notice, but once she no longer plays her role, her perspective on her body acquires a more professional, dispassionate eye as she coolly and calmly examines it in the mirror after Barry has barricaded himself in the bathroom.

LIZ: Do my tits look too big in this?
GREG: Can tits ever look too big? Eh? (*Snorts.*)
LIZ: My breasts mushroom when I'm premenstrual.
GREG: They're fine. They're glorious....
LIZ: Do you think I look, you know, a bit brassy?... Breasty. Tarty.
GREG: You look marvelous. You're a stunner.
LIZ: Do you think I look fat? [163–4].

Liz understands the attraction and power her body has in her profession when working on male celebrities like Barry. It is one of her main weapons of distraction, much like the sheik outfit for Mahmood. Her dissection of her body in the mirror is not intended to be a come-on to Greg, even though his compliments indicate he has an interest in becoming more than just a co-worker. His comments, though, fall on deaf ears, as she does not seek compliments but instead a true assessment of her physical prowess, admitting that at certain times of the month her body's hormones can disrupt the façade she wants to present. Her eye offers a clinical and cool analysis of how she looks in the black dress she wears and how well her body works within its confines. Just as Lucy assesses Charles in *Pale Horse* with a clinically dispassionate voice in order to remove any possibility of romantic attachment, Liz offers the same assessment of herself after the completion of her mission. In effect, she provides herself with a post-mortem examination of her body as a means to prepare herself better the next time she has to use it for the same task. She sees her body as an important professional instrument and façade for succeeding in her profession.

Jane's ability to cut through the chaff of the conversation to get to the heart of the matter with Barry is no different though from Liz's own character. As Barry attempts to deflect being exposed for his faults, Liz manages to stop all of his complaining and whining with a basic and direct question, which puts all of his behavior in context.

LIZ: Are you a good father?
BARRY: I — I'm not a bad father...
LIZ: And yet here you are... [173].

Her telling comment succinctly places all of his actions, recovering alcoholic falling off the wagon, offering to procure drugs, groping a young woman and fleecing his agent of his fee, within the context of the type of behavior he models for his own children, especially after the article is published.

Perhaps the most telling aspect of Liz's character though occurs after she and Greg have confronted Barry and backed him into a corner of denial. They then begin to interrogate him about why his wife was in the hospital. How responsible was he in putting her there? What did he do to her? Barry reveals that he had nothing to do with her hospitalization; she entered the hospital because she had been stricken with cancer. The reaction of the two journalists to the unexpected news is quite telling. Greg's initial reaction is "fuuuuuck" (181), and he immediately retreats from pursuing the story any further. In his mind, capturing Barry with drinks and drugs is one thing, but intruding on the privacy of a family dealing with cancer is too invasive in terms of his journalistic ethics. Liz, though, offers a striking contrast reveling in the fact that it is a "good story" (181). Liz eyes the newsworthy possibilities in publishing the information about the wife, especially in light of her husband's behavior, and begins to brainstorm the angle in presenting the newly developing elements of the story. She hypothesizes: "Maybe he didn't even feel any pain. That's the kind of person he is. They had everything *and yet* ... even as she lay dying, he was in a five-star luxury hotel room snorting large amounts of fucking hard drugs ... eh? Propositioning young *women*. Eh?" (182). Her attitude perfectly encapsulates the attitude of tabloid journalist that so distressed Penhall, especially when illness plays a part in the story. As Conboy noted, the tabloids have bestowed upon "the mundane facts of illness and death a newsworthiness" (187). Liz argues that it is not their decision about the ethical nature of the story just because of his wife's illness. "Just because some relative — OK, his wife or whatever — may or may not be rather ill — which we don't know for a fact — it could well change — she might make a full recovery — she might be in remission as we speak — but does this make his behavior excusable?" (184). Personal tragedy does not factor in her rationale; rather, everything hinges on Barry's choice to behave in the way that he did.

Greg does not share her beliefs. He fears that they have entrapped Barry and that he will sue. Liz has no trepidation about the merits and legality of what they have done, telling Greg if he feels that way then "why don't you just go after him and lick his arsehole?" (189). She then dismisses his professional ability to handle the stresses of their job: "If you can't stand the heat then go back to the *Wandsworth Guardian*" (189). As Jane, Liz relied on feminine stereotypes to get her story, but now as the journalist who must write it, Liz indicates why she is the most powerful character in the play, showing that she has a killer instinct for getting a story and following it through. Unlike Penhall's other characters, who find their means of employment threatened or lost during the course of the play, Liz bucks the trend. In his entire collection of plays, including the yet to be discussed *Landscape with Weapon*, his characters struggle with their work, whether as restaurant/bar owners, doctors, newspapermen, information technology experts, dentists or inventors. Liz is the only female character to not only be happy with her job, but also excel at it, and with her determined work ethic she will continue to succeed. There is no economic struggle on her part, no political environments in which to navigate, no oppressive, dangerous community around her place of work having an effect on her ability to succeed and no private baggage of family members and their history weighing her down. She is only defined through her public realm as a journalist and nothing more. Perhaps because of her freedom from distractions in the world around her, she succeeds where other Penhall characters fail. Despite her success, it is worth noting that she excels in a profession that relies upon subterfuge, lying and entrapment. Because of her lack of ethics, she thrives, unlike Greg who has a lapse of sympathy and loses his job. She rationalizes her behavior as completely acceptable because of the inappropriate choices that her victims, like Barry, make. Clearly, Penhall, through the character of Liz, makes a compelling argument about the satisfactory nature of work. Only those untroubled by their unethical behavior are destined to succeed, while those with a conscience struggle to deal with the complexity of the world and their own place in it.

Liz's mindset and ensuing success becomes clear in the final scene when she and Barry once again meet in the same hotel room under the auspices of her offering Barry condolences over Valerie's death. Barry, still irate over their previous meeting, accuses Liz for being culpable in the final days of his wife's life.

> BARRY: Her last few weeks ... you took away her ... will to ... her dignity, you see. The strain, you see. The stress. You don't know what it did to her...

LIZ: Well, ... she was probably quite ill before I came along...
BARRY: She wasn't fucking dying before you came along! [192].

While Liz's character has not changed as she still feels no sense of responsibility for what transpired, Barry seems to have learned from his experience, as he emotionally shares memories with Liz about the difficulty of Valerie's final days and angrily defends his wife's memory. After smoothly deflecting Barry's anger, Liz reveals the real reason for their meeting. She proposes that she write a new article, a follow-up to the previous one, disclosing his anguish in dealing with his wife's death. As before, Liz takes on a role in order to accomplish her goal, but in this case she now adopts the role played by Greg, as she manipulates Barry's ego. Needless to say, Barry, once again, is snookered by her, as she fawns: "I think it's a very special story and what's more a, a very moving story and I would like very much if you could find it in yourself to allow me to share, to *share* this very *private* story..." (197). In perhaps her greatest exploitation of the comedian and his family, she uses the death of Valerie as the reason why he should allow her to tell their story for public consumption. Even though Liz's last conversation with Valerie involved the wife's disavowal about having cancer (she said she had Irritable Bowel Syndrome) before hanging up on the reporter, Liz plays again the role of the understanding female, making up statements of love for Valerie that she knows that he wants to, needs to hear, even if it is impossible that Liz would have knowledge of any of the things she tells him about Valerie's feelings for him.

LIZ: I know how much she loved you. I know she *adored* you ... deep down. I know she *forgave* you. She didn't want to leave you.
Pause.
BARRY: She...? How do you know?
LIZ: It's *obvious*. She loved you to bits [198].

Liz and her newspaper, which had been antagonistic toward him, now volunteer to be a facilitator in his redemption of character, from being a sinner to being saved. The interest on the part of the paper, though, is not about aiding Barry in his grief and rehabilitating his character. It is instead part of the pattern of storytelling within the tabloid machine. Conboy noted: "Celebrity lives are often represented as two-dimensional rollercoaster rides between elation and depression" (187). Liz has told his story of depression and now it is time to share his elation of being a survivor and putting one's life back on track.

While Liz's behavior and attitude have been unethical and represent the worst of not only tabloid journalism but also human nature, Penhall does not allow Barry to escape unsullied, even though the audience feels sympathy for his dilemma. In the final scene he confesses his understanding of how much suffering and pain he has caused his family, and he shares a heartbreaking story about aiding Valerie in her final visit to the village near their home to say her last goodbyes. The earlier Barry with his attitude and deprecating wit has vanished, replaced with a more caring, understanding man. However, this image is undermined as Barry is swayed by first Liz and then her editor on the phone to make money off of the selling of his wife's story. Penhall's play ultimately suggests that the extensive tabloid nature of the country has not only infected the reporters, their bosses and the reading public but also the victims of the elaborate stings, who become willing partners and are equally culpable in the manipulation and corruption of people's lives in the paper. If the victims themselves do not fight against newspaper reporters like Liz, then what chance is there for the profession of tabloid journalism to fade away?

8

Landscape with Weapon *and* Post–September 11 Drama

In 2007, the year of *Landscape with Weapon*'s premiere, a continuous flow of post–September 11 films premiered, most receiving their share of critical praise but miniscule return at the box office. While a few films, released the year before, directly addressed the events of September 11, including Paul Greengrass' *United 93* and Oliver Stone's *World Trade Center*, the majority of the films released in 2007 focused on the declared "war on terror" military incursions into Afghanistan and Iraq as well as the effect the prolonged war had on soldiers and their families. These include Gavin Hood's *Rendition*, Paul Haggis' *In the Valley of Elah*, Michael Winterbottom's *A Mighty Heart*, Robert Redford's *Lions for Lambs*, Brian De Palma's *Redacted* and James C. Strouse's *Grace is Gone*. While all earnestly examined the political and personal ramifications of the post–September 11 decisions, none found an audience of steady viewers, suggesting that cinematic audiences did not want to see films that addressed the current political situation in the Middle East.

However, the one film to buck the economic struggles of post–September 11 material, becoming both a critical and worldwide box-office juggernaut, was Jon Favreau's *Iron Man* (2008), based on the Marvel comic book superhero, which earned 600 million dollars worldwide. Robert Downey, Jr., starred as Tony Stark, a hard-drinking, multibillionaire, notorious playboy weapon manufacturer, who loves the explosions that his weapons create and the economic power and sex appeal they bestow upon him. Challenged at one point by a reporter about the necessity of his profession, he makes a point that George Bernard Shaw's Captain Shotover in *Heartbreak House* (1920), another inventor of weapons, would corroborate, saying, "I guarantee you the day weapons are no longer needed to keep the peace, I'll start making bricks and beams for baby hospitals" ("Memorable Quotes"). One of the signature visuals from the film is an entire Afghanistan mountain range blowing up behind an energetically smiling, drink-wielding Tony Stark, as he shows off his latest weapon of mass destruction to the American military. The film, for all its summer popcorn cachet, its huge merchandising potential and a surprisingly grounded performance of the superhero by Downey, Jr. (no Spiderman or Batman angst here), would not have been possible without the post–September 11 mindset that hovered over the cultural world. Artists had been exploring means to address the rapid political and ethical shift of the world's landscape, where governments obfuscate information, terrorists disappear into mountain ranges and missions are not accomplished, even though government leaders say they are. Hidden behind the superhero flourishes, computer wizardry and expensive sports cars is a story of Tony Stark's revenge against a group of extremist Middle Eastern terrorists, who have held him hostage in a cave for months on end and threaten to kill him unless he makes them the same weapon that blew up the Afghanistan mountain range. Tony Stark accomplishes what no governmental military outfit has been able to do since September 11: pick and choose targets within the challenging terrain of Afghanistan and then decimate the enemy all by himself. While the film is a rousing take against the hubris of the military complex and a salute to the imaginative nature of and the successful implementation by the individual (albeit one of the richest individuals in the world), it never really explores any of the larger questions surrounding the ethical nature of military weapons and their creation. His company's manufacturing of weapons is merely an effective narrative device, which also allows for the explosions expected of a summer blockbuster.

And yet, the Iron Man suit that Tony Stark invents becomes a paradigm-shifting technology in the war on terror. His suit and its accoutrements allow for him to do what no one has done before: bring peace. This concept of the paradigm-shifting weapon that can bring about peace in the Middle East resonates heavily with Penhall's *Landscape with Weapon*, which also focuses on an inventor of weapons (however, he is not a ladies' man or the economic powerhouse that Stark is) and the effect his invention can have on the Middle East peace process. Like Stark's suit, his weaponized drone technology represents the missing piece for sedating the problems in Iraq and Afghanistan and any other place in the world where problematic political leaders might exist. Penhall's play addressed the ethical conundrum surrounding weapon technology that *Iron Man* failed to take seriously and did so a full year before Favreau's film premiered.

Penhall was not the only theatre practitioner to respond to the new world order in the first decade of the new century. Just like the movie industry, the theatre also responded to September 11 as well as the later military response in Afghanistan and Iraq. Unlike the film industry, which, by virtue of its means of production, takes time to respond to political, social and economic issues,[1] New York and London stages quickly responded to the September 11 attacks, as Anne Nelson's *The Guys*, about the firefighters who died at the World Trade Center, premiered in Manhattan in December 2001, a mere three months later. In May 2002 London theatre offered two premieres that commented on September 11. On the Olivier Stage at the National Theatre Peter Hall's production of a new translation by Colin Teevan of Euripides' *The Bacchae* stressed the narrative's depiction of an arrogant Western leader who fails to heed the prophetic warnings about his city's destruction at the hands of a mysterious and influential Eastern leader with devout followers. Drawing the play's violent climax in line with the destruction on September 11, the circular floor of Allison Chitty's set shattered, cracking wide open. Fire and the sounds of rage emanated from the jagged hole torn into the Theban town and the Olivier stage space. Hall's production reminded his audience how much the shock of the present can be found in the dramatic narratives of our collective pasts. Arrogance and vengeance never disappear. On the northern side of the Thames, the Upstairs Theatre at the Royal Court premiered Christopher Shinn's *Where Do We Live*, which details the lives of a group of New Yorkers in the weeks leading up to and after September 11. The play's position was not the violent cacophony of Hall's production, but instead the ability to soldier on with one's life even after the most devastating of events occur.[2] Later in 2002 in New York City Neil Labute's dark examination of the day after the towers fell, *The Mercy Seat*, premiered. In the play he presents an adulterous couple's contemplation of using the destruction of the Twin Towers as a means to run away together and start a new life, since the wife of the male believes he was at work in one of the towers when the plane hit.

While many playwrights relied on a fictionalized narrative format to address the political and military realities of the events that followed, a number of British playwrights, led by commissions from Nicholas Kent, artistic director of the Tricycle Theatre, embraced the format of verbatim plays, also known as documentary plays, to address the post–September 11 world.[3] In their book on verbatim theatre Will Hammond and Dan Steward noted the reason for the rise of verbatim theatre in the first decade of the new century: "The world seems to have become a more serious place, and we want our theatre to help us understand it" (11). Verbatim theatre did just that by providing a new context for addressing the pressing military situations threatening Britain and the world. Just as audiences had expectations about the type of new plays presented at the Royal Court, the Bush and the National Theatre, the Tricycle, with its reliance on verbatim theatre productions, starting in the 1990s, carved out its own niche for theatre goers seeking plays that used documents, transcripts, papers, interviews and other documents to tell stories about the real world. Some of the more important pieces to directly address the political landscape after September 11 include Richard Norton-Taylor's *Justifying War* (2003), which replays segments of the Lord Hutton inquiry into the death of David Kelly, who leaked information to the BBC about the dubious nature of statements made by Blair's government about the true threat Saddam Hussein posed to his neighbors; Victoria Brittain and Gillian Slovo's *Guantanamo: "Honor Bond to Defend Freedom"* (2004), which examines the situation surrounding five British citizens being held as enemy combatants at Guantanamo; Norton-Taylor's *Called to Account: The Indictment of Anthony Charles Lynton Blair for the Crime of Aggression against Iraq: A Hearing* (2007), which asks what a trial of Tony Blair for war crimes might look like, using testimony in support and against Blair's decision to invade Iraq, where every night the audience makes up its own mind up about his guilt; and Robin Soans' *Talking to Terrorists* (2005), which was actually a Royal Court production and features the theatrical distillation of interviews with terrorists, their victims and experts on terrorism. There were other playwrights who combined the tenets of verbatim theatre with fictional material. Gregory Burke's *Black Watch* (2006) mingled material gathered from members of the Scottish military force that served in Iraq with invented scenes. David Hare found the verbatim technique an attractive means of exploring the political nature of the lead up to the war in Iraq with *Stuff Happens* (2004). After having cut his teeth on the format with *The Permanent Way* (2003), about the National Rail Service crisis in Britain, *Stuff Happens* blends actual transcripts and interviews with fictionalized, behind closed doors conversations of American and British political leaders.

Many of the playwrights crafting verbatim theatre pieces believed that the press had failed in their duty to question the political decisions being made post–September 11, as the information was being entirely controlled by the governments. Hare stressed that verbatim theatre "does what journalism fails to do" (Hammond 62). Soans argued for the importance of verbatim theatre, saying: "The arts are more than mere entertainment. In my view they should be the vessel which houses the conscience of a nation; they should ask the difficult questions others would rather leave unasked" (17). Penhall had a differing opinion about the direction of political theatre addressing post–September 11 issues. When it came time for him to write his own post–September 11 play, he was not interested in using the suddenly popular avenue of verbatim theatre as a means of political theatre. He professed his disregard for the rise of verbatim theatre, stating, "I'm really dubious of writers who get their ideas from the library" (Maxwell). At a Platform interview with Aleks Sierz at the National Theatre, during the run of *Landscape with Weapon*, he explained why he opted for a fictional exploration of the Middle East problem, stressing that he doubted any playwright could really say anything new that a journalist stationed in and reporting from Iraq had not already said. In addition, he argued that there are two inherent problems with playwrights taking on such a politically fraught subject because, one, playwrights do not get out in the world enough and, two, since theater types are, for the most part, liberal leaning, their bias makes them less reliable on the subject. He decided that in his own political work he would approach the issues in Iraq from a completely new perspective, the perspective of a weapons designer.

In *Landscape with Weapon* Penhall's uses the relationship between two brothers as the grounding element of the play. Ned is an engineer on the precipice of seeing the prototype of his paradigm-shifting invention, which allows weaponized drones to enter Afghanistan mountain caves or even the London Tube, manufactured. His brother Dan is a dentist experiencing an economic windfall as he offers his patients the opportunity to have Botox injections while getting their teeth cleaned.[5] In the rented Earl's Court flat of Ned, one of two locations for the play's action, both brothers reveal their projects to one another and each is horrified with his sibling's plans, arguing about the ethics of each other's professional endeavor. In the next scene Ross, who is negotiating with the British Ministry of Defence for capital investment in the project, visits Ned. In the course of their discussion about the final paperwork for the project Ned, who is new to weapon design and manufacture, learns that the government will have a controlling share over the intellectual property for the invention, inducing concern for him over which governments will be given access to the technology and how they will use it. He is especially concerned about the Americans gaining a controlling share in the invention and selling it to any nation they want, whether legally or not. Despite his concerns, he indicates he will sign the papers when the time comes. The final scene of the act features the two brothers eating curries and arguing over the political ramifications of Ned's invention, especially in regard to the conflict in the Middle East, specifically Iraq. Each brother fails to convince the other of his perspective, and the argument turns personal. The two end up in a fight across, next to, and, eventually, on top of the dining room table with food flying everywhere. At the end of the scene Ned decides that he will not sign over his intellectual property rights, thus grinding the upcoming manufacturing of a prototype to a halt.

The second act moves the action from the private space of Ned's flat to the more public, industrial space of the manufacturing plant, where Ross tries to bribe Ned to sign the contracts. Her offer fails to sway him. Ross receives a phone call from the company chairman informing her that Ned has been made redundant because of his unwillingness to pursue the invention any further and, in turn, Brooks, an intelligence agent for the British government, is being sent by the Ministry of Defence to "convince" Ned into signing the document. Brooks coerces Ned to sign over the rights through threats and the revelation that a file exists on all aspects of his life. Ned, though, does not follow through on the agreement and programs a bug into the weapon, making it defective, and then vanishes. Brooks drags Dan to the weapons factory in order to find out where his brother is. After Brooks explains the various types of ways to torture people, Dan immediately gives up his brother's location, Dan's Italian villa, to the intelligence man. The final scene of the play once again returns to Ned's flat where Dan performs a dental checkup on his brother's teeth. After his experience with Brooks, who found Ned in Italy and then tortured him for the information about how to debug the weapon, Ned is paranoid, concerned about his brother placing tracking devices in his teeth, worried about being followed, and suspicious of his phone being bugged. The scene ends with Dan inviting Ned to come to his home for dinner in an effort to get him to reconnect with his family and begin the process of living a normal life, while Ned wonders about what useful invention he can create in the future, since weapons are all that he has known.

As with his two previous plays, Penhall does not base the piece on any specific autobiographical incidents from his life.[6] Instead, he wrote his most politically minded play to date, focusing, in part, on the developing nature of technology and our essential reliance on it within our geo-political conflicts. The fact that Penhall decided to address the engineering of weapons technology is significant as he is an admitted technophobe. "Technology freaks me out. On a deep subconscious level I mistrust it; I don't understand it" (Klein 82). However, connected to technology is the initial conflict in the play about Ned's loss of his intellectual property rights over his invention. Prior to writing the play, Penhall was negotiating with producers over a screenplay he had written, when he discovered that a friend of his, who was a weapons designer, was also in the process of negotiating with a manufacturer over a weapon he had designed. Penhall remarked that "we both realised that we were going to lose our intellectual property rights. We were being screwed by these companies in more or less exactly the same way.... Except that I was doing a crummy movie designed to part people from their cash and he was doing a weapon designed to kill people" (Maxwell). The conversation with his friend started his interest in exploring not only the inventor's lack of intellectual control in the weapons industry but also the previously unknown factor of the thrilling nature of discovery that comes with designing weapons, which he learned has its own upside. He realized that "it's fun making things go bang" (Maxwell). In his interviews with designers he learned of the ethical quandary behind the creation and manufacturing of their inventions. One of the designers told him, "If I thought my weapon was going to be used in Iraq I would probably have to walk away from the job" (Maxwell). The designer's comment perfectly captured the ethical quandary behind the invention of such devices. While there is the marvel of the creation process, the actual application of the final product is beyond the ken of the creator. As Ned says about the inventions of Da Vinci, the inventor's "flying machine was never made ... his war machines were never manufactured. He never had to worry about a plane full of passengers dropping out of the sky" (82). In addition to the conundrum surrounding weapons design, his research also unearthed questionable ethical aspects of intelligence gathering. In the production's program, Penhall described a dinner conversation he had with a Homeland Security agent who talked of the great adrenaline buzz he experienced when he would follow suspects and then use Sodium Pentathol on them. As the agent spoke, Penhall surprisingly found himself drawn to the powerful position of control that the agent's profession bestowed upon him and the attractiveness of "Trailing some fucker through Kansas in a big old car and tracking them down and subduing them" (*Landscape* program). However, he then noted his concern about his eager willingness to conduct such an act on another person. He said, "It's kind of testimony to the strangeness of people. We're contradictory and paradoxical and complex" (*Landscape* program).

Landscape with Weapon reconnected Penhall with the Royal National Theatre. Just like *Blue/Orange*, his new play premiered in the Cottesloe Theatre in March 2007 and the director was once again Roger Michell, who in the interim had directed the 2004 film version of Ian McEwan's novel *Enduring Love*, using Penhall's screenplay adaptation. Since this was Penhall's first new play in three years and it featured the same venue and director as his international success and Olivier Award–winning play *Blue/Orange*, there were high expectations surrounding its premiere, as indicated by Dominic Cavendish's review in *The Daily Telegraph*. "If anyone was going to produce a scorching, blinding, lacerating play about the arms industry, I'd have put smart money on that someone being Joe Penhall." However, he went on to write that "*Landscape with Weapon* strikes me with all the force of a mild disappointment…. It's no dud, but it fails to detonate quite as it ought." That sense of expectation and the failure of the play to match the reviewer's anticipation were intrinsically connected to a number of issues within the play, ranging from the sudden change in Ned's mindset about his intellectual property rights at the end of Act 1 to the play's politics. Penhall's claim in the play's program about the complex, contradictory and paradoxical nature of the human make-up carried little weight with the reviewers who sought clear rational lines of decision from Ned, not complexity and ambiguity. Benedict Nightingale of *The Times*, who praised the play as being "always absorbing and sometimes as lively and funny as Penhall's *Blue/Orange*," perhaps summed up best the reaction of many critics to the conundrum surrounding Ned's sudden change in motivation. He asked, "Would such a man suddenly decide to withhold his patent when he twigs that, shock horror, his invention will be part-owned by America and maybe sold to the Israelis and Saudis?" And yet, he also questioned the dramatic plausibility of the entire fulcrum upon which the play rests, namely an "articulate, undeniably balanced debate about 'acceptable' weaponry, conscience, the scientist's moral responsibility and, topically, the Iraq war and Middle East politics." In terms of the characterization of Ned and the problems inherent in his decision, the point was moot for *The Independent* reviewer who thought the issue was solved through the performance of Tom Hollander. He created a "geeky misfit who by the end has become a lonely, haunted and tragic figure, his excellent Ned convinces you that here is a man who has been too wrapped up in Da Vinci-like dreams of discovery" (Taylor). Kate Bassett of *The Independent on Sunday* was effusive in her praise of the play, noting that she could "feel the whole Cottesloe audience freeze" when Ned explained the advanced technological internal guidance system that would allow his drone to navigate cleanly through the London tube system. She reckoned that "It is a variation on Faust and also a kind of Shavian or Ibsenian play of ideas, grappling with shabby ethics in an alarmingly contemporary context." She felt that the play's strength was its focus on character, namely Ned's, rather than politics, noting that "what might have become an arid debate about armaments, ultimately turns into a human tragedy as Ned is left a mental wreck."

Other reviewers were more interested in dissecting the politics and arguments of the play. *The Daily Mail* noted that while the play does "raise fascinating issues with unsettling implications, ... not all the arguments stack up in Joe Penhall's new play about the arms trade" (Marmion). Michael Billington also commented on the argument at the play's heart, but he differed from Kate Basset on Penhall's presentation of his characters, writing, "I relished the debate without believing in the characters." Christopher Hart, the reviewer for *The Sunday Times*, like Billington, found the debate to be "engaging," but identified the play as a failure in terms of political theatre because "the play's sensibilities strike you not so much as right or wrong, but as seriously lacking in complexity, maturity and breadth; emerging from a tiny, tiny little world where everybody thinks exactly the same, agrees with each other ardently and credulously reads the same newspaper." Hart went on to admit that as he watched the play, he found the concept of drones flying around foreign countries, keeping tabs on suspicious and possibly dangerous leaders (he cites President Ahmadinejad of Iran as a prime example), as actually a good thing for national security, rather than a bad thing as the play posits, admitting his reaction was "not the reaction Penhall intended at all, I fear." *The Sunday Telegraph* found problems with the political posturing of Penhall's liberal-leaning bias toward "the Left-wing chattering classes," since Tony Blair's Labour government's decided to send British troops to Iraq. The reviewer went on to note: "This has created an obvious practical problem for angry, young playwrights who ... don't want to go completely off message" (Walker). He then directly took Penhall to task, specifically on the choice to look at weapons manufacturing: "Penhall has fashioned a play that is designed to take out only selected targets—middle-class Tory types involved in arms manufacture—while leaving their Labour paymasters still standing" (Walker). Other reviewers found the play quite bracing in its intellectual examination of the issue of weapons manufacturing, intellectual property rights and the struggle between the personal and public. *The Observer* found the world of the play: "repellent, threatening, fascinating" (Clapp). Mark Shenton of the *Sunday Express* wrote, "This is an important and bracing intellectual drama that brilliantly humanizes a moral conundrum" and in turn Penhall has "thrillingly animated another fictitious, but all too plausible, debate of moral conscience."

Shenton's use of the word "debate" accurately describes the structure of the play that Penhall crafted. *Landscape with Weapon* lays out various positions on the use of Ned's paradigm-shifting weapon in the war on terror and prompts the audience to decide its own position in relation to those arguments, similar to what Penhall did in *Blue/Orange* when he offered differing medical diagnoses about Christopher's mental state. In *Blue/Orange* the set was arranged like a boxing ring, allowing the audience to watch the two doctors duke it out over the fate of Christopher. Rather than having the audience on all four sides of the stage, for *Landscape with Weapon* William Dudley created a long, thin set, which split the audience in half, permitting each side of the house to see the other through the playing space. The set design for both Penhall plays facilitated Kritzer's argument about the efficacy of political drama in challenging the mindset of individual audience members, as "the theatrical dialogue must stimulate internal dialogues in which audience members themselves use the new perceptions and ideas made available in the performance to challenge perceptions and ideas they had previously recognized or accepted" (11–2). While Penhall's play provided the argumentative dialogue that debated the merits of the British government's involvement in the manufacturing of an ethically problematic weapon that could bring peace to the Middle East, the set provided an extra layer to the internal engagement of each audience member because as he heard the differing opinions on the stage in front of him, he simultaneously saw the other half of the audience through the playing space. Thus, he could tell if other audience members shared his same perspective in relation to the issues raised on stage via head nods, facial reactions and body language. The play and its theatrical presentation, then, provided each audience member with a myriad of different perspectives concurrently: a character's reaction on stage (up to three different ones in a few scenes of the play), the reaction of audience members on the other side of the theatre and the audience member's own reaction. Unlike *Blue/Orange*, which introduced material that was not at the forefront of the audience's familiarity, the relationship between schizophrenia and race, *Landscape with Weapon* contributed to a conversation that had been ongoing for a number of years. Audience members had already formed opinions about the American government, weapons of mass destruction, the political situation in the Middle East and the British government's rationale for entering the fray. Audience members would see the play and their fellow audience members as supporting or opposing their held perspective, and in doing so they might have their preconceptions challenged by their own internal dialogue among all these elements as they engaged with the production.

Penhall deftly manages the introduction of the hot button political topics within the play, but interestingly he does not immediately introduce the issue of intellectual property rights and weapons technology for the war on terror. Instead, he slowly escalates the questionable ethical choices of the characters by first introducing Dan's decision to include Botox injections within his dental practices. The argument between the two brothers about the procedure hinges on why Dan does it and what value Botox actually offers. These same questions will then be echoed as the two turn to Ned's invention and then finally to the British government's use of torture to extract from Ned the way to debug his invention's prototype. Along the course of the play the audience is challenged exponentially in terms of its own ethical threshold as Penhall directs the conversation from the personal (cosmetic surgery) to the public (drone weapons) to the controversial (the government's use of torture).

The opening scene of *Landscape with Weapon* once again highlights Penhall's ability, within the first few pages of his play, to establish character and thematic direction. His opening, in this case, is disarmingly funny and well-paced in introducing Ned, the cerebral, slightly out-of-it inventor, and Dan, his self-interested, money-making, but exhausted dentist brother. Both, in a sign of sibling rivalry and one-upmanship reveal that they are on the cusp of great professional successes. While Ned is reluctant to discuss his breakthrough as it involves violating the Official Secrets Act, Dan proudly trumpets that he has come up with a new procedure of offering Botox injections to his dental patients while their teeth are being cleaned. He crows: "I'm probably the first in the country. Nobody else is doing it this way" (13). While Dan considers his combination of dentistry and cosmetic surgery groundbreaking, his brother immediately questions the ethical choices Dan is making as a doctor, asking whether he is disobeying his Hippocratic oath. After all, how can he inject poison into someone's face? Ned's query is one that many people have about Botox and its inclusion cunningly allows for Penhall to begin engaging the audience, collectively through the physical components of the production and individually through a challenge to the preconceived notions held by each audience member on the topic. Celebrities who have had Botox are a tabloid staple and a familiar topic of discussion for almost everyone. Most people have an opinion about the merits of its use. Penhall's play establishes that the convincing naysayer is Ned, while Dan's retorts are not so effective in defending the procedure. In response to his brother's attacks about injecting Botox into his patients, Dan argues that he is just taking what he is due: "I paid my dues, it's time I got something back. Why the hell not?" (14). However, it quickly becomes clear that the larger element driving his interest in Botox is financial. He can charge 325 pounds for each session, plus he does not even have to be present as his nurses have all been trained to make the injections. In addition, he has created a training session for other dentists, so he can make money teaching them how to do the same procedure. The injections and the training sessions provide him with the opportunity to increase his already impressive economic position and power. He and his wife had previously purchased a villa in Italy. Because of the success of this new procedure, he has now added a pool and purchased "a brand spanking new, fully imported American Jeep from America" as his means of transportation around London (16). Ned scoffs at his brother's need for a Jeep in Shepherd's Bush, to which Dan weakly notes that there are a number of potholes in that part of town. He continues to defend the choices he has made because "there's a point to what I do. It pays the school fees" (16). Through his defensive statements, Dan appears as a selfish, money-interested, comical character. He provides an unnecessary service to people who are caught in the veil of vanity about aging. He subscribes to a philosophy of ethical egoism where everything he does through work is to better his own situation and life, with a focus on his material appearance and growth. Ned even wonders whether Dan is injecting himself, noting that his brother looks a little wooden. While he provides a necessary service in terms of his patients' teeth, he takes advantage of people's weaknesses about appearance for the sake of making money and bettering his economic position. As he reveals to his brother later in the play, his family life is not exciting. He and his wife have not made love in months, and his job entails having to stare into the smelly mouths of people. He desires something, anything that will offset the misery of his life, and for him it is the material gains that he can acquire through providing his patients with this cosmetic procedure.

Ned's posturing about his brother's new business plan initially positions himself as better than Dan, especially since he feels his profession provides a greater long-term positive effect for society. Disregarding the secrecy surrounding his project, Ned touts that while Dan's service is temporary — the Botox eventually breaks down, teeth get dirty, his invention will change the way the world operates militarily and politically. In response to Dan's statements that he does what he does for the sake of school fees, pools and Jeeps, Ned responds:

>Well, that's not why I do what I do.
>DAN: Why do you do it then?
>NED: Because I believe in it [17].

Ned, the consummate inventor, categorically believes in the good of what he does. At the center of his creations is an artistic basis. His ability to draw from and be inspired by art and, in turn, convert his invention into a reflective component of the aesthetic continuum resonates for him. This element of his character becomes clear when Ross comes to his flat to finalize the contracts for the British military's fiscal investment in the manufacturing of his invention. She notices on his computer a jet plane. He excitedly explains that he is in the process of devising a new outer skin for jets that can cool itself, solving the problem of overheating. The basis for his invention stems from his study of Islamic art, as he bases the principle of his invention on a common Islamic pattern. His inventions stem through his unique observations of the world around him. His understanding of how to solve the current limitation of drone surveillance units — their inability to go inside any buildings or caves — came to him after watching birds fly over the Thames. He eagerly explains to Dan that he noted that birds possess an innate ability to respond to one another as a whole as they fly. The entire flock shifts its flight pattern accordingly as each bird communicates with others about their flight path. Using that same concept, he created a drone surveillance system that would allow the drones to communicate and direct one another in their flight pattern when they are not in direct contact with the Global Positioning System. John Monk noted, "What appears to have motivated [Ned] is the pleasure he gets from creating machinery which, for him, has an entrancing behaviour" (119). Monk's use of the term "entrancing" is an apt one because for all of Ned's brilliance in weapons technology he possesses a naiveté about the end result of his invention. He describes to Dan how his drone inventions will work in the field: "Some are conducting surveillance — some are finding targets, some are taking out supply lines— some are repelling enemy fire — a rebel cell — a nest of safe houses— an entire town — picked clean — they eat it up like locusts on a stick of corn! It'll make guided missiles look like nutcrackers ... it'll be like a symphony in the sky!" (20). While Ned is clearly animated about the potential of his invention, Ned is completely horrified, calling his brother's invention a weapon of mass destruction. Dan can only see the successful implementation of the tasks programmed into the drones, rather than the effect such tasks will have upon human targets. A disconnect exists between the excitement of invention and the reality of implementation.

Ned, though, defends his creation against his brother's horrified dismissal precisely because of the pragmatic nature of its workings. Ned believes it will make war safer, keeping soldiers out of the line of fighting and making the targeting of the enemy far more precise. In addition, the drones can enter previously inaccessible spaces. Attempts to get Saddam Hussein failed because he only had to go inside his palace to avoid surveillance and possible military targeting. Architecture hindered the West's military technology. With Ned's invention that is no longer the case. The groundbreaking nature of his technology makes Ned cavalier, and a bit naïve, with his pronouncements about the actual performance of the weapon in a real life situation. He tells Dan: "Hey — I know it's, you know, evil-and-bad-and-sick-and-twisted but the world is full of bad, bad people, Dan. An' if they weren't so frigging *bad*, we wouldn't have to kill them. (*Long pause.*) Don't look at me like that! It's true!" (41). Ned believes in the utilitarian use of his weapon. It serves the greater good because the targets will be much more focused, meaning less civilian casualties than currently occur with the technology being used. From Ned's perspective the ethical dilemma posed by his brother over the use of such a weapon does not exist because he has already rationalized its use. He suggests to Dan: "What this weapon does is, it forces governments to eradicate mistakes— no, don't laugh — I'm trying to teach you something about the way the world really works. The real world, for real, in real life" (43). However, Ned's concept of real life does not completely jibe with the political reality of the role governments play in the creation and distribution of his invention. When he protests to Ross about the Americans managing the technology, including the weapon relying on the American-created GPS instead of a European one, Ross disabuses his naiveté about the political reality of the world: "Did you really think you could work with American engineers but not the American military? Did you really think the government would fund it without wanting to control it?" (38).

The reality that Ross explains to Ned is precisely what differentiates the two brothers' perspectives about the invention. Ned's work has been isolated and specifically focused on the scientific, mathematical, engineering and avionic challenges of the weapon, as he has traveled back and forth from job sites in Britain and the United States. The real-world application of his invention has been distant from his mindset. In other words, he has not been able to see the size and scope of the forest as he has only been looking at the individual trees. Dan, though, will not let his brother remain in such a naïve position about the long-lasting effect of his invention, and when Ned professes to Dan that he knows the reality of the real world and Dan does not, Dan offers his own sense of the reality of the military involvement in Iraq that is not as cavalier or grandiose in its presentation, describing the situation of a soldier who received a head wound in Iraq: "All he wants is a shepherd's pie and to kiss his girlfriend on the lips ... and he can't because he hasn't even got a gullet.... He'll have the entire World Cup squad in his mouth by now — craniofacial, temporomandibular, a prosthodontist.... There's soldiers coming home now with injuries so horrific and strange we don't even know what weapon was used" (44–5). Dan's example is far more personally directed, arguing about the situation of individuals, rather than the more idealistic and philosophical considerations that exist in Ned's support for his weapon.

While Dan's situation and his Botox arrangement is played for laughs at and about him, Ned's invention and its possibilities change the sibling dynamic and challenges the audience in relation to their response to the brothers. Dan, who was comical, now becomes a more even-keeled, serious critic in response to Ned's excited comments about the potential of his device to be a paradigm shifter, along the same line and importance as "the wheel, the internet, computers, liquid paper, the Beatles and the atomic bomb..." (39). Whereas Dan's medical scheme looks to better his own personal situation, Ned believes he has found a means of self-betterment, intellectual challenge and a device to bring peace to the world. However, in reaching such a state, he has isolated himself from not only the political world around him, but also his family. In contrast to Dan, who is married, has kids, and has some semblance of a life, Ned has nothing. The flat where much of the play takes place is rented because his wife left him and he had to find somewhere new to live. His sister-in-law disapproves of his profession and refuses to let him see his niece and nephew. When Dan asks if their mother knows what it is that Ned has invented, Ned becomes highly defensive, indicating that he has received critical comments from her as well.

> NED: What's it got to do with her?
> DAN: I just think she might like to know about this.
> NED: She's not interested in this.
> DAN: What do you mean?
> NED: She's not interested [23].

The importance of family has been an issue tantamount to all of Penhall's work. It is no different in *Landscape with Weapon*. When Dan is unsuccessful in convincing Ned of the highly problematical nature of the weapon he is touting and the technology he is praising, he consistently returns back to how Ned's invention disrupts the obligation one has to one's own family.

> DAN: You don't have kids yet, perhaps if you did you might not do what you do.
> NED (*beat*): What do you mean?
> DAN: I mean you'd find it quite hard to explain probably [25].

Neither brother though has much success moving each other from their positions. The first act ends in one of Penhall's more memorable theatrical moments as the two brothers, unable to bridge their ethical differences surrounding the invention and their politics, turn to personal attacks on one another and end up in a food fight (water, rice and curry go flying all over Ned's flat and on some occasions onto the audience) and then a wrestling match on top of the kitchen table. The sequence is surprisingly comedic, as the two middle-aged brothers resort more to heavy breathing and ineffective fight positions (a lot of rolling around on the table in a clinch in the National Theatre production) rather than any type of truly threatening behavior toward one another. However, during their grappling, something happens to Ned and when Ross calls, breaking up their clinch, he backtracks from his previously stated position and announces that he will now no longer give up his intellectual property rights. In doing so, he makes it impossible for the Ministry of Defence to fund the prototype.

One of the most problematic aspects of the play hovers precisely around this moment at the end of Act 1 with the alteration of Ned's perspective from being gungho about his project and its manufacture to his sudden decision to forgo its development. How does one explain this change in temperament? Is it merely a plot machination on Penhall's part as the action needs to move from its more private space to the more public space of the second act? Is there a motivation to be found for Ned's change of temperament? In a National Theatre platform discussion, conducted by Emma Freud on the Cottesloe Theatre set, Tom Hollander, who played Ned, was asked these questions and how he approached the sudden change in his character's mindset. Hollander identified the following viewpoints on Ned as being helpful in deciding how to play that moment. First, the arguments that Dan makes to Ned during the course of their two scenes together in the first act make Ned confront aspects of his job and invention that he has not had to contemplate, being that he has worked in isolation for so long. Second, as discussed earlier, Ned was so entirely consumed by the various design elements for the piece that it was not until he reached the negotiation stage with the Ministry of Defence via Ross that he began to consider the larger issues involved with its production and ensuing availability to other countries. For Ned the entire process has been an exciting, intense, intellectual exercise, but through his discussion with Ross he begins to understand the reality of the political ramifications involved with the bureaucracy of its creation as well as the expectations of the government, which Ned finds increasingly absurd. Demonstrating this latter aspect, Ross, at one point, tells him that the government now wants him to include a technician-friendly application that indicates which weapon has been activated.

> NED: Do we want this to be so easy to use that any old bunch of dummies can fire it? It's not Space Invaders.... It's precision technology. It *should* be difficult to use.
> ROSS: All they want is an indicator to show which weapon is selected.
> NED: If they don't know which weapon they've selected, then they shouldn't be operating it [31].

Ned's myopic view that only intelligent individuals will be involved with the use of the weapon's technology bumps against the reality of marketing plans and color brochures as the government wants to make the device as easy to use as possible so it can be sold to a variety of governments. Third, Hollander admitted that he had to convey early on in the performance that Ned is a bit odd and off-center, in order to make the naiveté of his mindset and subsequent change of perspective believable. Finally, he stated that ultimately the audience must accept Penhall's scenario, so that it can engage with the larger ethical questions surrounding the material. *Landscape with Weapon*'s program offered Penhall's perspective on his character's sudden change of heart, noting that the invention "will be sold and used to prosecute a war he considers to be morally dubious, arguably illegal, and he's increasingly uncomfortable about that." John Monk, in his article about engineers and ethics, considers, almost exclusively, the issue of Ned's sudden change of mind by looking at the character from the exclusive perspective of an engineer. Monk interprets Ned's position change as signaling his awareness that the production of his invention "may result in a machine that can be used for ends that the designer would find repugnant. And in doing so reveals that he acted in the hope that things would turn out the way he would find acceptable" (120). He suggests that Penhall's play argues that "engineers do have to worry about how they deploy their skills and talents because their designs may be made and go on to materially affect other people's lives" (120).

Perhaps the most interesting reason for Ned's change is the one that is only slightly hinted at in the text. A few moments before Ned and Dan devolve into their food fight, Dan asks: "What do you think Dad would say?" (46).

While Dan has used various family members as a means of gauging Ned's understanding of other people's reactions to his invention, his question about their father provides Dan with the last opportunity to change his brother's mind. As rehearsals started, the original version of the script contained a great deal more material about the sons' relationship with their father. Penhall explained: "I was originally interested in exploring the father and ... Roger Michell urged me to fill it out and make the father theme a major part of it" ("Re: Final"). As the rehearsal process ensued, the material in relation to the father was repeatedly excised (Penhall remarked, "It was hopelessly flabby" ("Re: Final")), almost twenty minutes of performance time, so that by the time of the final performance, only a few references remained to the characters' father, who died of cancer. Ned's response (the provoking of the fight) after Dan asks him about their father suggests guilt on Ned's part for not being there for his father as he battled the cancer, since he was busy converting the blueprint of his drone invention to actuality. Ned's change of heart, then, stems not only from the elements discussed above but also from a more personal recognition of how he felt that he let down his father because of his commitment to the invention rather than to the final days of his father's life. However, it is precisely this emotional reaction in Ned's character that Penhall decided needed to be excised from the final script. He explained: "It's not good if Ned has some sort of sentimental motivation for his actions. It's the equivalent of what Mamet calls 'the day my puppy died' speech. It's better than we simply assume that he's the black sheep, disapproved of by his family" ("Re: Final").

With the start of the second act, the play moves from the private discussion surrounding Botox and Ned's invention to a much more public and political circumstance as the action shifts into the weapons plant where Ned works. The conversation no longer takes place between family members but now becomes one where Ned, and later Dan, finds himself up against the government. While Dan and Ned were fairly even matched, in this situation they will be overwhelmed by the power of the British government as represented by the intelligence officer Brooks. Throughout the course of the second half of the play Brooks embodies the post–September 11 governmental mindset where threats, coercion and torture are necessary and acceptable policy options in protecting the safety of one's country and citizens as well as maintaining one's status quo of importance and position in the world pecking order. In creating this scenario, Penhall deftly increases the ramifications of the ensuing arguments. Whereas the audience confronted their own perspectives about cosmetic procedures and esoteric, hypothetical weaponry, in the second act they confront one of the most vitriolic debates of the new decade: the viability and legality of torture.

With the production of *Landscape with Weapon* Penhall found his play positioned with three other plays, written by his contemporaries Roy Williams, Mark Ravenhill and Martin McDonagh, all of which confront the question of torture. The least direct comment on torture occurs in the Royal Shakespeare Company commissioned *Days of Significance* (2007) by Roy Williams, which retools William Shakespeare's *Much Ado About Nothing* by focusing on a group of violent, drunk, partying, oversexed twentysomethings on the Saturday night before two of them are sent to Iraq. While his opening and closing acts offer political reactions on the English homefront to the conflict, his second act, set in Iraq, features a group of four English soldiers pinned down in an alley after a shootout with insurgents, prompted by one of the soldiers killing a little boy. The scene is bookended by two powerful, videotaped entries to a girlfriend by one of the soldiers. The first is coarse but playful, while the second one depicts a darker, angrier side to his stay in the war zone. Williams' second act powerfully examines the nature of the war and its effect on those who serve there. In the third act we learn that one of the soldiers is now on trial, accused of torturing and killing an Iraqi prisoner. Janelle Reinelt noted *Days of Significance*'s similarity to the outrage produced by the situation at Abu Ghraib: "Ben's crude attempt to communicate and be remembered [by making the videos] is uncomfortably close to the kind of theatricality of the Abu Ghraib photographs" (318). Williams, though, is not interested in exploring the political and ethical ramifications of British soldiers in Abu Ghraib-like torturous acts. It is merely the back story, driving his main female character's dilemma of whether or not to attend the trial of her boyfriend. While creating a powerful and visceral vision of the war in Iraq, Williams ultimately sidesteps the controversial behavior of his soldier, and in turn the very real situation of soldiers torturing Iraqis, in order to present the outraged reaction of friends to his alleged crimes. Accusations about his behavior become the norm instead of an examination of what motivated his actions. The political anger of the homefront overwhelms a psychological examination behind the torturer's acts.

Mark Ravenhill and Martin McDonagh, in contrast, directly address the nature of torture and its uses for the purposes of politics and intelligence gathering, as both set their works in a totalitarian country where torture is an everyday reality. Ravenhill's *The Cut* (2006) looks at the psychological and familial effect of government-ordered torture and killing on the bureaucratic official who administers the acts. In addition, the play posits that some citizenry worship the ritual involved with the administration of "the cut," which is the official protocol involved with killing political prisoners. The first scene of the play features a conversation between a prisoner who wants to experience "the cut" and the official who wants to avoid administering the act, highlighting the accepted ritualization of torture as well as the psychological burden torture places upon the torturer. In the play's middle scene the torturer breaks down at dinner with his wife, overcome by his position and inability to share his private suffering with others. The final scene shows the table being turned as the official now becomes a prisoner due to a regime change. The new government refuses to use "the cut" on its political prisoners, instead believing in incarceration. However, the official tells his replacement, who, too conveniently, happens to be his son, that in time his paymasters in the government will resume "the cut" because they always do. Torture has become too ingrained in the culture of their country. McDonagh's *The Pillowman* (2003), the most successful piece critically as well as financially of the four, is a multi-layered look at the power of torture as well as storytelling. Set like *The Cut* in a totalitarian society, two police officers hold a writer and his mentally handicapped brother in jail for killing children. McDonagh presents two different scenarios behind the characters' use of torture. The first is the more familiar dramatic situation involving the police torturing the writer in hopes of finding a missing girl still alive. The second scenario though is unexpected. Through one of the writer's monologues he reveals that his brother was tortured over a number of years by their parents in the bedroom next to his own, which inspired him to become a better storyteller. Audience members and critics could not help but make parallels between the play and the war on terror policy of torturing enemy combatants. Eamonn Jordan wrote, "For some, democracy is the prize and not a weapon in the war-on-terror. McDonagh is entering indirectly this contemporary debate. Indeed, the interrogation techniques, notionally in the name of democracy, deployed by the American army in Abu Ghraib prison in Iraq find many parallels with the McDonagh play" (49). *The Pillowman*, while at times finding surprising humor in its use of torture, shows the brutality, suffering and long-lasting effects that torture has upon its victims as well as the torturer. However, in setting these two plays within totalitarian governments, Ravenhill and McDonagh create plays that work within a scenario already well familiar to audiences. It comes as no surprise that such totalitarian regimes would practice, have practiced and will practice torture. Torture is an expected part of the narrative and the characters' actions. Ravenhill and McDonagh work within as well as disrupt that shared expectation to great effect dramatically as well as comedically in their plays. However, politically their plays do not challenge the audience's preconceptions and beliefs about torture. True, they may be reminded of Abu Ghraib, as Jordan suggests, but the audience does not make the connection between McDonagh's bumbling, squabbling police officers and the various governmental agencies torturing enemy combatants in prisons around the world. Instead, the two plays merely reify the audience's expectations that citizens who live in a totalitarian system will, more than likely, have their human rights violated. The same recognition does not follow through to their own government's policies and actions.

And yet, before and after these plays premiered, as well as during the premiere, the most contentious debate among Western governments, philosophers, lawyers, politicians, members of the military, academics, journalists and the average citizen surrounded the "when" and "if" the use of torture would ever be acceptable. After the September 11 plane attacks, torture moved to the forefront as the most effective means of gaining information about potential future threats to the United States and other Western nations. Alan Dershowitz, a law professor at Harvard, wrote the controversial tome *Why Terrorism Works* (2002), arguing that in certain situations terrorists should be tortured. The primary scenario he based his argument upon stemmed from the case of the ticking time bomb, a popular ethical conundrum posed by philosophers and textbooks, which can be traced back to Utilitarianism founder Jeremy Bentham. The scenarios vary, but the essential components of the question are this: you have captured a terrorist who has knowledge about the location of a bomb that is set to detonate, killing thousands of people. Faced with this situation, do you torture the terrorist to acquire the bomb's location? Dershowitz argued yes, prompting an ongoing debate about the efficacy of torture. Among the supporters of Dershowitz have been Richard A. Posner, a judge, and Charles Krauthammer, a journalist for *The Washington Post*, both of whom have argued for the use of torture when lives are at stake. Krauthammer went as far as to state that "the argument is not *whether* torture is ever permissible, but *when*" (309). Part of the basis for their argument is that one is morally obligated to save as many lives as possible. Acquiring intelligence that will save lives and, in turn, protect the nation is what is most important, especially since the persons being interrogated, in the case of post-September 11 situations, are defined as enemy combatants, rather than prisoners of war, thus excluding them from the Geneva Convention's rules concerning the ethical treatment of prisoners.

Detractors to the argument for torture included Ariel Dorfman, a human right's activist, professor, and author of *Death and the Maiden* (1990), a play that examines the long-term consequences of torture; Elaine Scarry, a colleague of Dershowitz's at Harvard; and Andrew Sullivan, a journalist, who argued that "it is impossible to quarantine torture in a hermetic box; it will inevitably contaminate the military as a whole" (323). This latter idea is a prominent one for those who argue against Dershowitz on the theory of the slippery slope. Where does one draw the line about which terrorist is tortured? How does one stop the creep of torture when it comes to gaining information? What information ends up becoming torture worthy? This last question becomes of interest for Penhall in the second half of *Landscape with Weapon*, as his play presents a contemporary England where the rules of torture have slid exceedingly far from the narrow definition set out by Dershowitz and his supporters, where torture is only a viable device when lives are in imminent peril. Instead, Penhall posits a situation, similar to the one argued by Dershowitz's foes, where the use of torture has become an accepted policy when it comes to the acquisition of information, whether from terrorists or, even more frighteningly, its own citizens. According to his play, the government believes that whoever has knowledge preventing Britain from gaining ground in the war on terror is a potential target of torture.

As the inventor of the drone technology, Ned believes he should have control where the technology goes and which government uses it, extending his personal responsibility into the political landscape of its usage. With the arrival of Brooks, though, Ned's sense of importance in how his technology should be used is undercut, as Brooks unemotionally states that "the Americans think you're a 'Jew-hater'" (56). Brooks' comment upends Ned's ethical position and changes the dialogue from a discussion about the proper use and distribution of the device to questioning Ned's possible prejudiced motivations in not wanting Israel to acquire the technology. In addition, Brooks alters the focus from Ned's personal concerns about his weapon's use to the world's superpower's interpretation of Ned's motives. Brooks does not question Ned's political allegiances to Israel. Instead, an entire country, "the Americans," a populace of over 300 million individuals, are. Voicing his concerns one-on-one with Dan or Ross is one thing, but to be challenged and accused by a faceless behemoth of a country is a frightening position in which to find himself. Shifting the focus of the conversation is Brooks' first step in controlling Ned and their interactions, which will eventually evolve into threats, coercive statements, and later torture in order to convince Ned to agree with the British government's position. Ned's neophyte positions have finally met the reality of a political world that exceeds his understanding. Brooks' questions and comments continually keep Ned off-balance: asking if he is an atheist; telling him to put a kibosh on talking about the inspirational nature of Islamic art, which the Americans believe makes Ned appear friendly to Islamic extremists; and revealing that he knows explicit details from Ned's personal medical history, including a prescription for depression he received after his father died.

While no torture takes place in the scene, Brooks perfectly demonstrates the means of coercion at his disposal, as he closely follows the playbook of the Central Intelligence Agency's document *Human Resource Exploitation Training Manual*, which highlights the effectiveness of threats: "The threat of coercion usually weakens or destroys resistance more effectively than coercion itself.... A threat should be delivered coldly, not shouted in anger" (159). The power of Brooks' confrontation with Ned resides not in any display of anger or violence, which is a constant component of McDonagh's two police torturers, Tupolski and Ariel, who let their emotions run away with their anger at the writer Katurian, but instead in his calmness in asking penetrating questions and making accusations. Like Pinter's Nicolas in *One for the Road* (1984), the Nobel Prize winner's take on torture, Penhall's Brooks is an entrancing, entertaining and powerful character, no doubt inspired by Penhall's own attraction to the stories that the Homeland Security agent shared with him. Unlike Ravenhill's psychologically damaged administrator in *The Cut*, Brooks believes completely in the righteousness of his mistreatment of Ned and Dan. He has been given an assignment by his government. In order to complete the task, he will use torture, which he has done before, if necessary. Brooks' actions and state of mind represent the government's institutionalization of torture. Why should he feel guilt over his treatment of the two brothers, since he has been deputized to commit the acts necessary to acquire the needed information. As Michael Hatfield wrote about the effect of the institutionalization of torture on the frame of mind of the torturer, "It was the law that became responsible for allowing what it does rather than the torturer being responsible for doing what it is he did. Thus, the torturer does not have to believe he is cruel or immoral. He is a deputized agent of the law's wisdom" (147).

Whereas Penhall previously presented the British government, as represented by the National Health Service, as incompetent and negligent in its treatment of mentally ill patients, in *Landscape with Weapon* his criticism becomes far more damning as he presents a British government that actively condones and orders torture. In such a presentation he echoes Ariel Dorfman's statement that "the times, the country we live in, allow torture to be applied, as it always has been, in our name, by allies and so-called friends and partners" ("Tyranny" 5). Penhall crafts a situation where the idealistic and naïve political ideas of Ned come face to face with a British government that is bent on maintaining its position of importance in the post–September 11 political landscape. The weapon he created not only provides an opportunity for a great deal of money to be made through the selling of it to other countries, but also it makes the country an important political player, something it really has not been for some time. His invention would provide *gravitas* to a government and a military that has been seen as a toady to the Americans. The government covets the weapon and the political inroads it provides with their allies, making it a necessary acquisition, even if the government must cross ethical lines in ensuring their primary hold upon it. As Brooks explains to Ned, illegal actions by the British government are no longer covered up, but instead used as media opportunities, which allow the government to foster support from the public through the active publicization of their misdeeds. "We have an open and friendly dialogue about everything from cluster-bombing to rendition. We have a good dialogue with the press, we're happy to be held accountable every now and then. Hell's bells, we release photographs of prisoners who are victims of civil rights abuse actually being abused on a fairly regular basis now. It shows we're cooperating. It reassures people" (58). The government has learned to manipulate the media and its citizenry by creating a façade of contriteness, while continuing its questionable and illegal actions. In addition, in the era of post–September 11, governments have now created new terms, which allow for more freedom in abusing their ethical responsibilities, i.e., terrorists are called enemy combatants instead of prisoners of war and torture is narrowly redefined, so acts like water boarding are not considered to be of a torturous nature. Torture has taken on varying levels of gradation. Brooks tells Dan that because of the current climate of protest "we can't call it 'torture' ... we call it 'psychological coercion' ... but it is torture.... Believe you me" (75).

Penhall's play suggests that the condoning of torture in Abu Ghraib, Bagram, Guantanamo, and other secret prisons, called "black sites," allows for the incremental creep that torture detractors have argued is a residual attribute of permitting torture to occur for any reason at all. By turning a blind eye, the acceptability of torture's use increases and invites the kind of behavior that Brooks demonstrates. Thomas C. Hilde explained the ramifications of such a choice of policy: "The logic in the practice of torturing for information entails institutionalization of a program of torture, which is a much more radical political question than torturing one clearly bad terrorist bursting with critical information. Institutionalization follows from the use of torture as a means of gathering information" (206). As Dorfman wrote, torture is used "in the name of salvation, some superior goal, some promise of paradise" that only the information extracted from the prisoner can provide ("Are There" 110). Britain, through its immediate policies in reaction to the world of post–September 11, has embraced the institutionalization of torture, using it to not only keep the country safe against terrorists but also to achieve the possibility of political supremacy, by being the country to produce the weapon that brings peace to the Middle East, or in other words, Dorfman's phrase of "some promise of paradise." As Brooks tells Ned about the game changing nature of his invention:

> Because every time a suicide bomber strikes, every time a young soldier or a humanitarian aid worker or journalist or some poor fucking welder from Wolverhampton is taken hostage and beheaded and we don't do anything about it because they're being shielded behind civilians ... every time innocent villagers die because we dropped a five-hundred-pound bomb and it missed ... just remember that this is a solution. Technological or otherwise, it's a solution. A *chance*. Something which offers *hope*. And so, you see, I think it's actually *wrong* not to try [61–2].

Penhall posits a Britain that embraces a comforting philosophy of long-term peace and hope in order to ameliorate the short-term use of such physical and psychological coercion. Brooks initially succeeds in the second act's first scene in getting Ned to sign over his intellectual rights through his coercion of the inventor. However, soon thereafter Ned programs a bug into the system and then disappears. In doing so, the dynamics of the relationship between Brooks and Ned have changed. Ned is the only one who knows how to debug the prototype. One of the primary uses of torture is to extract information from prisoners who are resistant to sharing what they know. From the perspective of the government and, more specifically, Brooks, Ned's action and subsequent flight makes him an optimum target of torture. However, Brooks has to find Ned, and in order to do so he coerces Dan into revealing Ned's hiding place by describing to him in detail all the various techniques of torture that he can use to extract information from his prisoner. Dan immediately divulges his brother's location, his Italian villa, fearing the physical toll Brooks could exact on him. Brooks then travels to Italy and captures his prey. In strict utilitarian means, the torturing of Ned does not matter in relation to the larger possibilities of the good that will follow. Ned's rights pale when compared with the possibility of peace, and the emergence of a stronger British reputation. Penhall's play shows that the steps from accepting the torture of the hypothetical ticking-time-bomb terrorist, who threatens thousands of lives, to the torture of misguided inventor, whose invention has the potential to save thousands of lives, are few indeed.

At the end of the play the brothers are once more back in Ned's flat. Ned has become exceedingly paranoid, believing his brother is placing homing devices in his teeth (he threatens to pull them out with a hammer), his phone is bugged and he is being followed. The treatment at the hands of Brooks has changed his slightly rumpled inventor persona into an empty and broken man. And yet, the act that has been committed by Brooks on Ned, turning him into this state, becomes the unspoken item in the room. In fact, the actual act of torture is never described, instead it is implied through Ned's brief description of being detained in an apartment in a non-descript warehouse section of an Italian town. "No air conditioning, baking in the sun ... cold at night ... bleak ... desolate ... dessicated.... There was no furniture ... not a stick.... I spent a lot of time just ... standing around ... nowhere to sleep ... 'I need sleep!' I said. 'Let me sleep'" (81). Ned describes an oft-used torture technique of not allowing a prisoner to sit down combined with sleep deprivation. However, both Ned and Dan for all their prolonged discussions about the nature of their respective business successes never address the torture that both know took place at the hands of the British government. Instead, both remain silent. As Ariel Dorfman explained about the effects after one is tortured, it "corrupts the whole social fabric because it prescribes a silencing of what has been happening between [torturer and victim]; it forces people to make believe that nothing, in fact, has been happening" ("Are There" 111). The end of *Landscape with Weapon* reinforces Dorfman's notion as Ned and Dan try to move away from their recent experiences with Brooks and instead look to find some semblance of normalcy in their lives, with Dan inviting Ned to come to his home for dinner. However, Dan wants Ned to maintain his silence on what transpired, telling him, "tread carefully with Nancy and don't say anything provocative" (84). In order to be reincorporated back into society, Ned will have to suppress his experience in the apartment in Italy. He will have to act like everything is normal, even though he has seen firsthand that everything is far from it. Instead, the two brothers have become victims, like the characters in the plays by Pinter, Ravenhill and McDonagh. Ultimately, the play ends with an argument that is shared by a number of commentators on the nature of torture and said best, perhaps, by Kristian Williams: "a society committed to individual rights ought to guard them zealously, even excessively, keeping its government on a short leash where torture is concerned" (26).

Afterword

In 2005 Joe Penhall wrote and directed the short film *The Undertaker* for the BBC. The piece echoes the interest of his early plays by focusing upon a lower-middle-class male undertaker, played brilliantly by Rhys Ifans, who has difficulty communicating with people because of the nature of his job.[1] However, he manages to make a connection with the grieving daughter of the man whom he is prepping for a funeral. Over the course of an evening they talk in a bar about the nature of death. Upon her request to see her father's body, he takes her into the preparation room and afterwards they head up to his room above the mortuary to talk some more. While there, the clatter of metal objects hitting the floor startles them. They return downstairs, discovering that the corpse is missing and in the alley behind the building the corpse's clothes are scattered. Distraught by the absence of her father and unconvinced by the undertaker's argument that perhaps his body had already been claimed for burial, the daughter leaves. The undertaker sits in the alley befuddled by the chain of events and then catches sight of the nearly naked corpse walking into view through a doorway as it stares directly at him.

In *Pale Horse* Penhall introduced an undertaker at work, and the scene, as discussed earlier, is scientific and distanced, reflecting the world of the play and Charles's internal struggles to mourn. *The Undertaker*, in contrast, offers more emotion than Penhall's second full-length play, as the young woman cries before her father's corpse and the undertaker makes pained attempts to bond with the young woman. Upon seeing her halting attempt to hold her father's hand, the undertaker encourages her to do so. When she does, he then, in what he believes is an act of compassion, manipulates the wrist of the corpse so that the hand responds to her touch and immediately grasps it. For the undertaker, this maneuver was to provide her an opportunity to have a final response from her deceased father. However, for the young woman it is a shocking and distressing act to have the body seemingly respond to her touch and grab hold of her hand. When they return to the room a little while later, her father's body will be gone. The question then becomes — why does the corpse come to life? Is it because of the undertaker's behavior of manipulating the body? Is it because of the tears of the daughter? Is it because the corpse is not ready to go? Penhall never supplies a reason, leaving the ending of the fifteen-minute film in a state of ambiguity. However, in an interview that Penhall gave four years after the film premiered, he provided a possible explanation for the abrupt ending. "I directed a short film for the BBC and the deal was that that would be a pattern for a longer film" (Roddick), but the BBC's "ineptitude and confusion and chaos and childish behaviour" prevented any further development of the idea. Considering this explanation, *The Undertaker* features only a smaller section of a larger story, which might have explained the nature of the corpse coming back to life. Despite the uncertain ending, and Penhall's admitting on the director's commentary of the film that he is not completely satisfied with how the movie finishes, *The Undertaker* is significant as it features an enduring example of Penhall directing his own work.

Penhall writing and directing his own film, albeit a short one, is equally important when considering the arc of his theatrical career. Penhall had six plays produced between 1993 and 2000, meaning that Penhall had a new play premiering on a major London stage about every fifteen months. In the 2000s, though, Penhall had two plays produced over the entire decade, meaning that Penhall now had a new play premiering on a major London stage every five years. Penhall did not stop writing. Instead, the nature of his writing took a new direction. Even though only two plays were produced in the 2000s, he had six television/cinematic productions released, including two film adaptations of his plays (*Blue/Orange* and *Some Voices*).[2] While writing for television and Hollywood can be significantly more rewarding financially than theatre, Penhall discovered that his most rewarding experience with the final product of his writing came not from his theatre endeavors, but from the television series *Moses Jones* and the film *The Road*. Penhall has also admitted that he enjoys the challenge presented by writing screenplays, "especially a big thumping American road movie" ("Re: The Final Questions"). In fact, he has relished the opportunity to write in a form other than a playscript. He remarked, "I think a great writer should be able to master other forms. Look at Pinter, Shepard, Mamet … and of course F. Scott Fitzgerald, Faulkner, Hemingway. Mamet said films are more like novels … more interior. I agree" ("Re: The Final Questions").

In addition, Penhall, for the most part, has had a strong voice in the production of his screenplays, unlike the experience of many screenwriters. For Roger Michell's *Enduring Love* and John Hillcoat's *The Road*, Penhall was highly involved in the process, especially in regard to *The Road* where Penhall was on location and traveled with Hillcoat to meet with Cormac McCarthy to show him the final cut of the film. (Penhall's experience on the film and encounter with McCarthy was captured in his article "Last Man Standing" for the *Guardian*.) For *Moses Jones* Penhall was also a producer. However, not all of his projects have been of the same type of quality experience as he had with

Michell and Hillcoat, specifically his six years of work on *The Last King of Scotland*, which ended in acrimony. While Penhall appreciated the respect he was given on *Moses Jones* and *The Road*, he acknowledged that "it can be liberating and fun to just be a craftsman for hire. And if they fuck it up ... it's their future" ("Re: The Final Questions"). According to imdb.com, Penhall's productive relationship with Hollywood will not be ending soon, as he has numerous projects in pre-production, including one with the movie director Mike Nichols, whose films include *Who's Afraid of Virginia Woolf?* and, more recently, *Closer* (2004).

Does this then mean that Penhall has given up on the theatre? Not at all. In fact, *Moses Jones*, which is about a black police officer's investigation of a murder in a Ugandan community in London, was originally written as a play, featuring 20 characters, and workshopped at the National Theatre before Penhall decided to convert it into a television series. Instead, Penhall's position as a writer has changed from when he arrived in London in 1990. In the 1990s he wrote to make a living and his fiscal survival was heavily reliant on the production of his plays. He found himself in a position where he could not be picky with his scripts, admitting that very few of the plays that he wrote during this time period were scrapped.[3] *Blue/Orange* and his ensuing work in television and cinema altered his economic position. With this financial security came a more critical eye about the material he has pursued and the work he has presented. He noted: "Now I only put something on if it really demands it. If I think it's exceptional" ("Re: The Final Questions"). And, in turn, the plays he has written in the 2000s have featured his dedication in exploring new territory, as he has maximized his comedic side to full hilt in *Dumb Show* and written his most politically minded play with *Landscape with Weapon*. As for his next play? It is already written. It is called *Haunted Child* and will be premiering soon, marking Penhall's first theatrical contribution to a new decade, the 2010s. No doubt, Penhall with this latest play will once again continue to challenge not only himself by exploring a new topic but will also continue to be that "thorn in the flesh" looking to provoke his audience through his argumentative look at the way that British society and all of us live our lives.

Chapter Notes

Preface

1. Even though newspaper interviews and profiles with Penhall exist, mainly because of the pressure from his play's producers to promote the work, the number of interviews he has actually given is relatively few. Penhall's philosophy has been to eschew the spotlight, favoring anonymity. "If I had my way, I'd do ZERO interviews" ("Re: E-mail," August 31). He especially is not interested in dissecting the nature of his plays and their meaning: "I think the writers who have a lot to say on the subject of theatre and their own writing are subtly shaping their audience and the writers writing about them. They're subtly telling the world how to understand their work, which is a little manipulative and disingenuous" ("Re: E-mail," August 31). After all, he continued "what's the point of creating a complex and enigmatic work of art, designed to reflect something of the complex and enigmatic workings of the human heart and mind — only to debase it all with facile analysis?" ("Re: E-mail," August 31).

Introduction

1. Sunrise was an organization that, during the summer of 1989, managed to throw some of the largest rave parties throughout England.
2. Many of the rave culture sources interviewed in various cultural studies as well as histories of the Acid House are only identified by their first name.
3. The play premiered at the Citizen's Theatre in Glasgow in February 1994, moved to the Edinburgh Fringe Festival in August 1994, and then opened at the Bush in the same year. It transferred to the West End at the Ambassadors Theatre and later returned to the West End, after a four-month tour, playing at Whitehall Theatre.
4. With the rise of the rave scene and ecstasy came a drop in the selling of beer. In order to offset the loss, breweries came up with energy drinks, like Red Bull, which the ravers would consume to help them dance throughout the night-long festivities.
5. Bond became one of Kane's strongest supporters, writing a lengthy supporting piece in the *Guardian*.
6. Penhall relayed his first meeting with Townshend at a restaurant in Richmond.

I was there on my very best behaviour because he's teetotal now. I was determined ... not to drink and I wore a suit and all the rest of it and the first thing he said to me was "I think ... *Some Voices* is a fucking masterpiece" and my cool immediately evaporated and I got piss-faced ... and, um, really blew it. He was really nice about it. He sent me an e-mail the next day saying "although we were both on different spaceships I feel we were going to the same planet" [Coslovich].

7. Penhall claims that the editor hired him because he was partial to Australians.

Chapter 1

1. This same New Man behavior would be Americanized two years later in the Doug Liman–directed, Jon Favreau–written film *Swingers* (1996), where the main character, through the five messages he leaves

on an answering machine, begins and ends a relationship with a girl he had just met a few hours earlier at a Los Angeles bar.

2. Similarly, the United States had seen the same appearance of this type of male behavior through the actor Alan Alda, who played Hawkeye Pierce on the 1970s and 1980s American television show *M*A*S*H*. Alda's transformation of his character from a drunk, carousing, womanizing doctor in the first few seasons to the more nurturing and understanding Hawkeye in later seasons perfectly illustrated the change that was occurring not only in the United States but also Britain.

3. Nick Hornby's memoir *Fever Pitch* (1992), about his obsession with the continually disappointing Arsenal football club, and Irvine Welsh's infamous *Trainspotting* (1993) were two representative texts.

4. On being placed in such a category Penhall told Harriet Devine: "He's kind of opportunistic, Aleks Sierz — and he opportunistically wrote, 'Joe isn't really part of the in-yer-face crowd, but I want to write about him anyway.'... I just thought he could have picked a better name than 'in-yer-face'" (249–50).

5. In an e-mail Penhall admitted that a great of the details in the play are taken directly from his experience in the pizza parlor, even down to the baseball bat.

6. In an interview with *USA TODAY* Penhall acknowledged the freeing influence Mamet had for playwrights in terms of the characters that they created. "He was important in making blue-collar drama and inarticulate people sexy and good box office. There's a simplicity to his work that we connect with. You can write about a bunch of thugs, not the state of the nation" (Stearns).

7. Even though he never saw the play, it is worth noting that his description ended up as a blurb of praise for the work on the back of Methuen's second volume of Penhall's plays.

8. Ironically, these plays that were presenting such a negative look at the streets of London were being written at the exact same time that the moniker of "Cool Britannia" was saturating the world press, featuring London as the center of the cultural universe as well as the coolest city in which to live.

9. Teach enters Don's junk shop and says, "Fuckin' Ruthie, fuckin' Ruthie, fuckin' Ruthie, fuckin' Ruthie, fuckin' Ruthie" (Mamet, *American* 9). He then proceeds to angrily and profanely describe the disrespectful behavior of Ruth and Grace when he ran into them at a diner.

10. Ives also appears in Penhall's next play *Some Voices*, where he dies on the street a few days after having escaped from the mental institution.

11. The movie version from 1996, directed by Michael Corrente and written by Mamet, goes even further, suggesting a cleansing of Teach's violence as all three exit the shop into the pouring rain together, washing away the distrust and anger that occurred over the quest to attain the buffalo head nickel.

Chapter 2

1. An analysis by Linda M. Davies and Michael F. Drummond of Care in the Community policy noted, "An extensive review of published studies concluded that 'care in the community is generally cheaper than care in a hospital, although none of these studies indicates that it is better' and notes that 'the more expensive treatment may sometimes be cheaper for society'" (18).

2. Looking back in 2002 on his experience as a new writer at the Royal Court, Penhall told the *Guardian* in a question-and-answer session: "The Royal Court is like Willy Wonka's Chocolate Factory to impressionable young writers. You win a ticket and get fed into the system and prodded and poked and moulded and revved up and then they unleash you three years later and see what you've got and I've got no problem with that, chum."

3. Daniel Craig would once again appear in a Joe Penhall–penned film in the film adaptation of Ian McEwan's novel *Enduring Love*.

4. Ironically, Ian's attitude would be echoed by the newspaper covering the opening night of the play, as they spent more space on the controversial play and its young female author when more serious news received short shrift, including the

rape of a school girl. The resulting fireworks in the press about her play only reinforced Kane's criticism of Fleet Street.

5. Penhall, in a lengthy profile of Sam Shepard for the *Guardian*, admitted that Shepard's plays inspired him to become a playwright. "When I don't know why I'm doing it any more, it's Shepard I turn to. People have remarked on the influence of Pinter and Mamet on my work ... but for me, Shepard's always been the boss, no question" ("The Outsider").

Chapter 3

1. Penhall later used this incident as inspiration for the scene in *Some Voices* when Ray intervenes in the fight between Dave and Laura.

2. It is worth pointing out that these lines provide one of the few laughs in the entire play. Once Charles begins his downward spiral, the levity disappears.

3. This same kind of familial tension is teased at in *Some Voices* but comes to full fruition in *The Bullet*.

Chapter 4

1. At one point in the 1990s David Mamet had five plays running in London theatres at the same time.

2. It toured Britain, including a stay on the West End, and then the British Council selected the work to be a representative of contemporary English theatre as it toured Sweden, Ireland, Italy, Australia and Israel.

3. In the play's original production Mark's sexual encounter was with Princess Diana, which no doubt was the inspiration behind Ravenhill's initial working title of "Fucking Diana." After her death in a car crash in Paris, he changed the identity of the royal fornicator to her sister-in-law Sarah Ferguson.

4. A similar reaction dogged Sarah Kane's first play *Blasted* until its subsequent revival by the Royal Court during its Sarah Kane season.

5. This same instance was born out a few years later when Mark Ravenhill's *Mother Clapp's Molly House* (2001) premiered to the consternation of some National Theatre ticket holders as the play featured graphic homosexual sex acts on the Lytellton Stage. Such actions, deemed by the upset audience members, simply were not done at the National Theatre.

6. In reflecting back on *Love and Understanding* Penhall acknowledged another element to his focus on the middle-class British character. "The play anticipated current Royal Court artistic director Dominic Cooke's manifesto to re-examine the middle classes ... because working class culture, as written by well brought up middle class playwrights, was starting to look tried and bogus" ("Re: The Final").

7. In *Blue/Orange* he successfully merged both interests by focusing on the rapport between the doctors themselves as well as the relationship they have with their patient.

Chapter 5

1. It is worth noting that Charles is the only father character to appear onstage in a Penhall play. The rest of his plays feature absent fathers, including the father from *Some Voices* who abandoned his family, the disinterested father on the phone in *Pale Horse*, the unknown father whom Christopher seeks in *Blue/Orange* and the father who died of cancer in *Landscape with Weapon*.

2. Delighted by his son's success as an internationally recognized playwright as well as the fact that he was earning a paycheck "for venting my spleen" ("Re: The Final"), Penhall's father never had the chance to read or see the play, as he died before having the opportunity to do either one. Penhall wrote, "I never forgave myself [for writing the play] because if I was honest, I think [the play] might have upset him. But this is all supposition. Who knows?" ("Re: The Final").

3. Penhall, though, takes the struggling situation between father and sons further than Miller does as Robbie and Mike reveal that each has had dreams about murdering Charles.

4. In a wink at Chekhov, Mark Ravenhill has his sole female character Lulu from *Shopping and Fucking* recite the same speech from *Uncle Vanya* while auditioning, she thinks, for a position as a television

spokesperson; however, the power of the speech is comically undercut as she recites the speech topless to Brian, a drug dealer.

5. In his next play, *Blue/Orange*, he much more effectively incorporates the sociocultural aspects of race and schizophrenia within the dialogue of his two debating doctors, where it feels much more natural and fluid.

6. Penhall will use this same theatrical trick quite effectively in *Landscape with Weapon* using two brothers, both of whom end up being interrogated in back-to-back scenes. As one scene ends, a brother is in a chair facing his SIS interrogator. When the lights come back up, the other brother is in the same position facing the same adversary.

Chapter 6

1. Michael Frayn's *Copenhagen* had been the prior production in the Cottesloe Theatre.

2. In 1955 former Prime Minister Winston Churchill offered "Keep Britain White" as a potential winning conservative platform for the next election (James 371).

3. Imelda Whelehan's response to the term "institutional racism" provided an interesting perspective on how such a diagnosis of society's problems could actually prolong the racist situation in the country. She wrote, "It is clear that the acceptance of the idea that the white majority might be unconsciously racist could itself become the means by which people deny full responsibility for the consequences of their behaviour; anything prefixed with 'institutional' sounds impersonal and difficult to challenge" (154).

4. Despite Penhall's frustration with the simplistic classifications of his identity, he also does see the humor present in these situations, which appear not only in the comedic moments of the play, but have also happened in his own life. He explained that the cultural contextualization of his identity "reached its apogee when I was told flatteringly by a beautiful woman in Africa, 'You're African, welcome home.' So, it's not all bad..." ("Re: E-mail," August 31).

5. Through Penhall's crafty writing, Robert does, at times, make a convincing case for his diagnosis of Christopher's behavior as he draws upon various possible cultural parallels to explain the patient's actions. The most prominent one involves the title of the play. At one point Bruce hands Christopher an orange and asks him to tell him what color it is. Christopher says the orange is entirely blue, including the pulpy segments inside. Robert argues that Christopher's interpretation of the orange could be driven by cultural antecedents from his childhood, including a French poem by Paul Eluard called "The World is as Blue as an Orange." Such an exposure, Robert argues, could explain the association that Christopher makes about the fruit. Penhall intentionally muddies the interpretation of Robert's comments to challenge the audience's own perception of Christopher, especially through the strength of Robert's use of language: "Robert is particularly well-educated and eloquent. He's the one who can twist anything to win an argument, which in an era of spin struck me as the kind of dramatic truth it would be exciting to see" (East).

6. Perhaps the best contemporary play to address the complex issue of race, nationality, citizenship and sport is Roy Williams' *Sing Yer Heart Out for the Lads* (2002), which takes place in real time during England's loss to Germany in football, as a pub filled with a mostly white and a few black clientele becomes more belligerent about whether blacks can ever truly be considered English.

Chapter 7

1. *Pale Horse* offers a second female role, but the actress rounds out the cast by playing a number of different characters that are, with the exception of one, non-gender specific: a woman, general practitioner, police officer and bar patron.

2. Penhall's last play, *Landscape with Weapon*, also features an older female character, Ross. However, the role is written in a way that removes any sense of gender. Ross could be played by a man and the play would not be affected at all; therefore, *Landscape with Weapon* will not be discussed in this chapter.

3. In *Landscape with Weapon* Dan re-

peats the word "of" ten times in a row and later stumbles over the pronoun "I" 18 times before finishing his sentence.

Chapter 8

1. One exception is the compilation film *September 11* (2002), which was released a year after the attacks.

2. Shinn later wrote a play dealing with the domestic effect of the war in Iraq with *Dying City* (2006), which focuses on a soldier's girlfriend's reaction to his death and the ensuing meeting with her boyfriend's twin brother.

3. Verbatim theatre, which appeared sporadically in British theatre since the 1970s, became a preferred theatrical device for addressing the political unrest surrounding the West's engagement with the Middle East. According to Will Hammond and Dan Steward, editors of *Verbatim Verbatim*, verbatim theatre can be defined as follows:

> The words of real people are recorded or transcribed by a dramatist during an interview or research process, or are appropriated from existing records such as the transcripts of an official enquiry. They are then edited, arranged or recontextualised to form a dramatic presentation, in which actors take on the characters of the real individuals whose words are being used [9].

4. The prescience of Soans' topic came to fruition when, a week after it premiered, the July bombings of the London transportation system occurred.

5. Penhall revealed to an audience at the Platform discussion in the Cottesloe Theatre that the inspiration for the Botox procedure derived from Penhall's feud with a neighbor whose profession involved giving Botox injections. Penhall described the administration of Botox a "fucking racket." He decided to make fun of his annoying neighbor through Dan's foray into the cosmetic procedure.

6. It is worth noting that the professions of the two brothers are to be found within his family as his father was a dentist and his brother is an aeronautical engineer.

Afterword

1. The idea for the film stems from a newspaper piece he considered writing when he was a journalist — a day-in-the-life piece of an undertaker. In doing research for the article he shadowed an undertaker for a day.

2. Currently, a film adaptation of *Landscape with Weapon* is in pre-production.

3. In an e-mail, Penhall revealed that only three plays that he wrote during the 1990s were put away in a drawer.

Bibliography

Articles, Movies, Plays and Television Series by Joe Penhall

Penhall, Joe. *Blue/Orange*. Dir. Howard Davies. BBC Wales, 2005.
_____. *Blue/Orange*. In *Plays: Two*. London: Methuen, 2008. 1–118.
_____. *The Bullet*. In *Plays: One*. London: Methuen, 1998. 255–328.
_____. *Dumb Show*. In *Plays: Two*. London: Methuen, 2008. 119–200.
_____. *Enduring Love*. Dir. Roger Michell. Pathé Pictures, 2004.
_____. "Introduction." In *Plays: One*. London, Methuen, 1998. ix–xv.
_____. "Ionesco's Rhinoceros Is as Relevant as Ever." *TheatreBlog*. *Guardian*, 3 Oct 2007. Web. 15 May 2008.
_____. *Landscape with Weapon*. London: Methuen, 2007.
_____. "Last Man Standing." *Guardian*, 4 Jan 2010. Web. 5 Jul 2010.
_____. *The Long Firm*. Dir. Bille Eltringham. BBC Drama Group, 2004. Television.
_____. *Love and Understanding*. In *Plays: One*. London: Methuen, 1998. 165–254.
_____. *Moses Jones*. Dir. Michael Offer. BBC, 2009. Television.
_____. "The Outsider." *Guardian*, 14 Jun 2006. Web. 16 May 2008.
_____. *Pale Horse*. In *Plays: One*. London, Methuen, 1998. 91–163.
_____. "Playwright Joe Penhall Describes How He Juggles the Demands of Hollywood, Stage and TV." *The Independent*, 25 Mar 2010. Web. 5 Jul 2010.
_____. "Riddles of the Sands." *Guardian*, 21 Apr 2004. Web. 16 May 2008.
_____. *The Road*. Dir. John Hillcoat. Dimension Films, 2009.
_____. *Some Voices*. Dir. Simon Cellan Jones. Dragon Pictures, 2000.
_____. *Some Voices*. In *Plays: One*. London: Methuen, 1998. 1–89.
_____. *The Undertaker*. Dir. Joe Penhall. BBC Films, 2005.
_____. "Who Wrote This Again?" *Guardian*, 21 Apr 2001. Web. 16 May 2008.
_____. *Wild Turkey*. In *Plays: Two*. London: Methuen, 2008. 201–267.

Profiles of and Interviews with Joe Penhall

Coslovich, Gabriella. "Talent Right in Yer Face." *The Age*, 26 Feb 2002. *Newsbank*. 8 May 2008.
Ducas, June. "He Can Make Men Cry." *The Sunday Telegraph*, 15 Feb 1998. *ProQuest*. 8 May 2008.
East, Louise. "Colour Coded." *The Irish Times*, 20 Jun 2006. *Newsbank*. 19 May 2008.
Ellis, Samantha. "Gutter Swipe." *Guardian*, 1 Sep 2004. *LexisNexis*. 24 Apr 2008.
Fanshawe, Simon. "Aiming High." *Sunday Times*, 5 Apr 1998: Sec. 11: 10–1.
Hemming, Sarah. "'I Did a Lot of Soul-Searching as I Wrote This.'" *Financial Times*, 3 Sep 2004. *ProQuest*. 17 Apr 2008.

_____. "It's a Mad, Mad, Mad, Mad World." *The Independent*, 12 Apr 2000: Sec. 2: 11.
Hoggard, Liz. "Extraordinary Joe and His Cast of Plain Men." *The Independent on Sunday*, 20 Aug 2000: Culture 6.
Horsburgh, Susan. "Pandering to Society's Worst Instincts." *The Australian*, 23 Dec 2005. *Newsbank*. 8 May 2008.
"Interview with Joe Penhall." *Guardian*, 6 Jul 2002. Guardian.co.uk. 8 Jul 2004.
Kingston, Jeremy. "Fair to the Middling." *The Times*, 30 Apr 1997: 38.
Litson, Jo. "The Misfits." *Weekend Australian*, 23 Feb 2002. *Newsbank*. 8 May 2008.
Logan, Brian. "'If You've Got a Big Mouth, the Stage Is the Place to Be.'" *Guardian*, 12 Apr 2000. *ProQuest*. 9 Aug 2001.
Maxwell, Dominic. "Arms and the Thinking Man." *The Times*, 26 Mar 2007. *LexisNexis*. 16 Apr 2008.
Morgan, Joyce. "Playwright Matures into an Ordinary Joe." *Sydney Morning Herald*, 30 Jun 1998. *LexisNexis*. 15 May 2008.
Rees, Jasper. "Bard of the Baseball Bat." *Evening Standard*, 7 Apr 1998: 26.
_____. "Vexed Questions of Colour." *Daily Telegraph*, 30 Apr 2001. *ProQuest*. 8 Aug 2001.
Roddick, Nick. "Interview: Joe Penhall, Playwright." *Scotland on Sunday*, 13 Sep 2009. Scotsman.com. 27 Jul 2010.
Rizzo, Frank. "The Dissolute, Desperate Demand for 'Love and Understanding.'" *The Hartford Courant*, 25 Mar 1998. *Newsbank*. 19 May 2008.
Smith, Laura. "'Racism Can Drive You Mad.'" *London Evening Standard*, 5 Aug 2001. Thisislondon.co.uk. 25 Jul 2010.
Taylor, Paul. "Trust Me, I'm a Reporter." *The Independent*, 2 Sep 2004. *LexisNexis*. 16 Apr 2008.
Williams, Sue. "Where the Heart Is." *The Sun-Herald*, 21 Jun 1998. *LexisNexis*. 15 May 2008.
Wolf, Matt. "Power Games that Scar in a Psychiatric Arena." *The New York Times*, 24 Nov 2002. *Newsbank*. 19 May 2008.

Newspaper Reviews of Joe Penhall's Plays

Bassett, Kate. "Hot Spark of Compassion." Review of *Some Voices*. *The Times*, 24 Sep 1994. *LexisNexis*. 8 Aug 2001.
_____. Review of *Landscape with Weapon*. *Independent on Sunday*, 8 Apr 2007. Independent.co.uk. 24 Jan 2009.
Benedict, David. "Ben Elton Finds It's Hard to Top Popcorn." Review of *The Bullet*. *The Independent*, 12 Apr 1998. *LexisNexis*. 15 May 2008.
_____. "David Benedict on Theatre." Review of *Some Voices*. *The Independent*, 20 Sep 1994. *LexisNexis*. 16 May 2008.
Billen, Andrew. Review of *Love and Understanding*. *The Observer*, 11 May 1997. *LexisNexis*. 15 May 2008.
Billington, Michael. "Lifting the Curse." Review of *Blue/Orange*. *Guardian*, 14 Apr 2000. *ProQuest*. 9 Aug 2001.
_____. Review of *The Bullet*. *Guardian*, 13 Apr 1998. *ProQuest*. 6 Aug 2001.
_____. Review of *Dumb Show*. *Guardian*, 9 Apr 2004. Web. 16 Apr 2008.
_____. Review of *Landscape with Weapon*. *Guardian*, 7 Apr 2007. *LexisNexis*. 17 Apr 2008.
_____. Review of *Love and Understanding*. *Guardian*, 7 May 1997: Sec 2: 14.
_____. Review of *Some Voices*. *Guardian*, 23 Sep 1994. *ProQuest*. 6 Aug 2001.
Cavendish, Dominic. "Disappointingly Blunt Weapon." Review of *Landscape with Weapon*. *Daily Telegraph*, 7 Apr 2007. *Newsbank*. 17 Apr 2008.

_____. "Mind Games without Frontiers." Review of *Blue/Orange*. *Daily Telegraph*, 2 May 2001. *ProQuest*. 8 Aug 2001.
Christopher, James. "A Send-up of Life's Priorities." Review of *Love and Understanding*. *The Times*, 6 May 1997. *LexisNexis*. 16 May 2008.
Clapp, Susannah. "Brothers in Arms Made for Loaded Drama." Review of *Landscape with Weapon*. *The Observer*, 15 Apr 2007. *LexisNexis*. 17 Apr 2008.
Coveney, Michael. "Beware of Greeks Bearing Rifts." Review of *Pale Horse*. *The Observer*, 29 Oct 1995: Review: 10.
_____. "Making a Song and Dance out of War." Review of *The Bullet*. *Daily Mail*, 10 Apr 1998. *LexisNexis*. 15 May 2008.
_____. Review of *Blue/Orange*. *Daily Mail*, 24 Apr 2000. *ProQuest*. 8 Aug 2001.
Curtis, Nick. "He Falls at the Last." Review of *Pale Horse*. *The Evening Standard*, 19 Oct 1995. *LexisNexis*. 15 May 2008.
De Jongh, Nicholas. "Firing Blanks at Family Anguish." Review of *The Bullet*. *Evening Standard*, 9 Apr 1998. *ProQuest*. 6 Aug 2001.
Gardner, Lyn. "Losing, Boozing and Feeling Sad." Review of *Pale Horse*. *Guardian*, 19 Oct 1995: Sec. 1: 2.
Gross, John. "Tales of High Vices in Low Places." Review of *Dumb Show*. *Sunday Telegraph*, 12 Sep 2004. *LexisNexis*. 16 Apr 2008.
Hanks, Robert. Review of *Love and Understanding*. *The Independent*, 4 May 1997. *ProQuest*. 6 Aug 2001.
Hart, Christopher. "Flying in the Face of Real Politics." Review of *Landscape with Weapon*. *Sunday Times*, 8 Apr 2007. *LexisNexis*. 17 Apr 2008.
Hemming, Sarah. "Bitter Pills." Review of *Some Voices*. *The Independent*, 28 Sep 1994. *LexisNexis*. 16 May 2008.
Kablean, Carrie. "Catharsis Is a Bit of a Turkey." Review of *Wild Turkey*. *Sunday Telegraph*, 21 Feb 1999. *Newsbank*. 19 May 2008.
Kellaway, Kate. "Trust Me, I'm a Journalist." Review of *Dumb Show*. *The Observer*, 12 Sep 2004. *LexisNexis*. 16 Apr 2008.
Kingston, Jeremy. "Murder on the Menu." Review of *Pale Horse*. *The Times*, 23 Oct 1995: 14.
_____. "Raunch to Ranch in a Long Day's Journey." Review of *Wild Turkey*. *The Times*, 31 May 1993. *LexisNexis*. 8 Aug 2001.
Macaulay, Alastair. "The Bullet by Name, but Not by Nature." Review of *The Bullet*. *Financial Times*, 14 Apr 1998. *ProQuest*. 19 May 2008.
_____. Review of *Dumb Show*. *Financial Times*, 9 Sep 2004. *ProQuest*. 17 Apr 2008.
_____. "Thrilling Triangle that Gets Inside Your Head." Review of *Blue/Orange*. *Financial Times*, 17 Apr 2000. *ProQuest*. 9 Aug 2001.
Marmion, Patrick. "Almost a Direct Hit." Review of *Landscape with Weapon*. *Daily Mail*, 13 Apr 2007. *LexisNexis*. 17 Apr 2008.
Morley, Sheridan. "Where's the Sting in This Tale?" Review of *Dumb Show*. *The Express*, 8 Sep 2004. *LexisNexis*. 16 Apr 2008.
Nightingale, Benedict. "A Flawed Inventor Discovers Angst as He Takes Off to the Moral High Ground." Review of *Landscape with Weapon*. *The Times*, 6 Apr 2007. *LexisNexis*. 17 Apr 2008.
_____. "More than This Job's Worth." Review of *The Bullet*. *The Times*, 10 Apr 1998. *ProQuest*. 6 Aug 2001.
_____. "Paper Tigers Show Their Claws." Review of *Dumb Show*. *The Times*, 9 Sep 2004. *LexisNexis*. 16 Apr 2008.
_____. "Who Helps When It's the Shrinks Who Need Shrinking?" Review of *Blue/Orange*. *The Times*, 15 Apr 2000. *ProQuest*. 9 Aug 2001.

Peter, John. Review of *The Bullet*. *The Sunday Times*, 12 Apr 1998. *LexisNexis*. 18 May 2008.
_____. Review of *Love and Understanding*. *The Sunday Times*, 11 May 1997: Sec 11:14.
_____. Review of *Pale Horse*. *The Sunday Times*, 29 Oct 1995. *LexisNexis*. 15 May 2008.
_____. Review of *Some Voices*. *The Sunday Times*, 24 Sep 1994: Weekend Times: 5.
Potts, Robert. "Sons and Fathers and Their Fathers." Review of *The Bullet*. *The Times Literary Supplement*, 24 Apr 1998: 20.
Portillo, Michael. "Dirty Business." Review of *Dumb Show*. *New Statesman*, 27 Sep 2004. *LexisNexis*. 16 Apr 2008.
Rose, Colin. "Bit of a Turkey." Review of *Wild Turkey*. *The Sun Herald*, 14 Feb 1999. *LexisNexis*. 15 May 2008.
Rubnikowicz, Renata. "Ben Elton and Trench Warfare: A Night in PC World." Review of *The Bullet*. *The Observer*, 12 Apr 1998. *LexisNexis*. 15 May 2008.
Segal, Victoria. "Paper Over the Cracks." Review of *Dumb Show*. *The Sunday Times*, 12 Sep 2004. *LexisNexis*. 16 Apr 2008.
Shenton, Mark. Review of *Landscape with Weapon*. *Sunday Express*, 15 Apr 2007. *LexisNexis*. 17 Apr 2008.
Spencer, Charles. "A Death of a Salesman for Britain in the Nineties." Review of *The Bullet*. *Daily Telegraph*, 10 Apr 1998. *ProQuest*. 6 Aug 2001.
_____. "Squirming in the Gutter." Review of *Dumb Show*. *Daily Telegraph*, 9 Sept 2004. *LexisNexis*. 16 Apr 2008.
_____. "Whether or Not the Patient Is Mad, the Play Is Bad." Review of *Blue/Orange*. *The Daily Telegraph*, 17 Apr 2000. *ProQuest*. 9 Aug 2001.
Taylor, Paul. "An Ethical Battleground." Review of *Landscape with Weapon*. *The Independent*, 9 Apr 2007. *LexisNexis*. 16 Apr 2008.
_____. "The Mood Is Black, but Play Is Gripping." Review of *Blue/Orange*. *The Independent*, 14 Apr 2000. *ProQuest*. 9 Aug 2001.
_____. Review of *Love and Understanding*. *The Independent*, 6 May 1997. *LexisNexis*. 15 May 2008.
_____. Review of *Pale Horse*. *The Independent*, 23 Oct 1995. *LexisNexis*. 15 May 2008.
Walker, Tim. "Selective Anger." Review of *Landscape with Weapon*. *The Sunday Telegraph*, 15 Apr 2007. *LexisNexis*. 17 Apr 2008.
Wardle, Irving. "The Man Who Went Where Joyce Feared to Tread." Review of *Some Voices*. *The Independent*, 2 Oct 1994. *LexisNexis*. 16 May 2008.
Woddis, Carole. Review of *Blue/Orange*. *The Herald*, 27 Apr 2000. *ProQuest*. 9 Aug 2001.
_____. Review of *Love and Understanding*. *The Herald*, 7 May 1997. *LexisNexis*. 16 May 2008.
_____. Review of *Pale Horse*. *The Herald*, 26 Oct 1995. *LexisNexis*. 15 May 2008.
Wolf, Matt. Review of *Love and Understanding*. *Variety*, 2–8 Jun 1997. *LexisNexis*. 15 May 2008.
_____. Review of *Pale Horse*. *Variety*, 30 Oct 1995: 177.

Secondary Sources

Alberge, Dalya. "National Theatre Sends Black Actor unto the Breach." *The Times*, 17 Aug 2002. *LexisNexis*. 27 Feb 2009.
Alibhai-Brown, Yashim. *Who Do We Think We Are?: Imagining the New Britain*. London: Penguin, 2001.
Allen, Paul. "Is British Drama Racist?" *Guardian*, 17 Apr 2002. *LexisNexis*. 27 Feb 2009.
Aragay, Mireia and Pilar Zozaya. Interview with Dan Reballato. In *British Theatre of*

the 1990s: Interviews with Directors, Playwrights, Critics and Academics, edited by Mireia Aragay, Hildegard Klein, Enric Monforte, and Pilar Zozaya. New York: Palgrave Macmillan, 2007. 159–71.
_____. Interview with Ian Rickson. In *British Theatre of the 1990s: Interviews with Directors, Playwrights, Critics and Academics*, edited by Mireia Aragay, Hildegard Klein, Enric Monforte, and Pilar Zozaya. New York: Palgrave Macmillan, 2007. 15–26.
_____. Interview with Stephen Daldry. In *British Theatre of the 1990s: Interviews with Directors, Playwrights, Critics and Academics*, edited by Mireia Aragay, Hildegard Klein, Enric Monforte, and Pilar Zozaya. New York: Palgrave Macmillan, 2007. 3–14.
Aragay, Mireia, Hildegard Klein, Enric Monforte, and Pilar Zozaya, eds. *British Theatre of the 1990s: Interviews with Directors, Playwrights, Critics and Academics*. New York: Palgrave Macmillan, 2007.
Ariés, Philippe. *The Hour of Our Death*. Trans. Helen Weaver. New York: Oxford University Press, 1981.
"Author Discusses Stunning Success of First Novel. " *Morning Edition*, 26 Jul 1996. ProQuest. 22 Jul 2010.
Bayley, Clare. "A Very Angry Young Woman." *The Independent*, 23 Jan 1995: 20.
_____. "Playwrights Unplugged." *The Independent*, 24 Feb 1995: 25.
Benedict, David. "Missing in Action: Our Black Stars." *The Independent*, 1 Apr 1998. *LexisNexis*. 27 Feb 2009.
Beynon, John. *Masculinities and Culture*. Buckingham: Open University Press, 2002.
Bigsby, C. W. E. *David Mamet*. New York: Methuen, 1985.
Billington, Michael. Review of *Sexual Perversity in Chicago*. *Guardian*, 2 Dec 1977: n.p.
_____. Review of *Trainspotting*. *Guardian*, 18 Dec 1995: 2:10.
_____. "Short Shrift." *Guardian*, 16 Apr 2005. *Newsbank*. 17 Apr 2008.
Boles, William C. "The Rise and Fall of the Lad: Joe Penhall's Early Plays." In *Drama and the Postmodern: Essays Assessing the Limits of Metatheatre*, edited by Daniel Jernigan. Amherst, NY: Cambria Press, 2008. 307–325.
Blue/Orange Program. London: Royal National Theatre, 2000.
Calcutt, Andrew. *Brit Cult: An A-Z of British Pop Culture*. London: Prion, 2000.
Central Intelligence Agency. "Human Resource Exploitation Training Manual." In *The Phenomenon of Torture: Readings and Commentary*, edited by William F. Shulz. Philadelphia: University of Pennsylvania, 2007. 155–162.
Chaillat, Ned. Review of *Sexual Perversity in Chicago*. *The Sunday Times*, 2 Dec 1977, n.p.
Chekhov, Anton. *Uncle Vanya*. In *Uncle Vanya and Other Plays*. Trans. Betsy Hulick. New York: Bantam, 1994. 83–157.
Collin, Matthew. *Altered State: The Story of Ecstasy Culture and Acid House*. 2nd ed. London: Serpent's Tail, 1998.
Conboy, Martin. *Tabloid Britain: Constructing a Community through Language*. London: Routledge, 2006.
"Curtains Up." *Midweek*, 24–27 Feb 1997: n.p.
Curtis, Nick. "Random Tour of a Chamber of Horrors." Review of *Blasted*. *Evening Standard*, 19 Jan 1995. *LexisNexis*. 22 Jul 2010.
_____. "Spotting a Real Winner." *Evening Standard*, 30 Nov 1995. *LexisNexis*. 12 Jul 2001.
Davies, Linda M., and Michael F. Drummond. "Economics and Schizophrenia: The Real Cost." *The British Journal of Psychiatry* 165, no. 25 (25 Nov 1994): 18–21.
Dean, Anne. *David Mamet: Language as Dramatic Action*. Rutherford, NJ: Fairleigh Dickinson University Press, 1990.

Devine, Harriet. *Looking Back: Playwrights at the Royal Court, 1956–2006*. London: Faber, 2006.
Dorfman, Ariel. "Are There Times When We Have to Accept Torture?" In *On Torture*, edited by Thomas C. Hilde. Baltimore: The Johns Hopkins University Press, 2008. 109–111.
_____. "The Tyranny of Torture: Is Torture Inevitable in Our Century and Beyond?" In *Torture: A Collection*, edited by Sanford Levinson. Oxford: Oxford University Press, 2004. 3–18.
Dromgoole, Dominic. *The Full Room: An A-Z of Contemporary Playwriting*. London: Methuen, 2000.
Dubose, J. Todd. "The Phenomenology of Bereavement, Grief, and Mourning." *Journal of Religion and Health* 36, no. 4 (1997): 367–374.
Edgar, David. "Plays for Today." *The Sunday Times*, 7 Sep 1997. *NewsBank*. 22 Jul 2010.
_____. "Provocative Acts: British Playwriting in the Post-War Era and Beyond." In *State of Play: Playwrights on Playwriting*, edited by David Edgar. London: Faber, 1999. 1–34.
Edley, Nigel, and Margaret Wetherell. *Men in Perspective: Practice, Power and Identity*. London: Prentice Hall, 1995.
Edwards, Tim. *Men in the Mirror: Men's Fashion, Masculinity and Consumer Society*. London, Cassell, 1997.
Fanshawe, Simon. "Playing with Europe's Theatrical Traditions." *The Sunday Times*, 13 Dec 1998. *LexisNexis*. 16 May 2008.
Flynn, Eileen P. *Issues in Medical Ethics*. Kansas City: Sheed & Ward, 1997.
Foucault, Michel. *The Birth of the Clinic: An Archaeology of Medical Perception*. Trans. A. M. Sheridan Smith. New York: Vintage, 1994.
_____. *Discipline and Punish: The Birth of the Prison*. Trans. Alan Sheridan. New York: Vintage, 1995.
Freud, Sigmund. "Mourning and Melancholia." In *The Standard Edition of the Complete Psychological Works of Sigmund Freud; Volume XI:V, On the History of the Psycho-Analytic Movement, Papers on Metapsychology and Other Works*. Trans. James Stachey. London: Hogarth, 1957. 237–258.
Garner, Lesley. "Closer to the Truth?" *The Sunday Times*, 19 Jul 1998: Sec. 11: 15.
Gorer, Geoffrey. *Death, Grief and Mourning*. Garden City, NY: Doubleday, 1965.
Grosso, Nick. *Peaches*. In *Coming on Strong: New Writing from the Royal Court Theatre*. London: Faber, 1995. 1–79.
_____. *Real Classy Affair*. London: Faber, 1998.
Guilliatt, Richard. "Lost Chord." *The Sydney Morning Herald*, 11 Sep 2004. *Newsbank*. 25 Jun 2008.
Hammond, Will. Interview with David Hare and Max Stafford-Clark. In *Verbatim Verbatim: Contemporary Documentary Theatre*, edited by Will Hammond and Dan Steward. London: Oberon Books, 2008. 45–75.
Hammond, Will, and Dan Steward, eds. *Verbatim Verbatim: Contemporary Documentary Theatre*. London: Oberon Books, 2008.
_____. "Introduction." In *Verbatim Verbatim: Contemporary Documentary Theatre*, edited by Will Hammond and Dan Steward. London: Oberon Books, 2008. 7–13.
Hanks, Robert. "What's the Deal, Patrick?" *Independent on Sunday*, 11 May 1997: 14–15.
Harrison, Melissa, ed. *High Society: The Real Voices of Club Culture*. London: Piatkus, 1998.
Hatfield, Michael. "Legitimacy, Identity, Violence, and the Law." In *On Torture*, edited by Thomas C. Hilde. Baltimore: The Johns Hopkins University Press, 2008. 145–164.

Hemming, Sarah. "Look Forward with Anger." *Financial Times*, 18 Nov 1995: Weekend FT 17.
Hilde, Thomas C. "Information and the Tortured Imagination." In *On Torture*, edited by Thomas C. Hilde. Baltimore: The Johns Hopkins University Press, 2008. 197–215.
Hollander, Tom, Pippa Haywood, Julian Rhind-Tutt, and Jason Watkins. Royal National Theatre. Cottesloe Theatre, London, Eng. 29 Jun 2007. Platform, chaired by Emma Freud.
Homans, Peter. "Introduction." In *Symbolic Loss: The Ambiguity of Mourning and Memory at Century's End*, edited by Peter Homans. Charlottesville: University Press of Virginia, 2000. 1–40.
Hughes-Hallett, Lucy. Review of *Trainspotting*. *The Times*, 15 Aug 1993. LexisNexis. 12 Jul 2001.
Humphries, Glen. "Sunnyboys Back with a Disc to Remember." *Illawarra Mercury*, 23 Sep 2004. Newsbank. 25 Jun 2008.
James, Winston. "The Black Experience in Twentieth-Century Britain." In *Black Experience and the Empire*, edited by Philip D. Morgan and Sean Hawkins. Oxford: Oxford University Press, 2004. 347–386.
Jordan, Eamonn. "The Fallacies of Cultural Narratives, Re-enactment, Legacy, and Agency in Arthur Miller's *Death of a Salesman* and Martin McDonagh's *The Pillowman*." *Hungarian Journal of English and American Studies* 11, no. 2 (2005): 45–62.
Kane, Sarah. *Blasted*. In *Complete Plays*. London: Methuen, 2001. 1–61.
Keane, Jonathan. "Ecstasy in the Unhappy Society." In *Young Britain: Politics, Pleasures and Predicaments*, edited by Jonathan Rutherford. London: Lawrence & Wishart, 1998. 98–111.
Kenyon, Mel, and Phyllis Nagy. "Seasons of Lad Tidings." Letter. *Guardian*, 4 Dec 1995: 2: 7.
Klein, Hildegard. Interview with Joe Penhall. In *British Theatre of the 1990s: Interviews with Directors, Playwrights, Critics and Academics*, edited by Mireia Aragay, Hildegard Klein, Enric Monforte, and Pilar Zozaya. New York: Palgrave Macmillan, 2007. 77–90.
Kramer, Mimi. "Three for the Show." *Time*, 4 Aug 1997: 72.
Krauthammer, Charles. "The Truth About Torture." In *Torture: A Collection*, edited by Sanford Levinson. Oxford: Oxford University Press, 2004. 307–316.
Kritzer, Amelia Howe. *Political Theatre in Post-Thatcher Britain: New Writing: 1995–2005*. London: Palgrave, 2008.
Landscape with Weapon Program. London: Royal National Theatre, 2007.
Lavender, Andy. "West End Gets Smack in the Face." *The Times*, 13 Dec 1995. LexisNexis. 12 Jul 2001.
Leek, Liz. "NT Education Workpack: *Blue/Orange*." Nationaltheatre.org.uk. Royal National Theatre, n.d. 8 Aug 2001.
Levinson, Sanford, ed. *Torture: A Collection*. Oxford: Oxford University Press, 2004.
Lezard, Nicholas. "Too Close for Comfort." *Harpers and Queen*, Jun 1997: 32.
Little, Ruth, and Emily McLaughlin. *The Royal Court Theatre Inside Out*. London: Oberon Books, 2007.
MacDonald, Kevin. "Postcards from the Edge." *Independent on Sunday*, 28 Jan 1996: Sunday Review 18.
Malbon, Ben. *Clubbing: Dancing, Ecstasy and Vitality*. London: Routledge, 1999.
Mamet, David. *American Buffalo*. New York: Grove, 1976.
———. *Sexual Perversity in Chicago and Duck Variations*. New York: Grove, 1978.
Marber, Patrick. *Closer*. New York: Grove, 1999.

Martin, Terry, and Kenneth J. Doka. "Masculine Grief." In *Living with Grief after Sudden Loss: Suicide, Homicide, Accident, Heart Attack, Stroke*, edited by Kenneth J. Doka. Bristol, PA: Frances and Taylor, 1996. 161–171.
McAuley, Tilly. "Shopping and Foucault." *Gay Times*, Apr 1997: 15–16, 72.
McLaughlin, Emily. "Joe Penhall: Dumb Show Education Resources." *royalcourttheatre.com*, Royal Court Theatre, n.d. 18 Jun 2008.
"Memorable Quotes for *Four Weddings and a Funeral*." *IMDb.com*. IMDb, n.d. Web. 18 Jun 2008.
"Memorable Quotes for *Iron Man*." *IMDb.com*. IMDb, n.d. Web. 28 Jun 2010.
Men's Free Press Collective. "Hopes and Dreams: Creating a Men's Politics." In *Feminism and Masculinities*, edited by Peter F. Murphy. Oxford: Oxford University Press, 2004. 80–92.
Midgley, Carol. "RSC plays Chelsea at their own game." *The Times*, 20 Oct 1997: 3.
Miller, Arthur. *Death of a Salesman*. New York: Penguin, 1976.
Monk, John. "Ethics, Engineers and Drama." *Science & Engineering Ethics* 15.1 (2009): 111–123. *Academic Search Premier*. EBSCO. 1 Jun 2010.
Montforte, Enric. Interview with Mark Ravenhill. In *British Theatre of the 1990s: Interviews with Directors, Playwrights, Critics and Academics*, edited by Mireia Aragay, Hildegard Klein, Enric Monforte, and Pilar Zozaya. New York: Palgrave Macmillan, 2007. 91–104.
Nightingale, Benedict. "Mainline to Misery." Review of *Trainspotting*. *The Times*, 16 Mar 1996. *LexisNexis*. 12 Jul 2001.
Norman, Matthew. "Diary." *Guardian*, 10 Feb 1998. *LexisNexis*. 7 May 2004.
"Our Decade: New Lad Rules the World." *BBC.co.uk*, BBC Online Network. 9 Mar 1999. Web. 21 Mar 2006.
Oxenbridge, Jason. "Sunnyboy with a Clouded Brain." *The Gold Coast Bulletin*, 9 Oct 2004. *Newsbank*. 25 Jun 2008.
Penhall, Joe. "Re: E-mail—Sections from Penhall chapters." E-mail message to the author. 20 Aug 2010.
_____. "Re: E-mail—Sections from Penhall chapters." E-mail message to the author. 31 Aug 2010.
_____. "Re: Final Questions." E-mail message to the author. 16 Sep 2010.
_____. "Re: The Final Collection of Writings." E-mail message to the author. 6 Sep 2010.
_____. "Q and A." E-mail message to the author. 10 Aug 2010.
_____. Royal National Theatre. Cottesloe Theatre, London, Eng. 7 Jun 2000. Platform, chaired by Sarah Hemming.
_____. Royal National Theatre. Cottesloe Theatre, London, Eng. 15 May 2007. Platform, chaired by Aleks Sierz.
Phillips, Anton. "Why Is Racism So Rife in the Theatre?" *The Observer*, 10 Sep 2000. *LexisNexis*. 27 Feb 2009.
Phillips, Trevor. "The Stephen Lawrence Phenomenon: Icon for a Skeptical Age." *The Observer*, 10 Jan 1999. *LexisNexis*. 27 Feb 2009.
Pinter, Harold. *Betrayal*. New York: Grove, 1978.
_____. *The Homecoming*. *Complete Works: Three*. New York: Grove, 1990. 19–98.
Rando, Therese A. "Complications in Mourning Traumatic Death." In *Living with Grief after Sudden Loss: Suicide, Homicide, Accident, Heart Attack, Stroke*, edited by Kenneth J. Doka. Bristol, PA: Frances and Taylor, 1996. 139–159.
Ravenhill, Mark. "Plays About Men: Mark Ravenhill, Kevin Elyot, William Gaminara." In *State of Play: Playwrights on Playwriting*, edited by David Edgar. London: Faber, 1999. 48–51.
_____. *Shopping and Fucking*. In *Plays: One*. London: Methuen, 2001. 1–91.

Reinelt, Janelle. "Selective Affinities: British Playwrights at Work." *Modern Drama* 50, no. 3 (Fall 2007): 305–324.
Reynolds, Simon. "Filthy Mind." *The Village Voice*, 15 Sep 1998: 70–73+.
_____. *Generation Ecstasy: Into the World of Techno and Rave Culture*. New York: Routledge, 1998.
_____. "Rave Culture: Living Dream or Living Death?" In *The Clubcultures Reader: Readings in Popular Cultural Studies*, edited by Steve Redhead, Derek Wynne, and Justin O'Connor. London: Blackwell, 1998. 84–93.
Robb, John. *The Nineties: What the Fuck Was That All About?* London: Ebury, 1999.
Roberts, Alison. "The Gore Lore." *Evening Standard*, 26 Jan 1995: 25.
Roberts, Jo. "Beyond the Sunny Side." *The Age*, 3 Jan 2006. *Newsbank*. 8 May 2008.
Rutherford, Jonathan. "Introduction." In *Young Britain: Politics, Pleasures and Predicaments*, edited by Jonathan Rutherford. London: Lawrence & Wishart, 1998.
Shepard, Sam. *Buried Child*. In *Seven Plays*. New York: Bantam, 1984. 61–132.
Shone, Tom. "Close and Personal." *The Sunday Times*, 26 Oct 1997: Sec. 11: 17.
Shulman, Milton. Review of *Sexual Perversity in Chicago*. *Evening Standard* 6 Dec 1977: n.p.
Sierz, Aleks. *In-Yer-Face: British Drama Today*. London: Faber, 2000.
Soans, Robin. Untitled. In *Verbatim Verbatim: Contemporary Documentary Theatre*, edited by Will Hammond and Dan Steward. London: Oberon Books, 2008. 15–44.
Southwell, Tim. *Getting Away with It: The Inside Story of Loaded*. London: Ebury, 1998.
Spencer, Charles. "Patrick Marber (Oct 1999)." *Nationaltheatre.org.uk*, Royal National Theatre. 7 Oct 1999. Web. 16 Jun 2008.
_____. "Nightmare City." Review of *Trainspotting*. *The Daily Telegraph*, 4 Apr 1995. *LexisNexis*. 12 Jul 2001.
_____. Review of *Blasted*. *The Daily Telegraph*, 20 Jan 1995: n.p.
_____. "You'll Be Sick with Laughter." Review of *Trainspotting*. *The Daily Telegraph*, 18 Dec 1995. *LexisNexis*. 12 Jul 2001.
Spicer, Andrew. *Typical Men: The Representation of Masculinity in Popular British Cinema*. London: I. B. Tauris, 2001.
Stearns, David Patrick. "Staging an Invasion." *USA TODAY*, 10 Apr 1998. *LexisNexis*. 15 May 2008.
Sullivan, Andrew. "The Abolition of Torture." In *Torture: A Collection*, edited by Sanford Levinson. Oxford: Oxford University Press, 2004. 317–327.
Taylor, Paul. "Courting Disaster." Review of *Blasted*. *The Independent*, 20 Jan 1995: Sec. 2:27.
Thornton, Sarah. *Club Cultures: Music, Media and Subcultural Capital*. Oxford: Polity, 1995.
Watkin, William. *On Mourning: Theories of Loss in Modern Literature*. Edinburgh: Edinburgh University Press, 2004.
Watson, Ariel. "Cries of Fire: Psychotherapy in Contemporary British and Irish Drama." *Modern Drama* 51, no. 2 (Summer 2008): 188–210.
Welsh, Irvine. *Trainspotting*. In *Trainspotting and Headstate*. London: Minerva, 1996. 11–62.
Whelehan, Imelda. *Overloaded: Popular Culture and Future of Feminism*. London: The Women's Press, 2000.
Williams, Kristian. "Legitimizing Torture." *Commonweal* 132, no. 21 (2005): 20–26. *Academic Search Premier*. EBSCO. 1 Jun 2010.
Wolf, Matt. "London's Unnerving Nihilists." *American Theatre* Sep 1997: 44–45.
Yates, Robert. "I'm Interested in Violence. But that Doesn't Make Me Tarantino." *The Observer*, 2 Nov 1997: Review 11.

Index

Abu Ghraib 171–2, 176
Adamson, Samuel 18
advertising 20, 77, 80
Alda, Alan 184
American Buffalo (film) 184
American Buffalo (play) 32, 35, 38–9, 184
Angels in America 69, 95
Arena 26
Arnott, Jake 135
Ashes and Sand 43, 55

The Bacchae 157
Basic Instinct 147–8
The Beauty Queen of Leenane 1, 16, 18, 30
Betrayal 93, 94
Bettany, Paul 87–88
Bey, Catherine 63–4
The Big Life 118
biographical information on Penhall 21–4, 31–2, 40–3, 63–4, 85–6, 101–2, 103, 114, 122, 139, 160, 186
black theatre 117–8
Black Watch 158
Blasted 15–6, 18–9, 21, 43, 55, 57, 137, 184–5
Blue/Orange 2, 5, 24, 49, 86, 123–34, 136, 139, 148, 163, 180, 185, 186; inspiration for 114–5; plot of 115; reviews of 115–6; set design of 118–9; title reference 186; writing of 114–5
Bond, Edward 18, 19, 183
Botox 163–5, 187
Bradwell, Mike 87–8
Brassed Off 31
Brittain, Victoria 157–8
Bruises 18
Bukowski, Charles 23
The Bullet 5, 22, 48, 98–100, 104–13, 145–6, 185; characterization of Richie 87–8; inspiration for 101–2; plot summary of 100–1; reviews of 102–3

Buried Child 5, 98–100
Burke, Gregory 158
Bush Theatre 3, 10, 12–4, 17, 22, 42–3, 86
Butterworth, Jez 19, 29, 44

Called to Account 158
Care in the Community 41–2, 47–50, 54, 116, 126, 184
Castlemorton 7–9
The Censor 18
Chekhov, Anton 31, 96, 107–8, 186–6
Churchill, Caryl 29, 43
Churchill, Winston 186
Clocks and Whistles 18
Closer 4, 18, 30, 81–3, 84–5, 93, 95–7
Codron, Michael 18
coercion 170, 174–6
community of men 33–9
community of mourners 59–61, 64, 74–5
Cool Britannia 184
Craig, Daniel 45, 184
Criminal Justice and Public Order Act (1994) 8
Curtis, Richard 25–6
The Cut 171–2, 174

Daldry, Stephen 42–3, 44, 136–7
Darwin, Charles 61, 68
Days of Significance 171
de Angelis, April 43
Death of a Salesman 5, 103–7, 110, 185
dehospitalization 126–7
Dershowitz, Alan 173
doctors 2, 23, 51, 70–1, 85–6, 89–92, 116, 119, 121–2, 185; relationship with patients 123–133
Donmar Warehouse 102
Dorfman, Ariel 173, 175, 176, 177
Dromgoole, Dominic 13, 18
Dudley, William 118, 163
Dumb Show 5, 86, 135, 140, 141, 146–54;

inspiration for 136–9; plot summary of 135–6; reviews of 140–1; writing of 139–40
Dying City 187

Eclipse Report 118
ecstasy 7–9, 27–8, 183; *see also* Generation Ecstasy; rave culture; youth culture
Elmina's Kitchen 117–8
SS *Empire Windrush* 119–20
Enduring Love (film) 3, 161, 180, 184
ethics 24, 91–2, 93–4, 126–8, 137–9, 151–4, 160–1, 163–77

Fair Game 18
Fever Pitch 184
Four Weddings and a Funeral 25–6
Freud, Sigmund 61, 68
friendship 34–9, 72–3, 90–1, 144
The Full Monty 31

Generation Ecstasy 4, 9, 12–6; *see also* ecstasy; rave culture; youth culture
generational recycling 18, 48, 111
Gibson, Harry 10–1, 13–5
Gorer, Geoffrey 59–62
Grant, Hugh 25–6, 31
Griffiths, Peter 120
Grosso, Nick 29, 30, 33–4, 45, 79–80
Guantanamo 157–8
The Guys 156

Hall, Peter 157
Hammersmith Guardian 23–4, 41–2
Hampstead Theatre 42
Hare, David 158
Haunted Child 181
The Homecoming 5, 98–100, 147
homecoming plays 98–100

identity 21–2, 35–9, 68, 76, 122–4, 128–9, 130–1, 133, 146–9, 186
Ifans, Rhys 179
In-Yer-Face theatre 4, 17- 21, 30, 78, 86, 115, 184
institutional racism 5, 119, 121, 186
Iron Man 155–6

Jones, Jimmy 137
Justifying War 157

Kane, Sarah 1, 2–3, 15, 16, 18–9, 21, 55, 57, 137, 183, 185
Kent, Nicholas 157
Kenyon, Mel 29–30
Kerouac, Jack 23

Kinnock, Neil 80
Kureishi, Hanif 43
Kushner, Tony 69, 95
Kwei-Armah, Kwame 117–8

Landscape with Weapon 5, 86, 142, 156, 158, 163–170, 173–7, 185, 186–7; inspiration for 160–1; plot of 158–60; reviews of 161–62; set design of 162–63
language 50–1, 70, 71–2, 79–80, 93–4, 108–9, 124–6, 130–3, 148–9, 186–7
The Last King of Scotland (film) 134, 181
Lawrence, Stephen 5, 120–1
Loaded 28–9
London Metropolitan Police Force 5, 119, 121–2
The Long Firm 3, 134
Look Back in Anger 10–1, 44, 79
Love Actually 26
Love and Understanding 4, 22, 84–5, 87–97, 107, 144–5, 185; inspiration for 85–6; plot of 83–4; reviews of 86–7
Lucie, Doug 137

MacDonald, James 16
MacPherson Report 121, 132
Mahmood, Mazher 138–9, 150
Major, John 8, 81
Mamet, David 32, 38, 77–82, 114–5, 170, 180, 184, 185
Marber, Patrick 2–3, 29, 30, 81–3, 84, 95, 97
marriage 48, 70–71, 93, 110–3
masculinity 25–32, 35–9, 68, 112
McCarthy, Cormac 3, 22, 180
McDonagh, Martin 1, 2, 16, 17, 18, 171–2, 174
McEwan, Ian 3, 135, 161, 184
McPherson, Conor 2
Mendes, Sam 102
The Mercy Seat 157
Michell, Roger 118, 161, 170, 180–1
Miller, Arthur 5, 103–7, 188
Mojo 17, 19, 44
Moses Jones 3, 22, 134, 180–1
Mother Clapp's Molly House 185
mourning 59–62, 66–76, 179–80
musical talent (of Penhall) 22–3, 40–1

Nagy, Phyllis 29–30, 81
National Health Service 3, 5, 18, 23, 41–2, 51, 54–5, 58, 89–90, 116–7, 121, 125–7, 129–130
Neilson, Anthony 16, 18, 19, 29
New Lad 4, 28–30, 46, 78–9
New Man 4, 25–9, 31, 46, 183–4

Nichols, Mike 3, 83, 181
Nighy, Bill 115, 119, 128
Norton-Taylor, Richard 157
Notting Hill 26

Oleanna 81
One for the Road 174
Orton, Joe 22
Osborne, John 10–1, 44, 79
Oxley, Jeremy 40–41, 50, 52

Pale Horse 4, 20, 61, 65–76, 102, 107, 143–4, 151, 179, 186; actors preparation for 62; inspiration for 63–4; plot of 62–3; reviews of 64–5
paternalism 126–28
Peaches 30, 43, 79
The Pillowman 172, 174
Pinter, Harold 93, 94, 98–100, 147, 174, 185
Powell, Enoch 120
Prichard, Rebecca 18

Quadrophenia 22

race 24, 117–25, 128–9, 130–2, 186; governmental policy concerning 120–2, 186
rave culture 7–9, 183; *see also* ecstasy; Generation Ecstasy; youth culture
Ravenhill, Mark 1, 2, 4–5, 16, 21, 55, 57, 78, 80–1, 84, 95, 170–2, 185–6
Real Classy Affair 33–4, 79
Red Bull 183
redundancy 101–2, 107–11
Regent Theatre 77
religion 61, 64, 67–8, 69–70, 74
Rickson, Ian 44, 62
Riff-Raff 31
The Road (film) 3, 22, 180
Royal Court Theatre 3, 15, 16, 42–4, 62, 80–1, 82, 86, 102, 140, 157, 184, 185
Royal National Theatre 3, 14, 41, 42, 82, 85, 114–5, 117, 125, 128, 140, 157, 158, 161, 168, 181, 185
Royal Shakespeare Theatre 14, 20, 171

Saved 19
schizophrenia 40–2, 48–58, 114, 121–2, 126, 130–1, 133
September 11 156–7
Sexual Perversity in Chicago 4, 77–82
sexuality 20–1, 27–8, 77–84, 95–6, 111, 147–51, 185
The Shallow End 137
Shepard, Sam 56, 98–100, 185
Shinn, Christopher 157, 187

Shopping and Fucking 1, 4, 15, 17, 18, 55, 80–1, 82, 84–5, 93, 95–7, 185
Sing Yer Heart Out for the Lads 186
Slovo, Gillian 157
Smith, Rae 44–5
Soans, Robin 158, 187
Some Voices 4, 20, 24, 42–3, 45–58, 64–5, 72, 90, 102, 107, 116, 139–40, 142–3, 180, 183, 184, 185; inspiration for 40–2; plot of 44, 142–3; reviews of 45; set design of 44–5
Speed-the-Plow 114–5, 116
Stuff Happens 158
Sunnyboys 40–1
Sweetheart 79
Swingers 183–4
Sydney School of Art 21, 40

tabloids 55, 137–40, 151–4
Talking to Terrorists 158
technology 9, 60, 105–6, 155–6, 160, 165–8, 169, 174
Thatcher, Margaret 4, 26–7, 46, 49, 81, 120; governmental policies of 8, 15, 27, 40, 120–1
The Three Sisters 96, 107–8
torture 170–7
Townshend, Pete 22, 183
Trainspotting (film) 11
Trainspotting (novel) 9–11, 183
Trainspotting (play) 4, 10–5, 29
Tricycle Theatre 117, 157
True West 56

Uncle Vanya 107–8, 185–6
The Undertaker 134, 179–80, 187
Upton, Judy 45, 55

verbatim theatre 157–8, 187
violence 19–21, 35–8, 49, 63, 72, 73–4, 120–1, 137, 168; *see also* torture

war on terror 155–8, 165–8, 170–7
Welsh, Irvine 4, 10–2, 15, 183
Where Do We Live 157
The Who 22
Wild Turkey 4, 20, 33–9, 46, 52, 62, 107, 113; inspiration for 32; plot of 32; reviews of 32–3
Williams, Roy 171, 186
Winstone, Ray 62, 136–7
work 31, 33–9, 46–7, 48, 65–73, 88–92, 97, 107–110, 146–54, 164–8, 179

youth culture 7–10, 12–14; *see also* ecstasy; Generation Ecstasy; rave culture

www.ingramcontent.com/pod-product-compliance
Lightning Source LLC
Chambersburg PA
CBHW032059300426
44116CB00007B/810